Feltham provides the reader with a high  about the counselling trade. The hon counselling is turned on its own organis. Candid and clearly written throughout, th book.

David Pilgrim, Professor of Health and Social Policy, University of Liverpool

Sacred cows had better duck, and fast. In Colin Feltham's latest book, you won't find banal self-satisfaction about therapy's beneficence, or yet another yawn-generating formulaic textbook. Rather, Feltham's discursive panoramic perspective takes therapy writing to new, urgently needed levels of critical engagement. For therapy's own future good, we need our senior figures to have the courage to 'call' it just as it is, fast and loose if necessary. For therapy needs fearlessly honest 'critical friends' far more than it needs uncritical evangelists. And of all the writers I know in our field, Colin Feltham is perhaps the best placed to provide such critical friendship. While perhaps not agreeing with everything he writes, he does provoke us into *thinking deeply* – which is a truly wonderful gift. For therapy trainings that seek to produce critically minded practitioners who are sensitive to both therapy's strengths and its many lacunae, this book is seminal reading – and for *all* therapists, not only counselling psychologists. Feltham gets more radical and searching the older he gets – and we should all be grateful for it.

Richard House, University of Winchester, author of *In, Against and Beyond Therapy*, and co-editor (with Del Loewenthal) of *Against and For CBT* (both PCCS Books)

This critical examination of counselling and counselling psychology does exactly what it states on the tin. Colin Feltham provides an informed critical look at the key figures, theories, practices and research strategies associated with these professions. In doing so he raises numerous questions that many try to ignore, avoid or didn't even know existed. Overall, a provocative and enjoyable read.

Terry Hanley, University of Manchester, editor of *Counselling Psychology Review*

Counselling and Counselling Psychology
A critical examination

Colin Feltham

PCCS Books
Ross-on-Wye

First published 2013

PCCS BOOKS
2 Cropper Row
Alton Road
Ross-on-Wye
Herefordshire
HR9 5LA
UK
Tel +44 (0)1989 763900
contact@pccs-books.co.uk
www.pccs-books.co.uk

Counselling and Counselling Psychology: A critical examination

British Library Cataloguing in Publication Data.
A catalogue record for this book is available from the British Library.

ISBN 978 1 906254 58 2

Cover designed in the UK by Old Dog Graphics
Printed in the UK by Ashford Colour Press, Gosport, Hants

CONTENTS

Series foreword, Ian Parker — vii

Acknowledgements — viii

Abbreviations and acronyms used in the text — ix

1 Where did it all go wrong? Origins of human suffering, attempted remedies, and critiques — 1

2 Key figures in counselling psychology — 24

3 Problems of counselling theory — 46

4 Problems of counselling practice — 76

5 Problems of counselling research — 107

6 Problems of counselling and counselling psychology as professions — 135

7 Summarising and answering the critiques — 161

Index — 193

Dedication

With affection for my past and present students and colleagues who, in an impossible profession in a mad world, have their hearts in the right place.

SERIES FOREWORD

The value of critique

'Critique' is the crux of good academic work, and functions as the hinge-point between scholarship, professional activity and practice. Each theory is only as strong as its capacity to withstand sustained critical examination of the assumptions it makes about the world, and so each of these books have been constructed in such a way as to anticipate what would be made of their arguments by the most searching reader.

A founding premise of each book is that learning about a field of professional activity must also be to understand how theory and practice are linked together, and so the role of 'critique' in this process of linking ideas is to question what the impact will be of those ideas on the lives of people outside the classroom. To 'critically examine' an argument is a way of constructing a new practice which will help us understand the world and change it.

Ian Parker
Professor of Psychology
Discourse Unit
Manchester Metropolitan University

Acknowledgements

I am grateful for the guidance and challenge of the series editor, Craig Newnes, for his detailed suggestions, and for the real help given by Pete Sanders and all at PCCS Books. Special thanks are due to Mick Cooper and Sage Publications for permission to quote from *Essential Research Findings in Counselling and Psychotherapy*. Thanks too to Terry Hanley. I have over the years benefited directly and indirectly from senior colleagues and participants in relevant clinical and academic fields. I am particularly thankful for the openness towards critical thinking of Windy Dryden, and the radical writings of Richard House, as well as many others. I would also like to thank Gail Evans for her long-standing collegial support. While I am not always in agreement with the views of colleagues at the British Association for Counselling and Psychotherapy, I have always encountered among them a great deal of openness to dissonant views.

Abbreviations and acronyms used in the text

ADHD   Attention Deficit Hyperactivity Disorder

BACP   British Association for Counselling and Psychotherapy

BPS   British Psychological Society

CBT   Cognitive Behavioural Therapy

CHRE   Council for Healthcare Regulatory Excellence (now PSA)

CORE   Clinical Outcomes in Routine Evaluation

CPD   Continuing Professional Development

CSJ   Centre for Social Justice

DSM   *Diagnostic and Statistical Manual of Mental Disorders* (5th ed., 2013)

EAP   Employee Assistance Programme

EMDR   Eye Movement Desensitisation and Reprocessing

GAD7   Generalised Anxiety Disorder Assessment 7

HCPC   Health and Care Professions Council

IAPT   Increasing Access to Psychological Therapies

IPN   Independent Practitioners Network

NHS   National Health Service (UK)

NICE   National Institute for Health and Clinical Excellence (UK)

NIMH   National Institute of Mental Health (USA)

NLP   Neurolinguistic Programming

OCD   Obsessive Compulsive Disorder

PCA   Person-Centred Approach

PHQ9   Patient Health Questionnaire 9

PSA   Professional Standards Authority (for Health and Social Care), formerly CHRE

PTSD   Post Traumatic Stress Disorder

RCT   Randomised Controlled Trial

REBT   Rational Emotive Behaviour Therapy

REF   Research Excellence Framework (formerly RAE)

TA   Transactional Analysis

UPR   Unconditional Positive Regard

Where did it all go wrong? Origins of human suffering, attempted remedies, and critiques

If I could create an opening sentence that concisely captured the essence, approach and scope of this book, I would, but the task is a little more complicated than this wish for succinctness can command. So let me say that I am an insider in the field of counselling, that is, I am from a practitioner background and I have had extensive roles across the counselling and related academic professions over a period of more than 30 years. I may be thought of as a critical friend to those who are also insiders or aspiring insiders. But I am also drawn to the kind of critique that one philosopher refers to as 'exuberant skepticism'.[1] Hence my fondness and support for many counsellors and counselling psychologists is in tension with my scepticism about theory, practice and research. I am also of the belief that enquiries of this kind must be rooted in some historical overview, however brief that is. This chapter therefore begins with a view on the origins of human distress, before going on to overview the development of psychological therapy. I then encapsulate the development of problems and critiques before summarising the multi-perspectival critical approach taken throughout this book. Readers are of course free to skip to those parts of the book that most interest them.

It is all too easy to treat phenomena like psychotherapy and counselling as springing from nowhere for no particular reason but to do so here would seriously short-change our understanding. People did not of course abruptly manifest neurotic problems in late 19th century Vienna for which Sigmund Freud happened to be fortunately on hand, nor individual problems in living in the USA in the mid-20th century for which Carl Rogers found a radical remedy. The first element of critique we can set against counselling is that its literature and training do not on the whole analyse and address the likely origins and scope of our extensive psychological suffering and this failure has serious knock-on effects for counselling theory and practice. It is also true that not everyone will accept my own narrative and aetiological account, which is as it should be when anyone promotes critical thinking.[2] No account is objective or final and I am well aware that I have a particular position with which many others disagree. But it is exactly these foundational epistemological problems that need to be aired in the human and social sciences and applied professions generally.

Origins of psychological distress

The natural world of our planet does not automatically and non-problematically present to us everything that we need. Wild animals, who in many ways suffer far less than humans by virtue of having simpler lives and a less complex consciousness, nonetheless frequently suffer from savage predation, terrible injuries and diseases, and shortened lives. One striking feature of humanity is that we drastically reduced such suffering from predation many thousands of years ago by means of weaponry and cooperation. We gradually lessened threats to starvation via agricultural developments. We continue to eradicate or control diseases and extend the lifespan via medical research and practice.

Alongside all this our brain and consciousness have expanded enormously and it seems probable that something within this very successful expansion has also paradoxically created the foundations for psychological problems. For now I will sidestep complex problems of disputed nomenclature: let us say that there are strong arguments for the early evolutionary development of neurological distortions in our human make-up. Some theories focus on dietary effects on our brains, others on the need to store and utilise massive amounts of information for dealing with complex social interactions, in some cases leading to psychotic states. Evolutionary psychology and evolutionary psychiatry and psychotherapy have developed speculative theories about mismatches between early human development and current living conditions.[3] It is suggested that our physical evolution into upright posture necessitated hips narrow enough for extensive mobility, that also affected intrauterine life, birth complications and a long period of infantile dependency, all of which leave us susceptible to problems to this day.

Following the consolidation of agriculture, along with the taming and domestication of animals, and patriarchy, some 10,000 or so years ago saw the beginnings of an irreversible concentration of humans in towns and cities. Pressures against unchecked emotion, and increasing dependence on symbols and rituals were paralleled by violence and its suppression. Dense living conditions coupled with environmental challenges to neurodevelopmental processes of planning, imagination, and cooperation all combined to accelerate language and thought. With these, however, came the ability to deceive others and a tendency towards self-deception. It is impossible to date the splitting of human consciousness into parts but the body–mind dualism probably predates Descartes by centuries if not millennia; and in some (disputed) accounts we are split into the threesome of reptilian, mammalian and neocortical brains. In this admittedly crude précis of what I have elsewhere called anthropopathology[4] we may see the deep roots of many of our contemporary social and individual problems and their intractability.

Many alternative explanations exist for the human condition in which our psychological problems arise. Some look back to a golden age and an original human goodness from which we have fallen. Some regard the industrial era as the starting point for extensive human woes. David Smail, for example, explicitly locates the origins of human distress in capitalism and the status quo.[5] Existentialists say we are simply 'thrown into existence'. Postmodernist discourse dismisses the idea that any one explanation is better than others. What is interesting here is that these all lead to different foundations for models of psychological therapy. Whether views about our evolution and development are implicit assumptions or explicit theories, all are influential in shaping therapeutic theory and practice. You can argue that we are all free to make good, fluid choices and to alter our behaviour as necessary, to re-author our lives, change our scripts and schemas, finish our unfinished business and so on. Or you can observe that something in our nature makes decisions unclear, change very difficult and relapse a constant reality. One of very few models of counselling and therapy that acknowledge the negative pull of evolution is compassion-focused therapy. In spite of BACP's long-standing requirement that course models account for the 'nature and development of human beings', this is usually very poorly explicated.

The psychologist Steven Pinker argues that some genetic explanations for entrenched political and religious sympathies may be valid.[6] Such views are of course anathema both to modern liberals who want to stress the realities of (relative) free will, social learning and cultural optimism, and to those who like to insist on their version of determinedly selfish human nature, its origins and consequences. But since we can see how stubborn views and temperaments are concerning politics, religion, optimism versus pessimism and extraversion versus introversion, we might bear in mind the possibility that our loyalties, hatreds and zones of indifference have deeper roots than mere rationality or wilful error.

Research is inconclusive on most of the severe forms of psychological distress, the common view being that both psychosocial and biological factors are involved in causation. We are told that perhaps one in four people suffer from some kind of psychological problem and that mental health problems, especially depression, rank very high in worldwide tables of illness and disability. Talking therapies can bring a degree of comfort and resolution to some sufferers but not predictably. Likewise for medications. The lives of millions are chronically wretched and we do not know whether research and treatment are gaining ground against psychotoxic biological and socioeconomic forces that cause and compound the various well-known forms of psychological distress. Mild to moderate and intermittent psychological problems are often helped by talking therapies, though again predictability of outcomes remains low. To what extent counselling can be considered a good thing for providing optimism or objectionable for holding out false hope is an open question.

Brief history of psychology and psychological therapy

Early mythology, religion and philosophy, and later proto-psychiatry have all arisen as attempts to address human suffering and problems in group and individual living. On the one hand, all these remain extant in various forms and have many supporters and followers; aspects of them can also be found in many models of counselling. On the other hand, we must ask to what extent early epistemologies have been made redundant by much later scientific findings and more sophisticated evidence and theory. The imagery and emotion characterising early mythology and religion persist in our contemporary consciousness and yet are also overtaken by the rationality of philosophy and science, and all these aspects of consciousness have problematic as well as purposeful features. It is no accident that our current models of counselling are often divided into those dominated by imagery and metaphor, emotion and reason. Nor does it take much archaeological and anthropological investigation to appreciate the deep and enduring roots of human tribalism and our difficulties in letting go of mistrust of others' ways of life and detaching ourselves from unhelpfully anachronistic loyalties. We are, as Anthony Stevens puts it, 'two million-year-old selves'[7] and our group affiliations have similarly long pedigrees.

Aesculapius (c. 2900 BCE), perceived as a god or magician, reportedly visited sick people in their sleep. Astrologers, sorcerers and magicians were common and according to some writers are the forerunners of all later religious healers, counsellors and psychotherapists. The Bible has many examples of insanity, considered to be caused by sin and possession by evil spirits.

Hippocrates (4th century BCE) is thought to have been the first to shun the idea of supernatural causes, to separate medicine from philosophy, and to categorise different kinds of insanity. Aeschylus first referred to *iatroi logoi* or 'healing words' in about 500 BCE. The Greeks, Zeno, Epicurus and Epictetus, and the Roman Seneca were known for their practical philosophy. In the Dark Ages the insane were often considered visionaries but were also feared and hated. From about the 13th century special hospitals appeared, compassion gradually increased (if alternating with abuse). At the end of the 18th century Pinel introduced his classificatory system, and Tuke established The Retreat in York. Vagrancy and 'lunacy' were entwined concepts. The point of these few historical examples is simply to demonstrate that counselling (if under different names) has a very long past and that its ingredients have always included a mixture of religion, myth, superstition, medicine and philosophy. We are still susceptible to this mixture today.

Psychological thought has been said by some to have commenced with Pythagoras in about 530 BCE. Others nominate Hippocrates and Galen. In the 19th century CE, Wilhelm Wundt moved back and forth between introspection and experiment in his development of psychology, William James studied the stream of consciousness,[8] and yet others like Galton, Pavlov and Binet sought to promote psychology as the 'science of mental life'. Curiously, just as psychology has downplayed its roots in philosophy, so psychotherapy and counselling have downplayed or remained ignorant of theirs in philosophy. Ellenberger made some attempt to acknowledge the powerful contributions of early Greek philosophers.[9] More recently some cognitive and existentialist counsellors have acknowledged similar (and more recent) sources. Seldom does a contemporary philosopher bid for philosophy to be acknowledged as therapeutic but Martha Nussbaum's *The Therapy of Desire* does just that, drawing scholarly attention to Hellenistic ethics including texts by Aristotle, Epicurus, Lucretius and Seneca on emotion, attitude, love, Scepticism and Stoicism.[10]

The British Psychological Society was founded in 1901 and clinical psychology dates from the 1950s when it coexisted and negotiated with both psychiatry and psychoanalysis. Analysing the claims of psychologists to be engaged in natural science based on valid experimental procedures, R.B. Joynson concluded long ago that psychology improves little if at all on common sense.[11] Academic, so-called scientific psychology is still often fiercely distinguished from 'folk psychology' by academics. Probably a majority of academic psychologists are either wary of psychoanalysis (which can also be referred to as psychoanalytic psychology and sometimes depth psychology) or downright dismissive of it. Yet in spite of BPS and Health and Care Professions Council (HCPC) controls over professional titles, no one can ban the use of various adjectives to imply linkage with or endorsement by 'psychology'. In some UK universities, programmes of analytical (Jungian) psychology are found and perhaps tolerated or humoured, as well as integral (Wilberian) psychology, and transpersonal, personal construct, humanistic, feminist, coaching, and positive psychologies. In rare cases university-based psychologists like Ian Parker reject conventional psychology altogether, moving through so-called critical psychology to a politicised position demanding radical changes in its practice.[12]

A significant moment in the development of the talking therapies was the Foster Report in 1971, which analysed scientology (itself with roots in Ron Hubbard's *Dianetics*, published in 1950) and warned of its dangers as a pseudo-psychotherapy. This was followed in 1978 by the Sieghart Report which first spurred action on the regulation of psychotherapists. This was the same time frame in which BACP had its origins. We should note that while no professional body has ever come up with a precise definition of counselling and psychotherapy, anxieties about distancing from scientology and establishing themselves as kosher, ethical professions (rather than dangerous cults) remain.

Both psychoanalysis and psychotherapy sound as if they are psychology-related (not to mention psychiatry-related) and to the public ear may be hard to clearly distinguish. But the former two disciplines have developed mainly outside the world of psychology and psychologists. Cognitive psychology and cognitive behavioural therapy fit into the ethos of academic psychology far better than most of those on the above list, except for personal construct and positive psychologies (and to some extent coaching psychology, for its commercial sector market opportunities). I believe it is fair to say that academic psychology by its controlled cerebral nature and its alignment with conventional culture cannot usually accommodate messy studies of emotional, dramatic, subjective and spiritual phenomena and countercultural values. This is not to say it cannot embrace experimental studies of, say, emotional states or claims to transpersonal experience, but it cannot do so via purely subjective participation, having nailed its colours to the mast of a putative objective science of human behaviour. Hence, clinical psychology largely supports psychological therapy but can only do so for as long as it sits on pillars of empirical evidence.

A striking peculiarity of the world of most of the talking/ psychological therapies (in the UK at least) is that these have developed somewhere outside of or in uneasy coexistence with academia, in a zone of combined entrepreneurial and folk-psychological interests, yet at the same time they remain just outside the zone of deeply suspect therapeutic and healing arts like psychic counselling, angelology, astrology, crystal therapy and scientology.[13] Almost certainly there are little discussed gender, class and cultural factors at play here. It has often been said that part of the success of counselling is simply due to the friendlier sound of the word when compared with psychotherapy or clinical psychology. Class and snobbery may operate here, with some people conversely being reassured by the scientific and professional ring of the latter terms.

Perhaps we can say that the psy-professions have 'evolved' according to perceived social needs, professional self-interests, and within a certain time and place. While they continue to evolve and adapt, great difficulty exists in rational, transparent revision and planning. By some entropy-like principle, they all become more complex in time, and are forced to reinvent themselves frequently as well as being forced by competition for resources and credibility to resort to more and more desperate and absurd tactics for survival. Representatives of all the psy-professions do not say, 'We're all after the same enhancement of mental health so let's abandon our historical baggage and pretences, and our pecking order, pool our resources and radically reshuffle'. Instead absurd battles over definitions, expertise and titles abound. And due to this state of affairs we seem doomed to live with obfuscations surrounding what is psychotherapy and what is counselling, for example. Every so often definitional battles (with muted background anxieties about jobs and salaries) erupt, sounding all too much like Hans Christian Andersen's tale of the emperor's clothes or like the silly arguments in Jonathan Swift's *Gulliver's Travels*. In many other circumstances we would call these behaviours childish and dishonest yet here we appear to take the implausible seriously.

Rather than wearily repeating such perennially unresolved definitional battles, I often use certain terms interchangeably and readers will realise that many texts illustrating our critical themes bear the titles of psychotherapy, counselling and/or counselling psychology. Differences of view about these are legion and the picture becomes even more complicated if we note that what passes as psychotherapy in the USA is frequently practised as counselling in the UK; the British Association for Counselling and Psychotherapy makes no distinction; the person-centred approach usually makes no distinction; and many training courses and textbooks happily use both terms in their titles. Brief dynamic psychotherapy can be shorter than some counselling; Frank Lake's pastoral counselling (or clinical theology), concentrating on maternal-foetal distress syndrome, was nothing if not deep; cognitive behavioural psychotherapy probably lacks the depth that may be found in person-centred counselling; counsellors are often found working with complex and deep issues, just as many psychotherapists are found working in counselling agencies. An entire sideshow of literature about alleged distinctions is however available.[14]

Brief history of critiques of therapy

Provisional explanations for the workings of the universe, nature and society have been constantly revised. Both the practices and theologies of religions have had to adapt to new knowledge and social changes, while trying to retain founding revelations. The Buddha found the religion of his time wanting, Jesus critiqued

Judaism, and so it goes. Ancient Greek philosophers competed with each other, and philosophy down the ages has produced swathes of criticism and reformulations of earlier philosophies. If accounts of the evolutionary embeddedness of our many flaws are true, then understandably whatever we do to attempt to correct our problems, we carry forward those flaws: there is always a fly in the ointment.

A significant article by Albee in 1990 summarised several critiques[15] of the mental health professions. He spoke of the 'unbridgeable gap between the enormous number of people with serious emotional problems and the small number of therapists available' in the USA (p. 370/124). One NIMH calculation at that time had it that 19 per cent of the population had a diagnosable psychiatric condition. This excluded diagnoses like psychosexual problems, and also family members affected by all this distress. Given the necessarily small proportion of therapists and the typical length of therapy, none but the affluent would receive therapy. Therapy 'does nothing to reduce the incidence of distress in the population'.[16] All in all, psychotherapy was in his view futile. Now this account nicely segues into the UK experience. Since the 1970s we have had a growing mass of counsellors, with counselling often being perceived, rightly or wrongly, as a kind of accessible, short-term folk psychotherapy.

The 'happiness czar' Lord Richard Layard's well-known government-backed initiative in 2006 to train and install legions of CBT therapists to deliver evidence-based cost-effective therapy within the NHS's new IAPT scheme appears to refute Albee's charge of futility (different continents and 20-plus years notwithstanding). Indeed Layard's associated campaign to promote happiness and the 'science of happiness' will in his fantasy also go some significant way to reducing distress in the population. Unfortunately Layard is a health economist[17] with a naïve faith in CBT and an incomplete grasp of the talking therapies, as well as an astonishingly naïve view of the connection between national happiness and CBT, and its potency to effect enduring happiness. Amid much vacuous UK Government talk in the 2000s about creating happiness and wellbeing, the gap between rich and poor continued to increase and, as authors like Wilkinson and Pickett have made clear, political and economic overhaul is necessary.[18]

Paradoxically, while we in the psy-fields accept and even promote the idea that humans are riven by deep self-deceptive forces, and try to intervene clinically to expose and modify these forces, at another level we act as if these principles do not really impinge on our own and institutional decisions. Practitioners may labour hard with their individual clients to erode layers of anachronistic and irrational beliefs and behaviours and yet in their personal lives experience similar problems, and in their machinations within professional services and regulatory bodies sustain destructive, absurd and irrational beliefs and behaviour year upon year. Part of the problem here too is that we are not only subject to historical constraints that we barely recognise: we are also constrained by the socioeconomic milieu in which we live – capitalism – and by the ongoing negative influence it has on us.[19] Every form of counselling rests on principles of individual resourcefulness, on the belief that whatever your circumstances you have sufficient autonomy to make a positive difference to your own life and possibly to the lives of others. This is a seductive, motivating belief. All theories of counselling contain or assume a large measure of individual freedom, yet this is highly questionable. But counselling is part of a liberal society of believers in self-determination, democracy, anti-determinism, and nobody is in a position to convince over-optimistic counsellors that their own and their clients' choices are more constrained than they think.

Some key critics and their perspectives

Freud had many critics in his own day, such as Karl Kraus, and psychoanalysis has borne much of the brunt of criticism due to its relatively long history. The Nobel Prize-winning biologist Peter Medawar made a judgement on psychoanalysis that still resounds down the decades and might be applied to most forms of talking and complementary therapies: 'doctrinaire psychoanalytic theory is the most stupendous confidence trick of the twentieth century'.[20]

Jerome Frank's *Persuasion and Healing* was first published in 1961[21] and although not strictly speaking a critique of psychotherapy, it was a cogent analysis of therapeutic claims and remains a classic text. Frank looked for common factors across diverse Western therapies but included some forms of religious healing. He concluded that for success clients need to have confidence in their therapist. The caring and empathy of the practitioner are reinforced by his social-professional status, which inspires confidence. These factors create the successful therapeutic relationship. The second ingredient is the sanctioned setting for healing, which forms part of the sense of a special ritual. The third is an optimistic myth (Frank's own provocative term) containing explanations for things going wrong and how they are corrected. The fourth ingredient is a set of tasks and procedures. Frank acknowledges that hope and belief are generated by therapists and these resemble placebos.

Paul Halmos's *The Faith of the Counsellors* [22] remains a landmark publication. In it, Halmos as a British sociologist showed a keen awareness of psychotherapy and counselling as rapidly expanding social phenomena. His analysis centres on the discrediting of politics in the mid-20th century along with the growth of many psychotherapies. Around that time religion, or at least traditional Christianity, had also started to decline. For all its flaws and pretences, counselling appeared to have a faith of its own based on love.

Several sociologists expressed discomfort at the perceived uncritical rise of the therapeutic with its emphasis on the self. Philip Rieff's *The Triumph of the Therapeutic*,[23] published in 1966, offered a sociological analysis of the decline of Christian moral authority and political engagement, summarised as the impoverishment of Western culture. Rieff regarded therapy as having altered the balance of society towards illusions of psychoaffective freedoms. Feeling, as an imperative, displaced moral commitment. Christopher Lasch in 1979[24] published his concerns with therapy's tendency to turn society inwards in *The Culture of Narcissism*. Like Rieff, Lasch lamented the loss of a sense of history, saw narcissism as a metaphor for the human condition, and spoke of the 'banality of pseudo-self-awareness'. Unlike Rieff he observed a 'flight from feeling', a 'cult of intimacy' and a false consciousness as part of a dying culture.

The sociologist Nikolas Rose began his analysis of the ways in which psychology has come to engineer our subjectivity into regulated forms of experience and behaviour by examining the psychology used in World War Two and afterwards in morale boosting. Contented workers, quality of working life and effective managers also required psychological input. Citizenship, family regulation, psychological testing, studies of attachment, mental health, education and social responsibility all culminate in the pressure to become an apparently free self, shaped increasingly by the values and practices of psychotherapy (and counselling). Psychological therapy is merely one among many psy-professions and 'technologies of the self'. We have succumbed to illusions of personal control and authenticity. The 'codes and vocabularies of psychotherapeutics' promise 'to make it possible for us all to make a project of our biography, create a style for our lives, shape our everyday existence in terms of an ethic of autonomy'.[25]

Philip Cushman's admirably ambitious book *Constructing the Self, Constructing America* chimes well with Rose's account, and also Halmos's. Cushman is himself a therapist but demonstrates an unusual awareness of the extent to which society came to be subtly shaped by therapeutic values and how blind therapists have been to their often adverse influence. 'Some therapists, especially those of the baby boom generation, having given up the hope of massive political change, chose psychotherapy as a profession for a number of humanitarian, altruistic, and personal reasons, including the hope that they could do well (financially) without doing harm (politically)'.[26] Cushman is critical of many psychoanalytic theorists but quite scathing towards humanistic therapies and the human potential movement as overly ahistorical, individualistic and lacking in critical thinking. Finally, Cushman recognises that 'psychotherapy is a rickety, ultimately impossible bridge, but it is one of the few dialogic opportunities available to us'.[27]

Frank Furedi, another critical UK sociologist, has kept up an attacking agenda for many years. Regarding therapy as a culture of emotionalism, he has questioned the growth of privacy, the diminished self, addiction to self-esteem and the idea of the vulnerable self at constant risk. Furedi is alarmed that everything from birth to death seems to have become subject to counselling interventions; he mocks the finding that there are now specialists for helping people cope with bereavement following pet deaths. He is more concerned with the effects of therapeutic expansion than with individual cases of therapy: 'individuals are not so much cured as placed in a state of recovery. They are far more likely to be instructed to acknowledge their problems than to transcend them.'[28] Interestingly Furedi claims that the medicalisation of distress (so objected to by many counsellors) comes not from the medical establishment but from below, that is, from groups of sufferers who benefit from gaining an identity, attention and even legal protection.

Katie Wright's *The Rise of the Therapeutic Society* is unusual, not only in being based on the Australian experience, but also in taking a balanced view. She analyses 'the destabilization of gender and the self; the legitimation of psychological expertise; professional therapeutic intervention into private life; the cultural diffusion of psychological models of reflexive selfhood; the ascendancy of the emotional realm; and, the disruption of the boundaries between public and private life'.[29] Wright's balance lies in asking whether therapeutic culture has not led to less denial about human suffering. Unlike Layard she is not naïve enough to suggest that any form of therapy has the potency to establish happiness on a social scale.

Apart from sociological critiques, in the late 20th century a number of serious critiques appeared that can be broadly divided into those indicting psychoanalytic models and those mocking humanistic models of counselling and psychotherapy. Among stalwart critics we have to number Hans Eysenck and David Smail, both from clinical psychology backgrounds, who for quite different reasons condemned the claims of most therapists. Eysenck's position was always that of the scientist dissatisfied with lack of evidence, while Smail's perspective was philosophical and political. In several publications Smail[30] built a case against pretentious therapeutic models while simultaneously arguing for the political roots of distress to be recognised and addressed. Largely well respected, Smail's work appears nevertheless to have been ignored by the counselling profession. Among enduring critics of psychoanalysis (and implicitly, psychodynamic counselling) are Adolf Grunbaum, Stuart Sutherland, Jeffrey Masson, Frederick Crews and Richard Webster. The humanistic therapies have often been lambasted for their so-called 'psychobabble' and narcissism.[31]

Taken together, the human tendency to suffer psychologically, to cling to tribalistic loyalties, to desperately seek remedies, to deceive and be deceived by shaky epistemologies, are all common enough to warrant deep scepticism in a field like the talking therapies. Therapy and counselling have certain similarities to the hopeful and salvational aspects of religion and politics. It is quite possible that many people are conned, perhaps are even willing to be conned, in counselling, and of course the placebo effect has been studied seriously as a possible contributing factor in the success of counselling. As we are sometimes told by positive psychologists, a thing does not have to be true in order to feel helpful and some illusions may be good for us.

A striking characteristic of counselling is its confidentiality. Usually confidentiality is regarded as so sacrosanct and axiomatically necessary that it sits above critique. One of the effects of confidentiality is that the very activity at the core of our discussion – two individuals sitting in a room discussing the distress or confusion that one is experiencing – is the most private, most subjective and least discussable, disguised case studies notwithstanding. Most writing on counselling is arguably about the peripherals of the profession, the theory, organisation and brouhaha of counselling and counsellors. There are grounds for thinking that Freud distorted his case studies and therefore for wondering to what extent others too may have done so. The highly charged atmosphere of counselling, like the confessional, creates secrecy and this secrecy easily becomes the soil in which great expectations, a sense of mystery, a priesthood of attendants and an edifice of training, research and publications grows. To use another metaphor, it is like a house of cards. If we could show that the actual face-to-face business of counselling is a much more humble, fallible, modest process than our publications suggest, the house of cards [32] – the counselling industry – might tumble. Indeed, it is possibly the reassuring edifice itself that feeds back into the counselling process placebo-wise to reinforce commitment and hope. The client alone with her counsellor, the religious adherent alone with his God – both when their faith is threatened – may well abandon reason and doubt and retreat back into the original faith.

The messy organic way in which psychiatry, psychoanalysis, psychotherapy, clinical psychology, counselling and counselling psychology have evolved leaves us with problems of nomenclature and communication. While there are historical and organisational differences between these professions, the overlaps are vast and are indeed a part of the overall problem of the field to be critiqued. Some regard counselling and psychotherapy as clearly distinct activities (and I shall examine this a little further in Chapter 6) but some, including myself, do not. I may therefore, as mentioned earlier, use any of the terms talking therapy, psychological therapy, therapeutic counselling. psychotherapy, therapy, counselling and counselling psychology (and occasionally psy-professions and psychopractice) with some degree of interchangeability in this book but attempt to be more specific when it really counts.

How and why to think critically

'Critical thinking' has recently become fashionable in higher education but it is largely a commodified, impotent form of critical thinking, as sophistry is to radical political philosophy. Academic authorities do not want students to be *too* intellectually restless. Similarly, 'critical theory' has become somewhat popular academically but its origins in the Frankfurt School in the 1930s were unsettlingly radical. But genuine 'critical theory explores the connections, overlaps, intersections, and interferences between the three spheres of economic development, psychic life, and culture'.[33] Counsellors certainly explore psychic/psychological life and try to be culturally sensitive, but are quite typically uninterested in economic aspects of the human condition.

Therapists are familiar with being attacked and have their own views on why people attack them. One might (perhaps should) question why anyone devotes his time to writing books criticising or deconstructing something instead of being more constructive.

We can, of course, learn a great deal from critique.[34] I want to say something here about forming an understanding of different positions from which critiques are formulated and what may motivate them. Consider the following groups of critics:

Uninformed critics – I have in mind here certain journalists, some sociologists and other pundits who seem to 'have it in' for the talking therapies and who miss no opportunity to parody them, while failing to have any true grasp of them.

Religious and political critics – These may or may not have a sound grasp of therapy but they usually have sincere objections and alternatives to it based on quite different worldviews.

Inter-approach critics – A great deal of critique entails practitioners and theorists from one therapeutic approach questioning, attacking or dismissing others, sincerely or otherwise, well-informed or not, often more openly in private verbal discussion than in the public domain.

Intra-approach critics – Here we have usually sincere practitioners disagreeing with colleagues over points of theory, practice or new developments, either reforming an approach or quitting it to form a new one of their own.

Disaffected intra-approach critics – This group (presumably small, possibly silent) consists of those who had a commitment to and an in-depth knowledge of a therapeutic approach or to the whole field, who come to reject it and possibly put talking therapy behind them altogether.

Interprofessional critics – I refer here to negative perceptions held by each psy-profession of others, for example, the classic psychoanalytic view that psychotherapy and counselling are mostly superficial; the counsellor view that psychologists often lack interpersonal sensitivity, etc.

Ex-clients/users as critics – A small but significant literature by people who have had (usually unsatisfactory) counselling or psychotherapy cannot be called uninformed *or* professional but adds up to a trenchant kind of critique.

Levels and nuances of critique

Rather than imagining critique as some evil intrusion into the wholly benign business of counselling, let us remind ourselves that counselling itself *is* a critique of the unexamined life and different models of counselling are inherently critical of others. A great deal of counselling is critical of everyday inaccurate listening and of the allegedly dehumanising biomedical model. Most counselling trainees will be required in academic assignments to read critically and show critical awareness of flaws in research design and reasoning.

Some critiques are informed by temperamental cynicism and ignorant dismissal of counselling. Some are based on temperamental iconoclasm and contrarianism, bucking against everything in a manner that may sometimes be immature. It is certainly possible for some critique to be driven by unconscious factors – such as many psychoanalysts have accused Masson of – but we need to exercise caution in such judgements. Some critiques, I think, are borne of a natural, innocent curiosity and scepticism. At another level, some critique comes from a disciplined philosophical scepticism, along with a spirit of something like investigative journalism and rigorous scholarship. For some minority, the only kind of critique that counts as weighty is the intellectually deconstructive kind associated with Foucault and other continental thinkers.

Critique can begin in various places. For example, we can examine relevant texts word by word and sentence by sentence to test authors' assumptions, comprehensibility, language use, rhetorical devices, emotional and authoritarian propaganda appeal, faulty logic, flawed heuristics, inconsistencies and so on. Such micro-textual analysis may be needed when closely analysing a research article, for example. Peer reviewers should be checking for these problematic authorial points as well as any flaws in research design. Book reviews are ideal vehicles for succinct critique but are often marred by the reviewer being either over-friendly towards a book (often an undeclared crony of the author) or venomously disposed to rubbish it. Wholesale rejection or endorsement of any article, book, lecture or conference presentation should probably be a rare event; most offerings containing at least some value based on counsellors' merits and demerits.

Quite how critical we are depends on some very basic positions. If we start from the status quo, accepting society as it is with little or no attempt to think about it critically, then we can legitimately argue that the flaws of counselling are not so great, that the enterprise is based on counsellors simply doing their best, plying their trade with as much clinical skill as possible, and committed to continuous improvement. Taking a large step back, we can instead argue that most human societies are flawed by industrial and capitalist mechanisms that cause epidemic psychological distress, and that counselling needs to become much more politically savvy. Taking a further, very large step back, some argue that human beings are deeply, fundamentally flawed by their evolution, biology and perhaps by ontological necessity, in which case the only remedies are probably medical or religious, or we may have to accept that there is no remedy. To some extent, counselling theory can attempt to take on board all but the last position. Writings about counselling rarely address such issues.

It is in the interstices of biological determinism, sociocultural freedom and humanistic-spiritual potential that one finds the sources of the greatest disagreement. Broadly speaking, biological psychiatry and natural science generally take the view that human beings have real limitations and pathologies that will probably respond favourably only to Western medical interventions. History can show that significant social learning and change do take place, for example, in sexist attitudes and violent behaviour, albeit often over long time spans.[35] Theorists and practitioners of counselling position themselves mainly in the humanistic-spiritual potential group, believing that significant individual change is possible beyond biological and social constraints. Hence the common antagonism found against the biomedical stance. The attractive strength of this position is in tension with its tendency to entertain beliefs in a wide range of putative freedoms and unverifiable mental (or holistic) states. The allegedly scientific psychology of the early 20th century was biased towards classical behaviourism, with little if any room for the mind, but gave way to the cognitive trend. The psychoanalytic tradition offers a somewhat ambivalent position on how free as opposed to how determined we are.

Perhaps we then move on to more systematic critiques. In the field of the talking therapies, we face the challenge of sorting assumptions and priorities. When an author writes about her favoured therapeutic model, for example, we might question its starting point. Does it offer to explain its view on human nature and the human condition or are these not relevant? Does it offer a convincing account of how psychological problems arise? Are these contrasted with any vision of the absence or prevention of problems? Is there a sense that the author has grappled with the question of epidemiology, that is, how prevalent psychological problems are? Is there a sense of history, scholarship, clinical acumen, fairness, awareness of other models? Even where an author chooses not to address all such matters, we might ask that she or he explains why not. Given the sprawling nature of our field, we are surely entitled to ask why yet further models are needed and what they add.

All the above are questions that can readily be put by counselling psychologists themselves. We then come to critiques that may be posed by external specialists. Rigorous philosophical analysis of assumptions, reasoning and language problems does not usually come from practitioners. Indeed counsellors may reject or ignore such analyses on the grounds that philosophers as non-clinicians do not really appreciate the fine-grained, moment-by-moment therapeutic phenomena involved (although a fair few philosophy-psychotherapy crossover texts exist).[36] It is also possible that sociologists, psychologists and neurologists may have critiques to offer based on factual inaccuracies or improbabilities. Those of us within the counselling psychology discipline should have the curiosity and humility to seek out and to consider such critical inputs, whether or not we finally agree with them. An overriding challenge here is to reflect on the extent to which we can remain open-minded about new information and perspectives that do not fit our preferred views and that may even threaten us. However idealistic this may sound, the first priority should always be clients' welfare rather than our own comfort or livelihood.

Some counsellors like to gently tease their clients that, equipped though they may be with their toolbox full of skills and techniques, they don't possess a magic wand that can banish their problems or change their personality. Psychodynamic theory includes wry observations of clients' 'magical thinking'. Yet counsellors do not apply rigorous tests of anti-magical thinking to themselves: subscribing to various incomplete and competing theories, they imagine that their professional conversations will have powerful and enduring effects on clients who will then, thus reconstructed, live significantly better lives. In the final chapter of this book I conclude with some thoughts on how counsellors might respond to critiques.

Endnotes

1. Kurtz, P. (2010). *Exuberant Skepticism.* New York: Prometheus.

2. Feltham, C. (2010). *Critical Thinking in Counselling and Psychotherapy.* London: Sage.

3. See for example Burns, J. (2007). *The Descent of Madness: Evolutionary origins of psychosis and the social brain.* London: Routledge; Buss, D. M. (Ed.). (2005). *The Handbook of Evolutionary Psychology.* Hoboken, NJ: Wiley; Gluckman, P., & Hanson, M. (2006). *Mismatch.* Oxford: Oxford University Press; Horrobin, D. (2001). *The Madness of Adam and Eve.* London: Corgi; Stevens, A., & Price, J. (2000). *Evolutionary Psychiatry: New beginnings* (2nd ed.). London: Routledge.

4. Feltham, C. (2007). *What's Wrong with Us? The anthropathology thesis.* Chichester: Wiley.

5. Smail, D. (1993). *The Origins of Unhappiness: A new understanding of personal distress.* London: HarperCollins.

6. Pinker, S. (2003). *The Blank Slate: The modern denial of human nature.* London: Penguin.

7. Stevens, A. (1993). *The Two Million-Year-Old Self.* College Station, TX: Texas A&M University Press.

8. Murphy, G. (1968). *Psychological Thought from Pythagoras to Freud.* New York: Harbinger.

9. Ellenberger, H. (1994). *The Discovery of the Unconscious: The history and evolution of dynamic psychiatry.* New York: Fontana.

10. Nussbaum, M. (2009). *The Therapy of Desire: Theory and practice in Hellenistic ethics* (3rd ed.). Princeton, NJ: Princeton University Press.

11. Joynson, R. B. (1974). *Psychology and Common Sense.* London: Routledge & Kegan Paul.

12. Parker, I. (2007). *Revolution in Psychology: Alienation to emancipation.* London: Pluto.

13. Carroll, R. T. (2003). *The Skeptic's Dictionary.* Hoboken, NJ: Wiley.

14. James, I., & Palmer, S. (Eds.). (1996) *Professional Therapeutic Titles: Myths and realities.* Leicester: British Psychological Society.

15. Albee, G. W. (1990). The futility of psychotherapy. *The Journal of Mind and Behavior, 11*(3&4), 369(123)–384(138).

16. *Ibid.*

17. Layard, R. (2005). *Happiness: Lessons from a new science.* London: Penguin. It may or may not be relevant but Richard Layard is not simply an economist. His father, John Layard (1891–1974) was a distinguished anthropologist who suffered from depression and consulted several therapists, including Homer Lane and Carl Jung. Lane ran into trouble after having sex with a patient. John Layard consulted Jung following a failed suicide attempt; Jung spent some time telling Layard about his own life, including his sex life with Toni Wolff, and later repeatedly told Layard how great he (Jung) was compared with Freud. Layard's wife Doris also had Jungian therapy. As a three-year-old, Richard was with his parents in Zurich. Lord Richard Layard is an old Etonian, an affluent man who argues for greater social equality as part of the 'science of happiness'.

18. Wilkinson, R., & Pickett, K. (2009). *The Spirit Level: Why more equal societies almost always do better.* London: Allen Lane.

19. Fisher, M. (2009) *Capitalist Realism: Is there no alternative?* Winchester: Zero Books. See also Richards, B. (Ed.). (1984). *Capitalism and Infancy: Essays on psychoanalysis and politics.* London: Free Association Books.

20. Medawar, P. B. (1975). Victims of psychiatry. Review of I. S. Cooper – *The Victim Is Always the Same. New York Review of Books*, January 23, p. 17.

21. Frank, J. (1967). *Persuasion and Healing: A comparative study of psychotherapy.* New York: Schocken.

22. Halmos, P. (1965). *The Faith of the Counsellors.* London: Constable.

23. Rieff, P. (2006). *The Triumph of the Therapeutic* (40th anniversary ed.). Wilmington, DE: ISI Books.

24. Lasch, C. (1991). *The Culture of Narcissism* (rev. ed.). New York: Norton.

25. Rose, N. (1989). *Governing the Soul: The shaping of the private self.* London: Routledge, p. 254.

26. Cushman, P. (1995). *Constructing the Self, Constructing America: A cultural history of psychotherapy.* Cambridge, MA: Perseus, p. 280.

27. *Ibid.,* p. 356.

28. Furedi, F. (2004). *Therapy Culture: Cultivating vulnerability in an uncertain age.* London: Routledge.

29. Wright, K. (2011). *The Rise of Therapeutic Society: Psychological knowledge and the contradictions of cultural change.* Washington, DC: New Academia, p. 5.

30. For example, Smail, D. (2001). *The Nature of Unhappiness.* London: Robinson, and Smail, D. (2005). *Power, Interest and Psychology.* Ross-on-Wye: PCCS Books.

31. See for example, Clare, A., & Thompson, S. (1981) *Let's Talk about Me: A critical examination of the new psychotherapies.* London: British Broadcasting Corporation; Kaminer, W. (1992). *I'm Dysfunctional, You're Dysfunctional.* New York: Addison-Wesley; Rosen, R. D. (1977). *Psychobabble: Fast talk and quick cure in the era of feeling.* London: Wildwood House; Singer, M. T., & Lalich, J. (1996). *Crazy Therapies.* San Francisco: Jossey-Bass. A more recent, concise and balanced critique is given by Totton, N. (2010). *The Problem with the Humanistic Therapies.* London: Karnac.

32. Dawes, R. (1994). *House of Cards: Psychology and psychotherapy built on myth.* New York: Free Press.

33. Buchanan, I. (2010). *Oxford Dictionary of Critical Theory.* Oxford: Oxford University Press.

34. Feltham, C. (1999) Facing, understanding and learning from critiques of psychotherapy and counselling. *British Journal of Guidance and Counselling, 27*(3), 301–312.

35. Pinker, S. (2011). *The Better Angels of Our Nature: The decline of violence in history and its causes.* London: Allen Lane.

36. For example, Heaton, J. (2010). *The Talking Cure: Wittgenstein's therapeutic method for psychotherapy.* London: Palgrave Macmillan; Howard, A. (2000). *Philosophy for Counselling and Psychotherapy: Pythagoras to postmodernism.* Basingstoke: Macmillan; and Mace, C. (Ed.). (1999). *Heart and Soul: The therapeutic face of philosophy.* London: Routledge.

CHAPTER 2

Key figures in counselling psychology

As in most fields of endeavour, counselling and its theoretical structure is characterised by the work and personalities of many admired founders or creators. Most of these came from Europe (many from Germany, Austria and Switzerland) and subsequently the USA. The vast majority have been men, indeed eminent white males, and a disproportionate number have been Jewish. Often referred to as inspired, talented or even geniuses, they usually had a small number of close colleagues and were followed by admiring 'disciples' and later by waves of loyal followers who developed and updated their original theories. Often early schisms characterised the history of distinct counselling and psychotherapeutic movements, male characters falling out with each other over matters of belief and ambition. The main focus of this chapter is on a small number of the key founders and the problems we are faced with when reading their biographies and accounts of their contributions to this field and to the history of ideas and science generally.

The huge overlap between counselling and psychotherapy makes for some difficulty in deciding exactly who to nominate as key figures. Given the large influence of psychodynamic counselling, Freud must certainly feature prominently here. Within the psychodynamic tradition, Melanie Klein and Donald Winnicott have contributed significantly to theory, training and practice. Given the influence of Carl Jung on the burgeoning transpersonal counselling movement, I will include some brief pertinent remarks on him. Some would argue that counselling is marked most prominently by certain humanistic founders and theorists. We could include here many American big names including psychologists like Abraham Maslow and European and American founder-practitioners such as Wilhelm Reich, Jacob Moreno, Roberto Assagioli and Arthur Janov. Reich was a hugely controversial figure whose ambitions to unite psychoanalysis and Marxism brought him great trouble, whose 'orgone accumulators' and probably far-fetched theories led to his imprisonment. Janov has been criticised for his enduring belief that he alone is correct, and for his unwillingness to cooperate with other professionals in the field of psychotherapy. But I will mainly concentrate here on Carl Rogers, then somewhat on Fritz Perls and Eric Berne, since the person-centred approach (PCA), gestalt therapy and transactional analysis (TA) are particularly well known within the ranks of counsellors and in typical integrative training courses. In the common tripartite organisation into psychodynamic, humanistic and cognitive behavioural models, I shall also make brief reference to Albert Ellis. I also include significant and sometimes colourful characters like Masud Khan and R.D. Laing for reasons given below. The above organisation is of course an editorial compromise that will not satisfy all readers.

As well as casting a spotlight on these individuals we would do well to ask what social and cultural conditions made it possible or necessary for them to arise. What conditions caused Freud to create psychoanalysis when and where he did? What was it about Austria, Germany and Switzerland in the late 19th century that led to the birth of psychoanalysis? Why has Jewishness had such an impact on the field and what subtle influence might Judaism have on theory? (Are most therapeutic models quasi-rabbinic narratives of suffering and hope?)[1] Why is psychotherapy so concentrated in Europe and North America? Why is psychoanalysis so concentrated on the east coast and the humanistic therapy movement on the west coast of the USA? Why are the founders almost all white males? We don't have answers to all these questions (although some are fairly obvious and some are factual) but I suspect they are all important and that the scholarship of posterity will provide answers.

Characteristics of leading figures

It is perfectly feasible that those who create systems or models of counselling are completely sincere and truthful in all their endeavours. In a spirit of enquiry and critique, what then should we be asking about them that is relevant here? Let me propose the following set of questions that we might pose or remember as we examine the lives and contributions of these founding figures:

1. What distinct personal experience and knowledge did he bring to the creation of his theory?

2. What motivated him to create a new approach rather than remaining satisfied with what existed?

3. From what sources did he draw his new ideas and material (experience, insight, experiment, inspirational innovation, scientific discoveries, etc.)?

4. To what extent did he benefit personally, financially and reputationally from his position?

5. What is the evidence that this is someone of integrity and unselfish dedication to the professional field and to the amelioration of human suffering?

6. To what extent did he involve colleagues in his work and attribute to them even-handedly significant roles and due credit?

7. In what ways did he himself embody or contradict the tenets of his clinical approach and the ethics of the profession?

8. With what degree of openness and honesty did he and his colleagues, followers and biographers present and revise data accurately, make findings transparent and cooperate with researchers?

9. In retrospect, how well does his contribution to knowledge and the advancement of practices designed to ameliorate human suffering hold up?

It would be disingenuous of me to pretend to believe that all, most or perhaps any of our key figures stand up to such scrutiny unscathed. Certainly Jeffrey Masson[2] came to the conclusion that one has only to scratch the surface of any and the flaws will appear. Anthony Storr ranked some psychotherapists alongside abusive religious leaders as gurus.[3] David Livingstone Smith, referring to himself as having been an insider in the psychotherapy and counselling profession for 20 years, claims that 'it is a sad fact that many psychotherapists are deeply troubled individuals whose lives are riven by emotional conflicts, psychological symptoms and chaotic interpersonal relationships'.[4]

According to Smith, neither suicides nor unethical breaches of boundaries and confidentiality have been uncommon in the profession. Between 1902 and 1938 when the Vienna Psychoanalytic Society existed, 9 out of 149 of its members killed themselves. Well-known therapist suicides have included Charles B. Truax in 1973, Bruno Bettelheim in 1990, Petruska Clarkson in 2006, and many lesser-known examples exist. In James Guy's analysis of therapist suicides, predisposition, work-related factors (isolation is key) and life events appear uppermost.[5] The suicide rate of therapists is probably somewhat higher than that in the general population and we must wonder about the link with the original attraction to the profession. Therapists have also not been outstandingly good examples of parenthood.[6] We can certainly argue that no one has to be expected to pass any such tests of saintliness. But we cannot ignore a certain onus of honesty.

We might as a matter of curiosity ask why we accord high status to some and not others. For example, Ron Hubbard, the founder of Dianetics and scientology, seems fair game for scepticism and for being written off as a fake by many. Harvey Jackins, (a one-time associate of Hubbard's), the creator of re-evaluation counselling, has been accused of abuse, authoritarianism, profiteering and quackery. Ronald Laing is depicted as a wild card who often behaved unethically but who retains a reputation as a serious figure in existentialist therapy and anti-psychiatry. Likewise, Fritz Perls is known to have behaved unacceptably with certain clients but that has had no lasting negative impact on gestalt therapy.

Some key figures fade from view altogether while others fascinate us for decades, and some attain a status that is akin to genius and quasi-sainthood (e.g., Freud and Rogers respectively). Why?

Sigmund Freud

The contribution of Freud (1856–1939) is so well documented and debated that it is difficult to produce a concise critical account that escapes repetition or accusations of bias or ignorance. The esteem in which Freud was and is still held by many sometimes amounts to setting him alongside key historical thinkers like Copernicus and Darwin. He is often referred to as a genius. But as Borch-Jacobsen and Shamdasani[7] argue from historical texts and archived material, Freud himself helped to cultivate this image in various speeches and papers. Furthermore, so much of the reputation and status of psychoanalysis (and psychoanalytic psychotherapy and psychodynamic counselling) rests on the person of Freud, his acclaimed self-analysis and his integrity, that we must consider how all this is to be evaluated. Look at the damning claim of Borch-Jacobsen and Shamdasani:

> Studies have shown to what extent Freud's 'observations' and case histories were at times selective, tendentious and even dishonest. Freud, one learns, did not hesitate to modify or to conceal this or that biographical element to fit his theory, to take liberties with chronology and translation, to present self-analytical accounts as objective cases supposedly interpreted through brilliant detective work, or to present imaginary therapeutic results whilst proclaiming the therapeutic superiority of psychoanalysis to other forms of psychotherapy.[8]

As these authors remind us, all such critiques are routinely rebutted by psychoanalytic loyalists on various grounds, preventing any progress in clarification and agreement on facts. It must be self-evident that if accusations such as the above are true – demonstrating that the man who allegedly single-handedly discovered the unconscious was often (or even sometimes) dishonest – then the very least of consequences should be lively scepticism.

Well over a century of clinical literature and practice and the financing and hopes of suffering individuals are at stake here. But this is not only about dishonesty; it is also about arrogance and absurdity. When a system of training analysis was instituted in 1912 everyone had to submit to it except Freud, which engendered a series of letters and accusations against and by Freud. Of Freud's singular exemption from the requirement to be analysed by another on the basis of his own self-analysis, Ferenczi said that Freud had the necessary strength to overcome unconscious forces 'for the first time in the history of mankind'.[9] Freud was here regarded not only as a genius or pioneer but virtually a superman, somewhat like Jesus Christ, being capable, unlike all other human beings, of resisting the pull of sin. This is an enormously important point to clarify. Does anyone seriously believe Freud to have been anything like an infallible superman above doubt? Freud allowed others around him to believe this nonsense, and the logic of his position allowed psychoanalysis to claim a chain of purity (the removal of neuroses) from singular originator to generations of appointed disciples, rather like the chain from Jesus through Peter to the present pope. Readers can formulate their own conclusions but clearly one obvious inference is that this was and remains nonsense and is no foundation for psychoanalysis, psychodynamic counselling or any other 21st century claim to science or to a legitimate model of psychological help.

Let's consider briefly a few other relevant phenomena that have their origins in the personality and machinations of Freud himself. Many others who were contemporary with Freud such as Janet, Breuer, Vogt and Frank hypothesised and put into practice notions of childhood sexuality, hypnosis, catharsis and talking therapy. Freud often claimed not to have read such theorists but the record suggests he did, and further that he was quite capable of plagiarism. According to Borch-Jacobsen and Shamdasani, Freud greatly discouraged criticism, indeed excluded from his orbit known dissenters, sometimes accusing Adler and others of paranoia – 'the pathologisation of dissent'.[10] Amid the proprietorial struggles, with Freud at their centre, there was constant rivalry and there were also accusations of damage being done to some clients.

We might retort that this is all mere historical flummery and of little significance to present-day psychotherapeutic and counselling practice which has changed hugely over the last century. We can certainly say that it is now irrelevant that psychoanalysis never needed the 'o' in the middle, being referred to more correctly by many as 'psychanalysis'. Even now some critics who should know better refer incorrectly to scream therapy (for primal therapy), to rational emotive therapy (which became rational emotive behaviour therapy in 1993) and to Rogerian therapy, inaccuracies that suggest ignorance and mockery. Similarly, we can suggest that the modern title 'couples counselling' should clearly be *couple* counselling. But aren't these extremely pedantic points? Of course a point like this is pedantic but I argue that in the often misty domain of psychotherapy and counselling, detail is important. If Freud falsified even some of his case studies, which we are told he did, then we are justified in worrying about the veracity of all case studies, since they form such a large part of the persuasive folklore of the profession. If Freud and his followers distorted theory to suit the purposes of establishing 'an international company based on franchises'[11] we are right to question the principles that underpin psychodynamic counselling.

As a man, we know that Freud was not attracted to therapeutic work for altruistic reasons, nor was he a lover of or optimistic about humankind. He was ambitious, fell out with collaborators, sometimes failed to acknowledge the work of others, and did not tolerate criticism. Some of his patients reported that he did not pay them full attention but appeared more interested in theorising than helping. He had a well-known addiction to cocaine and later to smoking, which led to fatal cancer of the jaw.

Carl Rogers

Rogers (1902–1987) was born into an almost fundamentalist Christian household in Chicago. Switching his studies from agriculture to history, theology and then psychology, he moved into working with children, encountered and rejected most behavioural and psychoanalytic ideas but was influenced by the theories of Otto Rank. Becoming a professor of psychology at 37, he gradually formulated his own ideas on non-directive counselling. He was doubtful about the power of psychiatrists and also battled with the professional psychology establishment. Unlike Freud and many others, Rogers was eagerly involved in empirical research, using audio-recordings to analyse and theorise the therapeutic process.

Rogers is held in great affection by most who knew him and by many counselling trainees and counsellors who never met him. He was 'known' to many through the training videos 'Gloria' and 'Kathy'. I have heard dozens of female students express their admiration for this man who appeared to be so warm and attentive to his clients. He is sometimes spoken of as avuncular, perhaps as the kind of father many women wish they had had and the kind of attentive partner they would like. He was also, of course, an eminent psychologist who created a wholly new approach to counselling/psychotherapy and advocated new approaches to marriage, education and other domains, and was nominated for the Nobel Peace Prize. Lionised and idealised, was Rogers too good to be true?

One of the few recorded negative reactions to Rogers as a person came from R.D. Laing. He described Rogers as 'one of the least personable people' he had ever met. Laing tried to 'get Rogers and his group to admit the darker side of human nature' and alluded to their 'California nice-guy bullshit'.[12] One apocryphal account has it that Rogers denied to Laing he 'had ever felt the evil rising within him'. Another commentator has spoken of him as 'guilty of innocence'. Rollo May, the existentialist psychotherapist, berated Rogers for ignoring the problem of human destructiveness, and in particular for failing to respond to the famous psychological experiments of Milgram and Zimbardo demonstrating common human violence. It may well be that his receiving research funds from the CIA for 10 years for sitting on the Society for the Investigation of Human Ecology was an example of simple naïvety, or not. David Cohen, in a critical biography that some have found offensively sensationalist, often using speculation and innuendo and lacking evidence (they say), suggests that Rogers had an on-and-off drink problem, was in later life unfaithful to his wife, was over-optimistic in his research with children and people diagnosed as schizophrenics, was out of his depth in treating a schizophrenic woman and was gullible when it came to the flaky writings of Carlos Castaneda and other early New Age pioneers.[13]

Cohen credits him overall as 'one of the most important psychologists of the 20th century'[14] despite his tendency for swapping 'the Id for Pollyanna'. Masson acknowledges Rogers' 'benevolence' but finds him extremely naïve in his grasp of work with schizophrenia and with traumatic events generally, as well as failing to speak out against the abuses of psychiatric patients.[15] The feminist therapist Betty McLellan recognises the importance of Rogers' contribution but is critical of his 'rather patronising tone, at times, and the beginnings of a language that was soon to develop into rampant psychobabble'.[16] Far less is written about Rogers than Freud but one can see the same split between uncritical hagiography and damning biography: one of the most important among men on the one hand, deeply flawed on the other.

The American psychotherapist Arnold Lazarus complained that on witnessing Rogers at work (mainly on video), he was always the same, always acting in the same relational style, which Lazarus took as a serious limitation. Most who knew Rogers attested to his genuineness, some finding him naïve and shy. Unlike Freud, he could not be accused of arrogance and deviousness. If anything we might see Rogers as simply appearing at the right time in American psychology, one of the hopeful humanistic psychologists of his time, with his heart in the right place. There are grounds for doubting, however, if his ideas and research on child development, schizophrenia, group encounters, education, relationships and conflict resolution will stand the test of time. Rogers' writings on the 'person of tomorrow' and the 'fully functioning person', on human beings as trustworthy, have a feel-good quality but lack realism and concreteness. The mythically saintly Rogers and his optimistic message require as much critical analysis as any other purveyor of therapeutic concepts.

It is because Rogers' person-centred approach has had such a huge influence on counselling in the UK from the 1970s that we must not uncritically accept him. As Masson puts it:

> An examination of the work of Carl Rogers reveals nothing of the kind of excess we found in some of the other therapists … He is not guilty of the kinds of abuse we saw in John Rosen or Albert Honig. Although he lacked the profundity of Freud and the sensitivity of Ferenczi, he was nonetheless representative of 'humane' psychotherapy as it is practised today in the United States. … The faults of Carl Rogers are not unlike the faults to be found in the average therapist.[17]

I am afraid to say that a large part of Rogers' charm may be based on his middle-of-the-road approach. Fond of generalising about organisms and humans as actualising, Rogers neither exhibited nor cited any biological detail in his theory. While ostensibly steeped in phenomenological method, he had, in the view of McCall, a rather weak grasp of phenomenology.[18] Having had great hopes of making a mark on the understanding and treatment of schizophrenia, the results of his research in Wisconsin led him to quietly retreat from these anti-psychiatric efforts. While seemingly at the forefront of humanistic therapy in the 1970s, Rogers managed to remain a low-risk-taking therapist whose clients achieved little of the emotional intensity of Reichian, gestalt, psychodrama or primal therapies. While increasingly attracted to the mystical, Rogers avoided both traditional Christianity and Buddhism[19] and while the person-centred approach is theoretically suggestive of the politics of radical anti-authoritarianism, we find little of the fiery Reich, of the politically articulate Fromm, or the oppression-addressing Jackins in the work or person of Carl Rogers. Arguably, the appeal of Rogers' PCA is in its moderately feel-good, very mildly challenging, intellectually non-demanding character.

And other prominent figures

Melanie Klein (1882–1960), clever and innovative as she was, had some serious problems including depression, narcissism and a bad marriage. She began analysis of her son Erich when he was five and later wrote about him in disguised form. She also analysed her son Hans. Many people described her as cold and ungiving. Her daughter Melitta, who she also analysed and wrote about, later accused Klein of brainwashing her clients into subservience and helplessness. Her son Hans died at 27, there being speculation about possible suicide. When Klein died, Melitta did not attend her funeral. Perhaps what today would be considered unethical practice and even abusive parenting was not so understood by the standards of the time. But the fact that Klein was advancing theories on object relations and child development and is hailed as a great innovator in this field does clash dramatically with many of the facts of her life. The practice developed in her name is often criticised for the apparent coldness of the therapist, which may reflect Klein's own personality.

Donald Winnicott (1896–1971) remains a much-praised figure in the psychodynamic world, in some ways portrayed as a rather saintly character whose paediatric work informed the development of theories of mother–child relations. Yet Brett Kahr[20] claims to have reliable information that Winnicott was sexually impotent in a 25-year marriage, that some of his patients committed suicide, and some of his clinical boundaries were very elastic. Kahr's work here is particularly interesting in pointing out the constraints on biographers of such figures caused by concern that their patients would be upset by negative revelations. Kahr hints that he had more such information that he felt he had to withhold. Gomez[21] suggests that Winnicott was a kind of Peter Pan figure, a loner, shrewdly self-interested, who remained oddly silent in his optimistic writings about the two world wars he lived through.

Masud Khan (1924–1989), trained by Winnicott, was an eminent, published and controversial psychoanalyst alleged to have ignored boundaries with trainees, had sex with them, had a drink problem, lied and was boastful. Famously, Khan is reported to have told Jeffrey Masson that he knew too much and if he talked openly about others in the psychoanalytic establishment it would bring about the end of British psychoanalysis. Khan is not of much importance to counselling but is included here to remind us that practitioners, both well-known and low profile, can be aberrant and their behaviour may not always come to light due to institutional collusion. Indeed, such is the pressure 'not to bring the profession into disrepute' and not to trust anecdotal evidence, that probably a great deal of negative common knowledge goes unheeded.

Carl Jung (1875–1961), at one time Freud's closest associate, became the originator of analytical psychology (also known as Jungian psychotherapy). His approach was far less influential than Freud's for many years but has enjoyed quite a renaissance. Its relevance for this book is partly to illustrate the characters of founders but more importantly to underline the trend in counselling towards transpersonal or spiritual themes.[22] A Swiss psychiatrist working with schizophrenic patients, Jung came to utilise mythology, theology, anthropology, alchemy, the Chinese *I-Ching*, and astrology for both theoretical and clinical purposes. Acknowledged as charismatic, he was sometimes considered telepathic, a great healer, and he was certainly intellectually fecund. But Jung has also been referred to as brutal, secretive, cold, borderline, anti-Semitic and racist, often talked about his own preoccupations directly with patients, bullied some, and had sex with some of them. He was ambitious to see his own therapeutic approach overtake Freud's psychoanalysis, which caused him to delay judging the Nazis' position. In line with contemporary counselling norms, Jung showed relatively little interest in politics but great fascination with spiritual matters. Undeniably highly imaginative, he had gone through a period of so-called creative breakdown. It is difficult to say whether Jung will be finally judged an attractive visionary, a megalomaniac, or a modest contributor to practical therapy and counselling.

Fritz Perls (1893–1970) is the pre-eminent founder of gestalt therapy. Disliked by his own father, he yet became an uncaring father himself by most accounts. He is also known to have had sex with some of his clients and possibly to have played some part in driving one or two to suicide. Even sympathetic biographers agree he was often needy, jealous, and a grandiose showman. His restless or energetic character took him travelling to many parts of the world and gestalt therapy itself is an eclectic amalgam of gestalt psychology, existentialism, Zen Buddhism, psychodrama, Reichian non-verbal techniques and Buberian dialogue, not to mention the psychoanalytic principles in which he first trained. A small point perhaps, but Perls was a lifelong chain smoker, even in clinical sessions (see him in the Gloria film).[23] Many regarded him as anti-intellectual and guru-like and he did indeed dress flamboyantly and often act unpredictably. When living in South Africa he had a luxurious house complete with swimming pool, not exactly a man of the people. He had four analyses, one of them with Reich, with whom he got on well but about whom posterity has serious reservations.

Subsequent generations of gestalt therapists distance themselves from the 'Perls-ism' characterised by his typically dramatic or 'boom-boom-boom therapy'. They also distance themselves from caricatures of gestalt therapy as technique centred, while many counsellors find the 'empty-chair technique' occasionally useful and non-problematic. Those loyal to Perls remember him as much more than the villainous aspects of his personality, as highly creative, tender and gracious.

Eric Berne (1910–1970) was analysed by Paul Federn and Erik Erikson and drew many of his ideas from them. A medical doctor like his father, he went on to found transactional analysis (TA). Divorced three times, Berne was perceived as quite different by different observers. While forbidding others to smoke, he smoked his pipe constantly. Controlling, shy, nasty, competitive, argumentative, moody and hostile are some of the adjectives used about him. Some say his own script was to find love evasive and an early death inevitable. Like Perls, Berne seems to have had great contrasts in his personality, including many positives. An arguably glaring contrast about Berne is that the man who disliked jargon and wanted to make therapeutic ideas accessible, the man who promoted the principle of human beings as fundamentally 'OK', spawned a model saturated with such an off-puttingly specialised language of psychopathology.

Albert Ellis (1913–2007) founded rational emotive behaviour therapy (REBT) after an earlier career as a sex therapist and psychoanalytic therapist. Overcoming childhood adversities himself, his personality seems to have been thoroughly stoical. He does not appear to have been quite the colourful character that many others here have been but he was always very outspoken, defending free, guiltless love and gay liberation from the earliest of days. He came to find psychoanalytic work slow and unrewarding and turned to philosophy to create REBT. He was extremely critical of other approaches and of clients who wanted therapy to shore up their neurotic ways, but in line with his philosophy/therapy he desisted from damning them. Often thwarted in love and embattled against some colleagues in later life, Ellis worked through illness, showed no signs of the grandiosity of fellow therapy founders and can only be accused of being something of a workaholic and rather too intellectualised for the taste of many others. Ellis preferred to do everything rapidly and consequently his clinical sessions usually lasted only 30 minutes. Some have found Ellis's style of REBT, as a variant of CBT, to be insensitive to more fragile clients. His work, especially in the form of the 'tyranny of the shoulds' and his stress on the importance of hard work (rather than endless talk) towards personal change, is familiar to most counsellors.

R.D. Laing (1927–1989) is important for us here as the leading radical anti-psychiatrist who moved beyond psychoanalysis to draw upon existentialism to establish principles of countercultural authenticity and autonomy. Laing is still significant as a spokesman for people with severe mental health problems or psychoses and he experimented with alternatives to hospital incarceration. He was outspoken, outrageous, occasionally violent, used drugs, drank too much, slept with some clients and often transgressed conventional boundaries. Opposed to the nuclear family but eloquent about suffering within families, Laing had ten children by four different women and has a mixed reputation regarding his sense of responsibility and integrity. His theories about schizophrenogenic families have not persisted and his radical non-interventionist views on mental illness are largely discredited. But notions of the divided self and the mad society probably have endured, and existential counselling certainly owes him a debt. The existentialist approach is one of few to use philosophy rather than psychology as a basis for its practice, and makes freedom, choice, courage, authenticity and acceptance of death central.

We might say that these generations of theorists and founders bore many of the signs of creativity mixed with disregard for social norms; many of them behaved like artists. Much of their work would be considered unethical today. Many of their characteristics undermine any fantasies we might have that those heading up therapeutic enterprises are saintly embodiments of their own concepts.[24] We can ask to what extent the uniqueness of each model reflects the personality of the founder in terms of creative extension or unconscious working out of their own personal problems. It is certainly obvious that huge differences exist, for example, Jung's, Perls' and Laing's charismatic personalities and sprawling theories stand in contrast to the quite sober personalities and fairly straightforward theories of Rogers and Winnicott. Judgements of different models are attempted on the basis of research but probably the majority of students, acolytes and followers judge them by how closely they match their own taste and personality needs. Unfortunately the average client has little knowledge of the theories and the figures behind them, nor much choice about who to see.

A conundrum for counselling psychology

The key figures in our field are predominantly men and a majority are American. But we might ask whether they are predominantly *psychologists* and whether they explicitly utilise psychology (and which variant of psychology). In fact many of the big-name founders are from backgrounds in medicine, neurology, psychiatry and psychoanalysis and even those with roots in psychology, like Rogers, did not follow the standard psychological tradition. Most of them are known as psychotherapists rather than counsellors or counselling psychologists. Counselling psychologists may attempt to promote themselves as respecting human subjectivity but they cannot easily shrug off the mantle of psychology as a science. Now, surely we could expect the ranks of counselling psychologists to include some prominent figures as counselling *psychologists*, that is, explicit users of what psychology is agreed to be? Contrast this situation with recognition of Daniel Kahneman, frequently referred to as 'the world's most distinguished living psychologist'. Do counselling psychology programmes refer much to Kahneman and his work? I doubt it.

Kahneman, in his bestselling *Thinking, Fast and Slow,* surely has some relevant lessons for our field. In his schema, System 1 refers to automatic and intuitive thinking and System 2 to effortful, deliberative thinking. Drawing on Kahneman's work on heuristics, we might say that people (counsellors and clients) are attracted to counselling on the basis of the 'affect heuristic', that is, it feels good, we like it, and these positive feelings can lead us into decisions to spend a lot of money on training or therapy and on defending our decisions against all counter-evidence. Kahneman reckons that psychological therapists are probably good at reading immediate cues in the clinical situation but not good at recognising their errors and limits in the longer term. Examining the 'hostility to algorithms' Kahneman puts it thus:

> The line between what clinicians can do well and what they cannot do at all well is not obvious, and certainly not obvious to them. They know they are skilled, but they don't necessarily know the boundaries of their skill. Not surprisingly, then, the idea that a mechanical combination of a few variables could outperform the subtle complexities of human judgement strikes experienced clinicians as obviously wrong.[25]

I do not know if Kahneman is right or wrong. I'm not sure if his views necessarily support CBT and its emphasis on rationality. But views like his (as formerly those of Hans Eysenck) may have even more significance for this field than the self-confirmatory belief structures of founders and followers of models of psychological therapies. Kahneman himself is from a background in mathematics and the psychology of economic behaviour and those of us who by personality and calling are intuitive, holistic thinkers are unlikely to welcome his appeal to impersonal calculations. But we may be wrong (and, as Kahneman suggests, we may thereby be acting unethically). Ultimately the key figures in addressing our species' epidemic of psychological distress could turn out not to be counselling psychologists themselves (predominantly System 1 thinkers who have a massive sunk-costs commitment to their profession) but System 2 thinkers who work at understanding long-term complexities. These could also include evolutionary psychologists.

Greatness, hierarchy and patriarchy

In spite of the overwhelmingly female majority membership of the counselling world we should not be surprised by its leadership being dominated by males. This presumably reflects gender patterns in other professions and disciplines. But we should be surprised that this has not received more critical attention. Men have sought and gained the limelight which includes, let us remind ourselves, relative fame, kudos, influence, wealth and international travel for the founders. We might want to depict Rogers as doing arduous but necessary globe-trotting in the course of saving the world but he enjoyed the travel and the adulatory buzz of it all. A fair proportion of leaders of psychological therapies have exhibited some of the features of charisma, eccentricity, craziness, dogmatism, abusive and exploitative behaviour, dishonesty, fraudulence and anarchistic traits. Of course we can argue that such failings have no necessary correlation with the greatness of their discoveries and creations. We can argue that in any field the genius runs some risk of peculiarity or madness. Perhaps in counselling, however, we need to think twice about accepting this state of affairs. We might also wonder why the flaws of the greats can be hidden for so long. A fear of reprisals, libel suits and unemployment might help to explain some of this. But the privacy surrounding counselling is also a central factor, as is the loyalty and collusion of followers. All these factors contribute to keeping leaders' foibles and failings hidden.

Let us now, however, correct the impression that our field is characterised by a small number of power-seeking men surrounded by mistakenly loyal or uncritical followers. There are the second- and third-generation torch-bearers, those who often vigorously promote an approach, the academics, trainers and researchers who take it forward and themselves gain much in the process. Less celebrated are the rather anonymous or shadowy ones, the chairs of professional organisations, the behind-the-scenes determined, obsessional and opinionated bureaucrats, the quiet wheeler-dealers who keep things afloat, and the quietly profiteering businessmen (EAPs are not run purely for love). There are the middle tiers of course leaders, lecturers and supervisors, many of them part-time employees. There are the unsung heroes, the modest ones who love the subject and activity of counselling and who try genuinely to take it forward and develop it for clients' sakes but who make little noise. And then there are the legions of foot soldiers, the poorly paid counsellors, the students and volunteers. It would be a crude generalisation to claim that everyone at the top of this rough hierarchy is male and everyone at the bottom female but I think there is some truth in this picture.

Were it not for the efforts of individuals like Richard Nelson-Jones in promoting the cause of counselling psychology within BPS, that development might have been sorely delayed. Were it not for Windy Dryden's vigorous, almost single-handed promotion of rational emotive behaviour therapy (REBT) in the UK, it would be little known here. Indeed Dryden may be largely credited with fuelling the boom in counselling literature from the 1980s. Were it not for Dave Mearns and Brian Thorne, the person-centred approach would have a much lower profile in the UK, or its development would have taken much longer. Psychodynamic counselling would probably have remained a very minor and inferior aspect of psychoanalytic practice without the energy and writings of Michael Jacobs. Similarly, existential counselling has been promoted most vigorously in the UK by Emmy van Deurzen. This is not to deny the wider support given by many others. But it is suggestive of a phenomenon whereby a few enthusiastic believers energetically spread ideas which then stick. One way of understanding the spread of therapies is to regard them as memes that, once past a certain point, propagate themselves ceaselessly. Or might we say that they have an actualising tendency of their own?

We can say this is simply the way of the world. We can dispute the picture given. We can remind ourselves of Anna Freud, Melanie Klein, Karen Horney, Laura Perls, Insoo Kim Berg, Marsha Linehan, Francine Shapiro and other significant female figures. You might object by demanding more evidence for the failings of the great, for their wealth, for things being wilfully hidden. You might even argue that this picture demeans the hard work, commitment and status of many lesser known figures. Perhaps I am wrong to claim such abuses of greatness and incorrect to portray a hierarchy of this kind. But over 30 years in the business of counselling paints this picture for me. What I infer from it is that counselling (and the talking therapies generally, as also most caring and helping professions) is part of the continuity of patriarchy and all its follies. Anthropologists and historians are not in complete accord on this but many agree that institutionalised male power, or patriarchy, has dominated most societies for something like the past 10,000 years. Patriarchal systems are characterised by hierarchy, usually by a chain of rank from God to ruling men, men in general, then women and children (with male children ranking more highly than girls). Familiar though we now are with corrective, critical feminist thought, explicit and organised objections to patriarchy probably go back only about 200 years.

Patriarchal features include privileging men over women domestically, so that women still perform most housework tasks. Women do most childrearing and care of the young and elderly. Women on the whole are the lowest paid whether as menial workers or professionals who do most of the 'emotion work' like counselling. Women are most subject to domestic violence, sexual abuse and rape. We are familiar with these facts. But we may think less about the flip side, which is that many men have probably suppressed their tender and emotional selves, often to the point where they do not even recognise they have them; they suffer accordingly and inflict this on others. Men privilege the intellectual, professional and practical domains. Men retain power in the churches and armed forces and arguably women make inroads into these professions only by taking on existing male behaviours. But it has also been argued that men drive rationality, science and technology in the conviction that these are the only ways forward. The politics and economics of our patriarchal civilisation arguably belittle the role of emotion, of everything from childbirth practices and childcare through human-scale education, work that honours human bodily and emotional needs, and so on.

It is far beyond the scope of this book to enter in any detail into the evolutionary, anthropological, historical, cultural and economic roots and consequences of patriarchy. But we can reasonably ask whether the volume and kinds of distress caused by our society are not patriarchal at root. We might fairly wonder if counselling is not essentially an intuitive, female-driven corrective that is thwarted and distorted by historical male forces and interests. Is it not possible that somehow men expropriate women's intuitive knowledge and reproduce it to their own credit? Were Winnicott and Bowlby really needed to tell us what most women have always known? We can certainly surmise that a large gap exists between academically oriented theorising and on-the-ground, face-to-face, everyday counselling. At the very least we must ask how far we can get with counselling as remedial in an intrinsically damaging capitalist society, that is, a society structured around having rather than being. How far can any serious critique of counselling get that fails to address questions regarding patriarchal traditions and assumptions? These questions take us beyond well-known feminist critiques of original Freudian and contemporary models of therapy, and beyond the creation of new feminist approaches which, however locally and urgently necessary, do not get to grips with the depth and extent of the patriarchal mechanisms pervading society, the professions and our own deeply internalised resistances to change. We cannot critique the so-called great men of our discipline without asking how and why we invest mythical greatness in them.

Endnotes

1. See for example Cooper, H. (Ed.). (1988). *Soul Searching: Studies in Judaism and psychotherapy.* London: SCM Press.

2. Masson, J. M. (1990). *Against Therapy.* London: Fontana.

3. Storr, A. (1997). *Feet of Clay: Study of gurus.* London: HarperCollins.

4. Smith, D. L. (2003). *Psychoanalysis in Focus.* London: Sage, p. 127.

5. Guy, J. D. (1987). *The Personal Life of the Psychotherapist.* New York: Wiley.

6. Maeder, T. (1990). *Children of Psychiatrists and other Psychotherapists.* London: HarperCollins.

7. Borch-Jacobsen, M., & Shamdasani, S. (2012). *The Freud Files: An inquiry into the history of psychoanalysis.* Cambridge: Cambridge University Press.

8. *Ibid.,* p. 2.

9. *Ibid.,* p. 51.

10. *Ibid.,* p. 85.

11. *Ibid.,* p. 102.

12. Kirschenbaum, H. (2007). *The Life and Work of Carl Rogers.* Ross-on-Wye: PCCS Books, p. 277.

13. Cohen, D. (2000). *Carl Rogers: A critical biography.* London: Constable.

14. *Ibid.,* p. 326.

15. Masson, J. M. (1990). *Against Therapy.* London: Fontana.

16. McLellan, B. (1995). *Beyond Psychoppression: A feminist alternative therapy.* Melbourne: Spinifex, p. 92.

17. Masson, J. M. (1990). *Against Therapy.* London: Fontana, p. 247.

18. McCall, R. J. (1983). *Phenomenological Psychology: An introduction.* Madison, WI: University of Wisconsin Press.

19. See for example Vitz, P. (1988). *Psychology as Religion: The cult of self worship* (rev. ed.). Grand Rapids, MI: William B. Eerdmans; and Brazier, D., & Brazier, C. (1993). *Beyond Carl Rogers.* London: Constable & Robinson.

20. Kahr, B. (1995). *Ethical Dilemmas of the Psychoanalytical Biographer.* London: Free Association Books.

21. Gomez, L. (1997). *An Introduction to Object Relations.* London: Free Association Books.

22. 'Jungism' is regarded as a charismatically led occult cult, by Noll (Noll, R. (1996).

The Jung Cult: Origins of a charismatic movement. London: Fontana). It almost certainly underpins much of the 'spirituality' found within counselling.

23. It may seem a moot point whether the practice of therapists' smoking is significant, since social disapproval of it has been acute only relatively recently. However, in certain humanistic therapies like primal therapy, smoking was regarded from the 1970s as a serious neurotic habit.

24. Spinelli, E., & Marshall, S. (Eds.). (2001). *Embodied Theories.* London: Continuum.

25. Kahneman, D. (2011). *Thinking, Fast and Slow.* London: Penguin, p. 228.

CHAPTER 3

Problems of counselling theory

The most glaring problem of counselling theory is anything but singular. It is the sheer multiplicity of theories. It may be an exaggeration to claim, as it sometimes is claimed, that there are over 500 or 600 different brand-name theories in this field[1] but it is relatively straightforward to count around 20 or 30 fairly well-known theoretical models and even this many, argue the critics, is far too many. But before proceeding, a word about terminology. In some scientific fields one speaks of a number of testable hypotheses and this number sooner or later diminishes as a result of testing. In the field of counselling this is not how things work. Usually a single figure and/or small team of enthusiasts concocts a new, distinctively named theory of counselling and then launches it with accompanying training courses, successful case studies (or these may not be bothered with at all), publications, an institutional centre and so on. It may or may not be empirically evaluated for effectiveness and compared with others. In essence, all such theories are hypotheses (sometimes known as core theoretical models, schools or approaches) but quickly become products. They are not drugs so do not have to be rigorously tested before being marketed; they resemble commercial products but are sold far more discreetly. Most are variations on pre-existing theories rather than genuinely new. Many have impressive multi-syllabic, often hyphenated names. So already here we see the problems of proliferation, lack of gatekeeping or product control, income-generating activities passing as discreet yet smoothly promoted, quasi-professional services.

We also need to look, however, at several other levels of theory. First, we have significant differences between all theoretical models, that is to say seriously different views on human nature, psychological functioning and malfunctioning, psychological intervention, the nature and extent of therapeutic influence and so on. Second, we have no real consensus on what any theory must contain in terms of its constituent parts (that is, from among theories of human development, psychological type or temperament, social contexts, psychopathology, ethics etc.). Third, we have no agreement on standards of measurement and acceptability of theory (for example, are scientology, astrological counselling, psychodynamic counselling, psychosynthesis, neurolinguistic programming, cognitive therapy etc. all equally commensurate and if they are not, what criteria do we use to distinguish them?). Fourth, we should ask where counselling theory sits alongside other disciplines such as mainstream psychology, sociology, politics, biology and so on. All in all, these questions pose difficult and seldom-faced problems for any activity like counselling psychology that is a clinical practice and profession taught in or validated by universities.

One aim in this chapter is to summarise key concepts from relevant major approaches. However, in keeping with the broadly humanistic and integrative ethos of the counselling world, my attention will be given mainly to the psychodynamic and person-centred approaches, with some comments on the problems of integrationism, eclecticism and pluralism. Critiques of CBT are now common and necessary but not focused upon much here due to limitations of space. However, it is fair to say that many integrative counselling training courses include aspects of CBT, Egan-based courses embrace social learning principles and CBT techniques, and some counselling courses are explicitly cognitive behavioural. Many counsellors undertake CBT workshops, often in order to improve their employment prospects and not necessarily out of enthusiasm.[2] Brief, solution-focused therapy is also popular with many counsellors, being one of the newer constructivist, strengths-based approaches that sit well alongside positive psychology. Although they have a significant presence, existential counselling, transactional analysis and gestalt therapy theory are not focused on much here.

Psychoanalytic theory

Psychoanalysis, psychoanalytic psychotherapy and psychodynamic counselling share the same origins in Freudian and related theory. All such theory has been greatly modified across the years and differing schools of psychoanalytic practice reject or take up different emphases.[3] Broadly speaking, the drive-conflict models have given way to models of developmental deficit or relational disruption. Psychodynamic counselling remains highly influential in the UK, with a number of private or voluntary training institutes, colleges and universities promulgating it as their core theoretical model. But it is also influential more generally, being *part* of the very language and fabric of all counselling language, training and practice. By this I mean that it is difficult to imagine any course or practitioner not being familiar with some of its central tenets. When I say 'familiar with' I do not assume that all have an accurate or in-depth understanding or sympathy with these tenets, but all will have at least some grasp of essentials. The task here is to identify and critique these tenets.

The unconscious

It has been said that without the concept of an unconscious there can be no psychoanalytic practice. Most of us can readily agree there are things about which we are not fully aware, or things we have forgotten or found hard or embarrassing to accept. Since the mind is restless, there is often 'something on top' (in full awareness) and other things below the surface that may float in and out of consciousness; things that are forgotten can sometimes be retrieved by concentration. Freud himself allowed for subconscious and preconscious processes. The multimodal psychotherapist Arnold Lazarus prefers to speak of non-conscious processes or material.

Philosophers such as Schopenhauer and Nietzsche (that Freud unconvincingly denied reading) had concepts akin to an unconscious. A contemporary of Freud's, Max Dessoir, spoke of an 'underconscious'. But in psychoanalytic thought the unconscious is a part or function of the mind that keeps painful and conflictual items from us, that deceives us, making us forget, repress, dream and joke about serious matters, or casts us into repeated relationship problems that our conscious mind is unaware of and would probably deny. What is stored unconsciously may completely contradict our self-image and cherished beliefs. For example, I may regard myself as wholly heterosexual yet have a homosexual dream (or vice versa); I may be a fundamentalist Christian yet dream I am conducting an abortion. But we cannot decide simply to look honestly at ourselves and accept all aspects of ourselves. Our minds trick us, they have reasons to, and it is only via dreams, jokes, slips of the tongue, inexplicable psychosomatic symptoms and transference within analysis, that we have any awareness of anything awry and even then we are powerless to correct matters.

The unconscious is not a physical part or region of the brain. It is not directly observable or open to experiment. Freudian dogma has it that only the psychoanalyst (himself rigorously analysed previously by another analyst, with the exception of the self-analysed Freud) in the analytic setting is able to comprehend, interpret and in a timely fashion utilise interpretation to bring about the client's insight into the workings of his or her unconscious, and this only across hundreds of analytic hours. Hence, psychodynamically speaking, you are doomed to a distorted and unhappy life indefinitely unless you seek and complete successful psychoanalytic treatment from a bona fide agent of psychoanalysis. Furthermore, every superficial or transient problem in living or *symptom* always signals deeper unconscious conflict. You may go to see a psychodynamic counsellor (or a counsellor whose theoretical affiliation you do not know but who turns out to be dogmatically psychodynamic) with a wish to quit smoking, to overcome the sadness of bereavement or deal with stress at work. Whatever your presenting problem or symptom, the psychodynamic counsellor (or the integrative counsellor who is trying to get a psychodynamic take on you), will start to formulate hypotheses about the origins of your problem in your childhood or perhaps in the tensions between your personality and events that are taxing you. The hypothesis of an unconscious and its habit of stirring up trouble cause the counsellor to listen for psychodynamic confirmation and probably to guide the conversation ever so subtly towards this. Even if you had no such deeper causative process, even if you had no intention of excavating your unconscious, even if no such entity as an unconscious can be shown to exist, and even if this procedure feels damaging and abusive, it is all a logical extension through decades of Freud's original dogma.

Consider this observation of a psychodynamic counsellor working in a university counselling service: 'Nearly everyone who comes to see us brings a reality problem to be sorted out and an unconscious to be explored, an anxiety to be relieved and a phantasy to be untangled, an acute need to be helped and a transference relationship to be tested out'.[4] The absurdity of translating psychoanalytic logic into interpretative practice can be summed up in the old joke: the patient who arrives for his appointment late is resistant; the patient who arrives early is anxious; the patient who arrives exactly on time is obsessive. This can be followed through in observing the way the patient or client enters the room, where and how he sits, what he wears, how he speaks and hesitates, and so on. Everything is up for interpretation. It is unlikely that many analysts actually act like hermeneutic wizards; it is quite likely that some analysts suspect lesser-trained counsellors of 'wild analysis' which includes compulsive and clever interpretations; it is overall very likely that the concept of and faith in the recognisable dynamics of the unconscious lead to unwarranted and distorted views and treatments of clients.

As Borch-Jacobsen and Shamdasani put it of Freud's dexterity in utilising the concept of the unconscious for his own purposes:

Everyone — colleague or patient, sane or raving mad, dead or alive — was subjected to the same deciphering from the same hermeneutics of unconscious desire. In this sense, we can well say that Freud's 'case histories' (*Krankengeschichten*) are no less mythical than the fabulous 'history of the psychoanalytic movement' narrated in his autobiographical writings or the history of humanity described in his phylogenetic and anthropological fictions. No matter where we look, we find the same rewriting of history, the same narrativising of arbitrary interpretations, the same transformation of hypotheses into facts.[5]

Many have questioned and totally refuted the concept of the unconscious. For the existentialist philosopher Jean-Paul Sartre, for whom we are all 'doomed to freedom', the notion of being unconsciously driven is akin to 'bad faith'. We may push certain things to the back of our mind and we like to claim that we cannot carry out actions we wish to because 'something' is holding us back. But this is simply rationalising our lack of authenticity and courage, making excuses for ourselves. (Smith, however, argues that Sartre misunderstood the meaning of the unconscious, and offers nine 'naïve objections' to the concept as well as further 'serious objections'.)[6] Plainly, 'the unconscious' can be considered a piece of superstitious nonsense on a par with belief in evil as an entity with a life of its own, say, or in the devil himself. But for psychoanalytic practitioners it is of course lucrative nonsense that also sustains an ego-enhancing sense of mastery.

Or it is sometimes claimed that terrible abuses in childhood or dramatic, life-and-death shocks in later life have to be repressed into the unconscious because they are too traumatic to be faced by the conscious mind. We may experience numbing, blankness of memory, flashbacks and nightmares but we cannot face and rid ourselves of such trauma. This is sometimes said to be evidence of the unconscious mind protecting us from overwhelming psychic pain. Yet some who suffer from post-traumatic distress say that they wish their minds *would* make them unconscious of their troubling memories. Given the diversity of human personalities, it is quite possible that some of us are besieged by and others are forced to repress such pain, but even if this is the case it casts serious doubt on the notion of a universally valid unconscious. Matters are further 'complicated', shall we say, by the adumbrations of Jung's collective unconscious, Assagioli's superconscious, and all manner of other related colourful theories that Freud would have no truck with and that do not translate across theoretical models or find much confirmation in either academia or common sense.

If the task of psychodynamic counselling (or its upscale grandparent psychoanalysis) is to make the unconscious conscious (and then only to convert unconscious misery into conscious unhappiness, as Freud put it), we can fairly ask if it reliably does this and if it's worth all the trouble and expense. To judge from the 100 or so years of psychoanalytic practice, from the lives of psychoanalysts and psychodynamic counsellors, we might conclude that there is no good evidence for such claims. Where are all the psychoanalysed people who are more conscious and less miserable than the rest of us? Certainly there are people who have learned to use 'therapy-speak' with apparent insight. But of those citizens who we admire for their moral or other personal qualities, how many got there due to any form of psychoanalytic (or other therapeutic) treatment?

Transference and countertransference

Transference is said to be the unconscious acting out of aspects of the workings of the client's conflicted mind in distorted perceptions of the therapist or counsellor. The client expresses positive erotic transference for the counsellor, say, which 'means' that deep down the client imagines (or 'phantasises') the counsellor as the good parent he or she never had, 'the person who loves me unconditionally, who listens to my every word, who really cares about me'. Alternatively, or alternatingly, the client may express negative transference, seeing malignancy, coldness or incompetency in all the counsellor says and does. The unusual conditions of the counselling environment (intense attention to the client, apparent fascination with all that he or she says, asymmetrical disclosure, lack of agenda, lack of judgementalism, absence of small talk) pretty much forces the typical client to be thrown back on their imagination, on saying anything that comes to mind, on idealising or denigrating the counsellor.

Now, transference is taken very seriously by a majority of counsellors, possibly all the more by those who harbour some self-doubt about their status and skills. Some counsellors admit that if they had the money they would train as psychoanalysts, because even if they don't really believe in it, the myth persists that in the hierarchy of mysterious depth psychologies, the analyst is king and the poor counsellor is a cheap imitation. While a majority of counsellors do have some personal therapy as part of their training (mandated by BPS but not by BACP), most cannot afford the thousands of pounds paid out by actual analysts in training. Hence, anxiety about less-than-total awareness of her own unconscious processes and the possibility that she is missing some ever-so-significant slither of transferential material in her client is enough to make the counsellor (whether person-centred or cognitive behavioural) hyper-alert to it and to take any suspicions of transference or countertransference to supervision. (Counter-transference, the 'flip side' of transference, is the practitioner's unconscious feeling towards the client and can be either an obstruction or a useful insight.)

Attachment and loss

Focus on early needs for security led to quite elaborate theories about different styles of attachment and the consequences of insecure and abusive early attachments. It makes sense to assert that babies and infants depend on caregivers for their physical survival and on the quality of attachment for their psychological flourishing throughout life. Those starved of affection or denied reasonable continuity of parenting or early care are more likely to flounder in various ways in later life. Attachment theory advanced by Bowlby and others has fleshed out in empirically grounded terms some of the more abstruse aspects of psychoanalysis. Theorists of bereavement experiences (including Freud) have added to our understanding of the effects of death and other significant losses. In practice terms this means that psychodynamic counsellors are alert to unconscious anticipations of and reactions to the counsellor's illness, holidays and any other breaks. Attachment styles claim to help explain why individuals react differently to divorce and separation (as well as why they choose the partners they do). Excessive independence can be a form of denial of the need for attachment.

What such theory is not so good at is accounting for individual differences in coping with loss. These may sometimes be explained by the earliest and/or compound experiences of loss and deprivation but innate differences in resilience are probably also in play, as well as other mitigating factors. It is not proven that all who have had early losses can only resolve these by talking about, re-experiencing and working through them. It is evident that theories about stages of grieving for losses have crumbled somewhat in the face of idiosyncratic realities. It is questionable whether all clients really need to go through the routine of having several therapeutic sessions in order to have a 'proper ending' but nevertheless this is a standard part of psychodynamic practice and the client can be made to feel defensive if she does not wish to pay for such a drawn-out, ritual experience. Stoicism, as built into CBT, is also a means of addressing loss, even if not approved by psychodynamic practitioners. Attachment theory elevates the relational and plays down the autonomous and solitary, indeed tends to define these as pathological. But it is becoming more evident that at least some small proportion of people are loners, even asexual. Psychodynamic theorising is also poor at making adjustments for sociocultural changes and familial variations.

Psychodynamic theory comes across to some as attractively complex, inserting itself into many nuances of our psychological lives that are not well understood or explained by other disciplines. In some ways it can feel more compelling than the arid and atomistic discourse of conventional psychology. Yet there remains a chasm between its theoretical complexity and any widespread, convincing evidence of its effectiveness. Presumably this is why so many former psychoanalytic practitioners (Reich, Perls, Berne, Janov, Ellis, Beck, et al.) left the fold to create what they saw as more effective methods. By comparison, the theory of the person-centred approach considered below is often considered lightweight, even superficial, which raises for us the question of how important or unimportant theory really is.

Let me give the last word here to Smith:

As it stands, psychoanalytic theory must be seen as an illusion that is perhaps
partly true and probably largely false, but even if in some far distant future
ingenious researchers manage to prove that psychoanalytic theory is totally
true (which, of course, would be logically impossible given the range of mutually
contradictory theories making up contemporary psychoanalysis), its present-
day advocates still do not have good reason for regarding it as such. Without
sound evidence at their disposal, advocates of analysis are inevitably *believers.*[7]

Person-centred theory

The person-centred approach (PCA) is extremely influential in
the world of counselling, in its own right and as an underpinning
for other models. Let us note at the outset that over the course of
its existence it has been known as non-directive counselling, client-
centred counselling/therapy and person-centred therapy or
counselling. It is sometimes incorrectly referred to as Rogerian
therapy, and complaints are made by some authorities on the
approach that it is often misrepresented by people who have
completed only basic counselling skills training courses taking it
as their title. I often hear people saying their course is 'basically
person-centred' or something similar. It is sometimes said to be
theoretically light (and to this is attributed much of its popularity)
but its proponents refute this allegation. Whether theoretical
lightness or complexity is any measure of the credibility and
effectiveness of a therapeutic approach is another matter. Although
critiques of Rogers and the PCA are far fewer than those of Freud
and psychoanalytic therapies, in any consideration of critiques of
the PCA we encounter the same kinds of rebuttals: mainly, it is
always felt to be misrepresented.

One can turn to existing critiques such as those presented by
Paul Wilkins,[8] an astute insider loyal to the PCA. Here we find
listed and rebutted the usual critical suspects. We would expect
from a well-known pro-PCA writer a refusal to entertain criticisms
constituting any serious threat but this scholarly text also confirms
for us that the task of the critic is always going to be tough. Although
the PCA dates from only about 1940, like psychoanalysis it has a

number of specialised concepts, terminology and revisions from across the years. There is almost a sense that criticism is impossible unless one is either prepared to suspend all other activities long enough to wade through piles of historical documents or face being shot down for failing genuinely and microscopically to understand the approach. Note that in the contemporary debate between atheists and religious believers, people like Richard Dawkins are routinely dismissed by the latter for an alleged lack of true and detailed understanding of religion. So it is here too.

Wilkins helpfully outlines standard critiques of the PCA for us. It stands accused of a shallow 'niceness'. It is a therapy for the 'worried well' and cannot address serious mental health problems. It is perceived as easy to learn. (Interestingly, while Wilkins refutes this charge, at the same time he has made it known publicly that he himself completed no formal training course in it, but after qualifying as a psychodramatist attended PCA workshops and read around the subject intensively.) Person-centred loyalists like to suggest that Rogers was and the PCA is 'revolutionary', yet critics often regard it as fitting all too smoothly and safely into statutory counselling agencies. It has an uncritical American-style focus on individual autonomy. It has a weak account at best of the origins of incongruence and psychopathology generally, and many of its practitioners are hostile to clinical assessment. Its so-called core conditions may be neither necessary nor sufficient. Non-directivity is often said to be mythical. The person-centred counsellor's habit of reflecting or parroting clients' words back to them is a well-worn criticism. Practitioners are also accused of often having sloppy boundaries. Finally, in the spirit of inter-approach critiques, the PCA has no concept of the unconscious and transference and therefore risks dangers of entanglement.

Wilkins addresses and refutes all these points skilfully and in some detail, much as we are used to seeing politicians skilfully fending off the criticisms of interviewers: the message is 'you are not going to get anywhere with your questions'. Rather than examining all these points, all of which in my view have some merit, I will concentrate on some major issues below.

The actualising tendency

Rogers was a psychologist of his time, he was ambitious to establish a new kind of psychology, and his theories show many traces of descriptive, generalised phenomenology and positively toned speculation rather than detailed analysis. Rogers applied his definition of the actualising tendency to all organic life. It is the motivational force that maintains and adds complexity to human beings and always moves towards fulfilment of potential. To some extent drawing on Maslow's hierarchy of needs, Rogers devised this principle as the key underlying base for everything else. It is inherent, active, holistic, prosocial. It is surprising that the looseness of such terms is not more often questioned. The actualising tendency is an all-purpose, imprecise concept, so vague as to fit almost any circumstances (except of course the deeply negative aspects of life). I know many person-centred practitioners personally and find some of them extra-sincere and honest (congruent), warm and attentive (respectful and empathic), decent likeable people. Yet I am mystified by their attachment to the dogma and gobbledegook of the PCA. Ultimately, I see no difference in terms of irrational beliefs between them and the psychoanalysts and the religious, all of whom are sincere in their attachment to and apparent full understanding of an in-group jargon that others remain baffled by.

Tellingly, Rogers and later person-centred adherents make copious use of agricultural and horticultural metaphors to help describe the actualising tendency. Since Rogers also endorsed 'the work of biologists such as Szent-Györgyi, who concludes that there is definitely a drive to perfection in all living matter'[9] we might be forgiven for thinking that Rogers was and the person-centred community is serious about any alignment of their theory with biology. Freud, for example, is sometimes regarded as a 'crypto-biologist' who sought to put his biological aspirations behind him.[10] However, one finds no reference to Darwin in Rogers' corpus of work, an omission that is startling both set against Rogers' agricultural background and the contemporary burgeoning of Darwinian literature generally and within psychology in the form of evolutionary psychology and psychotherapy. Although Rogers' theoretical edifice did not naïvely conceptualise all life as benign or nice, it seems fair to say that he placed very little emphasis on the savagery of the animal world, on the perennial hatred, violence and deception in human societies, on deep-seated and probably biologically driven psychiatric problems, and the universality of entropy and death, most of which now have (some of us think) plausible Darwinian explanations. Set against the Darwinian-derived portrait of humans as torn between stubborn evolutionary, genetic and neurological forces, Rogers' portrait seems to many (myself included) decidedly Pollyannaish and so *American*. Was Rogers and are his admirers more wedded to rose-tinted, liberal Christian, hippie and utopian visions than they like to think?

In practice, the actualising tendency of the client must logically meet that of the counsellor in a kind of win-win virtuous circle, according to person-centred tenets. Indeed all human beings, if driven by this prosocial actualising tendency, must always be close, or on a path of convergence, to the kind of congruence and relational depth extolled by person-centred counsellors. Close, were it not for conditions of worth[11] and other thwarting forces. We are surely entitled to ask whether this fantasy scenario of millions of actualising tendencies trying to converge, or in the case of counselling, just two converging, is realistic. The polar opposite fantasy is that human beings are always out to subvert and thwart congruence, pro-sociality and potential fulfilment. Somewhere in between we can posit a scenario of the blind leading the blind or the one-eyed human being as king in the country of the blind. If, as some of us suspect, the actualising tendency and other positive but woolly person-centred principles cannot withstand much analysis, perhaps we are entitled to propose self- and other-deceiving tendencies as universally at work.

The core conditions

In 1957 Rogers set out six necessary and sufficient conditions for therapeutic personality change. Three of these conditions have become known as the 'core conditions'. Taking Rogers at his word we must ask whether unconditional positive regard (UPR), congruence and empathy are indeed necessary and sufficient. UPR is presented as a *sine qua non* of the whole enterprise of counselling, not only of the PCA. We cannot help another unless we first of all accept him and manifest that acceptance so that he experiences it. We accept his humanity and individuality but not necessarily all his attitudes and behaviours. When working with a paedophile you would certainly not collude with his paedophilic attitudes or false repentance; you would not condone sexist and racist language used by a client, and you might well confront it. But in both these cases your radical acceptance of the client as a person would be maintained. Within a person-centred framework you would regard his actualising tendency as having been thwarted or distorted. Your UPR towards him, coupled with congruence, would show him that you connect with his own self-trusting processes and you can discriminate between these and the more twisted aspects of his thoughts and behaviour. Given sufficient time, commitment and relational depth, the client may come to be fully self-accepting and once again attuned to his actualising tendency rather than thrown off course by thwarting factors.

Person-centred writers have cautioned against the mere portrayal of UPR. It must be deeply and genuinely felt and communicated. But exactly how does one compartmentalise such an unconditional attitude from reservations about particular heinous attitudes and behaviours? It would be possible to tell the client that you hate what they have done but love who they (really) are. In fact it might be easier to voice this to certain clients than, for example, telling a somewhat boring client how boring she is. 'I love you but I don't love your boringness'? Perhaps 'I fully accept you and your presumed struggle with your own boringness'? But perhaps I am exaggerating the problems here. Most psy-practitioners, in my experience, are broad-minded, accustomed to working with a wide range of people, and are able to maintain basic respect for all. (This isn't to say that some clients are more or less warm and readily likeable than others.) But at the other end of the scale of rapport and attractiveness are clients who are especially good to work with, who are appreciative, articulate, insightful and rewarding. Does UPR then flow more naturally and eagerly?

UPR may sometimes be sufficient for therapeutic change to occur. The power of being accepted, for someone who has experienced a great deal of rejection in life, can be enormously impactful, perhaps even life-saving on occasion. But this can happen outside counselling, for instance when meeting a new friend or lover. It is also, of course, as Christian *agape*, or love, the basis of human and divine forgiveness, and it is probably more than coincidental that it had this place in Rogers' thought. Some missionaries from cults practise so-called 'love-bombing' which is arguably similar to UPR. No adherents of any counselling approach can claim UPR as their own, nor can its impact necessarily be claimed as anything more than fortuitous. But is UPR always necessary? Consider that on occasion confrontation (probably now one of the least used of counselling interventions), although unpleasant, can effect great change, possibly operating in the same way traumatic events can lead to positive post-traumatic growth ('cancer was the best thing that ever happened to me'). You would not necessarily want your surgeon to hold you in high regard, you would be justified in simply knowing that she is one of the best surgeons for your condition. So I believe the case for UPR being necessary and sufficient is complex and far from proven.

Congruence consists of the counsellor being true to herself, both in the sense of maintaining high levels of self-awareness and honouring one's own personality in relation to each client, and in the sense of refusing to take on any false professional persona. The counsellor enhances the sense of congruence by participation in personal development or self-awareness groups in training. She strives to be aware of how she feels (differently) about each client, generally and in a moment-by-moment way, and may or may not share how she is feeling with clients, making such decisions as she deems appropriate and timely. This is similar to the psychodynamic counsellor being aware of countertransference. As the client becomes aware of his presumed incongruence, he will also be inspired by the counsellor's congruence to take risks with his own.

Congruence, authenticity and the pursuit of the 'real self' are central to the human potential movement and the sensitivity of hippie values antagonistic to 'bullshit' and hypocrisy. There are good reasons – physiological as well as interpersonal and religious – to consider lack of sincerity or honesty harmful to health and society. The willingness of anyone today to be consistently deeply honest or congruent is often constrained by a culture of politeness combined with fear of reprisals in employment settings and close relationships; nor does capitalist culture prioritise honesty. Indeed historically many people have paid dearly for speaking their minds. It is an open question whether person-centred counsellors should be expected to exercise UPR, congruence and empathy at all times with all people, Rogers' commendation of the PCA as 'a way of being' suggesting as much. But as in life, so in counselling, one must surely be sensitive to possible fragilities in others and costs for oneself. Now, a big problem hanging over congruence and its centrality in the PCA is its relativity. No one is entirely free of incongruence, nor is there any reliable mechanism for congruence enhancement. At any one time a balance of congruence– incongruence is likely to operate. There is no evidence that anyone attains a state of optimal congruence from which they never slip back, yet this inevitable forward movement is usually implied, not only in person-centred literature but in most counselling texts. It may be more realistic to hope for eternal vigilance or mindfulness against inevitable setbacks.

I cannot deny the value I place on congruence (or honesty, or parrhesia) but I know how often I fall short of it. Brad Blanton's 'radical honesty'[12] affirms what we are all taught, that honesty is the best policy, yet everyday life constantly compromises us. Many clients value counselling precisely because in this unnatural arena they can potentially say whatever they like, however asocial, bizarre or risky. But we all know that everyday life is not like this. The optimal congruence permitted and encouraged in counselling can be brought into the real world, as in the Jim Carrey film *Liar Liar*. But it cannot be sustained.

Again, empathy is a quality that all practitioners aspire to and none would suggest that it is ever unnecessary. You must understand the client if you are to help him and it is plausible to suggest that the more deeply you can extend your understanding, the better. For many, feeling truly heard and understood clearly is powerful and sufficient for great relief to occur. Empathy works at many levels from simple factual understanding of the client's circumstances to the fine nuances of deep and complex feelings in the present and derived from the past. Emotionally intelligent people probably have some natural ability to be empathic and some training will likely enhance this. But as Albert Ellis has suggested, some clients thrive on being understood (along with being 'prized') but do not necessarily thereby improve therapeutically.[13] Given the principle that the core conditions interact, the congruent counsellor will become aware when her client becomes dependent on the comforting feeling of being understood and may voice this as a challenge. Nevertheless, the criticism that for some clients endless empathy will merely delay responsibility taking and due progress remains intact.

We should also ask why Rogers came up with these particular conditions. Would everyone on pondering over clinical sessions or audio-recordings come up with the same names for the same phenomena? Why six or three and not five or two? Why not interest or engagement, understanding, attention, compassion, re-moralisation, or love? Empathy and congruence do of course have a slightly scientific ring about them, as does unconditional positive regard. Rogers used other terms, such as respect, prizing, non-possessive, non-judgemental warmth or acceptance for UPR and realness and genuineness for congruence, but the multi-syllabic pseudo-scientific terms have stuck. And why are these conditions so popular in the counselling world, particularly among trainees? It is surely their simplicity that is attractive. Many non-person-centred therapists insist that the core conditions underpin everything they do but are obviously insufficient. Trainers within the person-centred community may object that they are deceptively simple, easy to misunderstand, extremely arduous to learn and implement, and so on. But this mantra-like trio, however distorted or variously interpreted, remains popular and influential.

Non-directivity

Honouring the client's organismic experiencing, his internal locus of evaluation and the general flow of experience means that the person-centred practitioner is extremely reluctant to take any control in sessions or even to interject in a manner that might nudge the client away from his own moment-to-moment train of experiencing. It has similarities with psychodynamic free association and the Kleinian abstinence whereby the analyst withholds her own response in order to allow the client's full rage or other feelings to build and erupt. The person-centred counsellor is not necessarily silent or even quiet, she is engaged, she actively uses empathic reflection to let the client know how she has heard him and to invite correction. She tries strenuously to avoid interpretation, curiosity and anything that might influence the client. It has been amply demonstrated however that even Rogers, skilful as he was, tended to reinforce clients' statements when they coincided with his own beliefs. Halmos among others has emphasised that non-directivity is a myth.[14]

Non-directivity is an aspect of the egalitarian ideal aimed at by person-centred and other humanistic practitioners. By meeting as equals, avoiding any exercise of power, counsellor and client are honouring the trustworthiness of human nature. There is no 'patient' but a free client met by an egalitarianism-loving counsellor. However, as Martin Buber objected in his famous dialogue with Rogers,[15] the client comes with troubles, meets the expectations of the counsellor regarding time, place and fees, and the counsellor does not freely give of her whole self but only her professional self. Although she may believe that she is meeting her client beyond artificial structures, the relationship is not essentially an I–Thou one, unless occasionally and accidentally.

But the biggest problem with any ideal of non-directivity is not its mythical nature. Insofar as one can interact non-directively, it is possible and in much counselling is standard practice to minimise questions and influencing. Most counsellors find themselves being trained for the unnatural behaviour of withholding questions and instead relying on empathic or clarificatory statements designed to facilitate the client's volunteering new information or clarification if he so wishes. A trainee supervisee once told me he did not know his client's name because the client had not mentioned it. Although it was hard to understand how this came about at all, the counsellor remained a little reluctant to ask for the name. It could of course be the case, however rare, that someone wishes to withhold their name but one could then at least enquire. It could also be the case (this is probable) that the trainee had misunderstood his trainer, and most person-centred counsellors would, I think, say 'I notice you haven't told me your name'.

There are two worse examples of where non-directivity can lead, however. One is the charge that it may be unethical to refrain from offering CBT or mentioning to a depressed client that there is significant evidence that CBT is effective for depression.[16] Since many person-centred counsellors are averse to assessment, diagnosis and influence, they may well avoid any temptation to use the term depression (or its now common euphemism 'low mood') or any sense of urgency. Additionally, the habit of waiting for the client to arrive at his own decisions can delay interventions aimed at addressing depression, which may worsen with time. The most dramatic example of dogmatic adherence to the principle of client self-determination and therapist non-directivity is found in David Reed's book *Anna*, about his schizophrenic wife who received treatment from anti-psychiatric Laingians. Anna burned herself to death during a psychotic episode.[17] This cannot be laid at the door of the person-centred community but very similar theoretical principles underpin it. It is sometimes objected that the PCA has moved on from early principles but strong anti-psychopathologising currents remain and non-directivity is still defended.[18]

A more prosaic observation can be made of the laissez-faire culture spawned by the 1960's and 1970's hippie movement. Rogers admired many of the manifestations of this movement, even if too timid himself to fully embrace it. Most principles of the human potential movement resonate with anti-authoritarianism, optimal freedom, non-directivity and self-regulation. Rogers' work has inspired child-centred education and liberal relationships. Having once been a believer in and 'practitioner' of child-centred parenting, I am now convinced by experience that most children do not flourish in non-directive conditions but need a judicious blend of age-appropriate freedom and guidance (and even sometimes prohibition). Cultural practices can and do swing to extremes and our current technical-rational, controlling culture has clearly moved beyond a wise mid-point. We may cite and paraphrase the

Goldilocks paradigm of the wisdom of being 'not too directive, not too non-directive' here to make the point.

The naming of different therapeutic approaches and the concepts within approaches, indeed the whole definitional problem in counselling could fill a (probably tedious) book. Names have marketing and public relations functions and often change historically, as we have seen. They are also woefully imprecise and the source of much confusion. 'Person-centred counselling' manages to imply both that it is warm and is something others are not, as if other therapies are not centrally concerned with the person of the client. (Rogers began using the term 'person-centred' in the late 1970s.)[19] But the person-centred approach is not about the whole person, as sometimes implied, since it has nothing to do with a person's medical needs, financial plight and so on. It might be more accurately called facilitated self-actualisation, self-trusting reinforcement therapy, empathy-centred counselling, or something similar. What it sets out to do is not to address the mythical 'whole person' but to impose a particular philosophy of so-called actualisation on clients. Many clients want and ask for counsellors' advice, guidance, techniques and ideas about how to change aspects of their lives. Some flexibly minded counsellors are happy to provide such a service but the purist person-centred counsellor is wedded dogmatically to belief in everyone's ability (and need?) to find their own way. Arguably, sometimes a fish is what you need, or directions to the nearest fish shop, not a series of fishing lessons.

Eclecticism, integrationism, pluralism

Beneath the official version of practitioners receiving rigorous training in one clearly identified, named model and retaining all its purity of delivery has always existed the unavoidable variety of different counsellors' individual interpretations of theory and techniques. Beneath the myths perpetrated by theorists, trainers and professional body bureaucrats insisting that each model has some sort of laser-accurate application, the reality may be that common tricks of the trade are used iteratively and intuitively.

Idiosyncrasies in counsellors' personalities and in their clients have necessarily called forth idiosyncratic practice. Early analysts warned against 'wild analysis' and the presumed necessity for purity of dogma and practice continues into our own day. Similar insistence on dogma can be seen in the early formation of religions and politics, and similar splintering into groups and individual interpretations can also be detected. Psychotherapy and counselling long ago attracted criticisms of degenerating into a mish-mash of haphazard practices. Yet are we really to imagine there exists on the one hand a group of loyal, skilled practitioners who remain true to the original therapeutic dogma and who deliver flawless therapy, while on the other hand there is a group of foolish and renegade practitioners who arbitrarily dispense with the established truths of dogma, who practise in an undisciplined way according to mere whim and hubris, whose clients are likely to be markedly damaged or served poorly? This latter group is the fantasised target of purists' accusations of haphazard eclecticism. So effective has their campaign been that few if any practitioners today refer to themselves as eclectics. Yet perhaps we should wonder if the anti-eclectics are unaccountably eclectophobic.

One or two senior figures have commended 'theoretically consistent eclecticism' and 'technical eclecticism' to distinguish an acceptable, formal practice of discerning selection of techniques but it is always implied that these are highly skilled practices that some rebel army of badly trained or simply unruly practitioners are incapable of. Arnold Lazarus's multimodal therapy is heavily based on assessment which leads to selection of techniques most likely to help the client. Lazarus has stressed that he is not an integrative practitioner but an eclectic, that he sees only conflict between the many competing theories and is content that his therapy is relatively theory-light. He also argues that the whole field is in the 'dark ages'.[20]

Integrationism and integrative therapy and counselling, on the other hand, have been held up as principled, elegant theoretical blends of different models. Acknowledging the wisdom of responding to different clients with subtle variations in technique, and also acknowledging the unwieldy variety of therapeutic approaches on offer (and the incredulity this must have in public relations terms), some have commended the creation of these new, blended models. One avenue to disciplined integration is for individual practitioners to train first in one approach in depth and then another, for example three years in transactional analysis and another three in person-centred. This is a rare, expensive choice except perhaps for a few affluent practitioners. The other, preferred model is the theoretical blending of two or more models, for example, of some object relations theory with aspects of personal construct and CBT theory into cognitive analytic therapy. A not-uncommon form of integration is to join the 'relational' (PCA or psychodynamic) with bodywork or social learning theory in the embodied-relational and Egan-based approaches.

It is now acceptable to refer to one's practice as integrative, to write case studies for accreditation purposes that are integrative, in fact a majority of counsellors and many courses refer to themselves as integrative,[21] and a professional integrative movement complete with conferences and research programmes has existed for many years. Yet the ongoing problems here are obvious. Why should we take every brand-name approach so seriously as to believe they require careful integration? Why, if integration is a pressing problem, does it take years to achieve (and in fact looks like never happening), comparable with interfaith and ecumenical movements in the Christian church? Why do new integrative approaches simply multiply in the meantime? Do we really think the eclecticism problem has gone away, especially when a distinguished American therapist like Sol Garfield referred to what he did as an 'eclectic-integrative approach',[22] a title that would barely be possible to use in the UK? When students have asked me how they should respond when asked by fellow professionals and clients as to how they style themselves and what to write in accreditation applications, we have discussed all these matters and most conclude that it amounts to a ridiculous and unhelpful mess.

Dogma, facts, dissensus, and lacunae

We might argue that each therapeutic approach has its central set of dogmas that are propagated in training and publications. 'This is what we believe here; this is how we do things; this is how we expect to see theory carried through into practice.' The founder has spelled matters out, these theories have been refined, and this is what we expect to be accepted (presumably barring some small space for minor disagreements and future developments).

By the admittedly problematic term 'facts' I refer here to areas of knowledge that are mainly non-contentious. For example, all training has to impart some knowledge on professional ethics and law. Such knowledge is usually available from the relevant professional body and for the most part applies equally to practitioners of every approach. Matters of professional boundaries, good practice, complaints procedures, contracting, advertising and so on probably comprise the less exciting but still essential items of training. Statistics concerning social contextual matters like mental health and race, gender, sexual orientation and disability may be regarded as factual, even when subjected to interpretation. Psychopharmacology may be regarded as factual in at least some of its basic chemical aspects, even if not in debates on its helpfulness and harm.

By dissensus I mean all those aspects of human behaviour, meaning and psychological health that are contentious. We cannot in this field presume that consensus exists on matters of assessment, diagnosis, psychiatric classifications, notions of psychopathology, normality, treatment and the like. We might well call this a minefield. We cannot use terms like human nature, mental health and psychopathology with any expectation of cross-approach agreement. One approach's *sine qua non* is another's anathema. This is especially true of positions on human distress (or what brings people to counselling), so much so that we cannot even agree on nomenclature: 'mental illness' is out; the euphemism 'mental health problem' is used sparingly; 'problems in living' is acceptable to some; other terms include presenting problem, client concern and symptom. 'Disorder' is anathema to humanistic practitioners, many of whom reject the idea that any such entities as schizophrenia, bipolar disorder, obsessive compulsive disorder even exist or that focusing on so-called deficits is at all helpful. 'Incongruence' of the client is as far as some person-centred practitioners will allow themselves to go towards acknowledging all this.

The lacunae I have in mind as regards most counselling training include genetic, evolutionary, neurological and socioeconomic factors. Some courses may touch on them, particularly socioeconomic factors (and especially the sensitive areas of race and ethnicity, culture, gender, sexuality, disability, class and religion) but barely. One good reason for this omission is that if a serious attempt were made to include all desirable topics, any course would simply grow to unwieldy and expensive proportions; and it might become self-defeating, encouraging students to question too much the assumptions on which counselling is built. But the gaps certainly tell us about counselling values and priorities. Despite protests to the contrary, counselling, psychotherapy and all talking therapies remain focused on what goes on in your head, and to a lesser extent in your body, emotions and relationships. They remain focused on how you have got yourself into this mess, as it were, how you construe your situation and what you can do to think, feel and do differently about it. Vanja Orlans and Susan van Scoyoc show that BPS's concerns here lead with subjectivity and intersubjectivity and first-person accounts.[23]

There are a few exceptions to this in some models of feminist, social and evolution-informed therapy but standard counselling training is, I think, focused on the individual and her or his autonomy and responsibility. Most counselling theory appears to have arrived at premature closure a few decades ago, its primary drive being to justify and add to the original formula rather than continuing to pose questions about the aetiology of human distress. Indeed we might say that this phenomenon of theoretical closure is what characterises all models of counselling: they become myopic instead of remaining genuinely open to new data. The question 'Why is there so much human distress of such an obdurate kind?' is ignored (because each approach already possesses this knowledge!) and is replaced by an agenda of confirmation-seeking via biased research and favourable theorising. Solution-focused therapy (along with all positive psychology models) may assert a claim to novelty in pointing away from 'problem-saturated' theory, and transpersonal models promise transcendence of social conditions and neurological curbs. Faith in a fuzzy notion of infinite neuroplasticity rules in all such models. But it is still faith.

I suspect that as well as this process of premature theoretical closure another phenomenon is at work. Such a mass of promising data is already available from different but relevant disciplines – for example, on deep history, evolutionary psychology, genetics and epigenetics, obstetrics, developmental/lifespan psychology, sociocultural influences and so on – that no one can hope to be familiar with it in any depth. We might add to the above list philosophies of science, of the mind, and of self-knowledge among others. Therapeutic theories are often appealing both to creators and students for their heuristic short cuts. Those interested in the vocational pull of counselling are not usually the most intellectually well equipped and intellectuals of the ideal polymath kind are not usually the most empathic. Counselling approaches are constructed rather hastily from quite limited data and emotional investment for fairly urgent, practical application. Difficult, complicated theory that delays or challenges therapeutic models is not welcomed. Popular, potted versions of neuroscience, say, like those purporting to show positive connections between early love and healthy neurological development, are sometimes embraced for their apparently confirmatory role. Those with a helping vocation cannot wait for knowledge gaps to be filled and refined and so resort to the kinds of heuristics so common in counselling theory (and also in self-help literature).

Cleaning up the theory problem?

What would it take to make necessary changes to counselling theory? Is it conceivable that we will ever see a taste or pressure for integration so strong that the multiplication of theories would go into reverse and head towards a singularity? In the short term it looks unlikely but in the long term, if counselling survives, we might predict that any funded version of counselling will necessarily become a convergent one. A laissez-faire pluralistic hermeneutics of human nature, behaviour and change could drift on for years and can be defended as free organic development or as simply subject to the play of market forces. But it does seem probable that a more formal development of counselling will take place.

For this to occur, first we would need to agree on a sound definition of counselling and its scope and aims. But how likely is this without simultaneously addressing the problematic of all overlapping and competing psy-professions, and without falling into the fiasco of the pseudo-discriminations the HCPC found itself in in 2010 (between supposedly deep work with severe problems and less deep work with issues of wellbeing)? How realistic is the prospect of re-examining the very nature of clinical and counselling psychology, for example, when the deep problematic of *psychology itself* would eventually have to be faced? If the mess of dissensus goes back centuries and involves fiercely held differences of view about human nature, psychological health and growth, and mechanisms of intervention and change, are we ready and able to change things radically now? Were we able to convene a well-intentioned committee to decide on simplifying and vastly improving mental health services, even then we would encounter great difficulties in agreeing on what mental health is and whether counselling is necessarily about mental health at all. I suspect that all concerned realise how insurmountable the obstacles are and tacitly agree to continue with business as usual. Because movements like counselling begin organically and continue with stubborn tradition, they resist radical alteration. Were we able to begin at the beginning, we would need to put aside personal, theoretical and professional self-interest and thrash out clear definitions, identify and abolish duplications, cleanse associated language of all obfuscatory jargon, and push through deep-seated mental health and clinical ideologies to the possibility at least of some tentative consensus.

If we agreed to base counselling or some other arrangement of psychological therapy on a clearly demonstrated need among a significant public, to be practised after basic training, what place would theory have in this? I suspect that first a rather light general theory of the personal emotional-cognitive integration of practitioners, plus some theory underpinning basic skills and a range of techniques would be required. Ethical, legal and other factual matters require little theory although an aptitude for critical thinking would be necessary here. A consideration of client presenting problems, how these are to be assessed and which skills and techniques may be indicated, might be the main valid place for theory and debate. An awareness of what may not lend itself to psychological therapy and require referral elsewhere would also entail theorising and debate. If we so wished, we could devise a generic training programme free from narrow brand loyalty or 'schoolism'. If we came to see counselling as more akin to a practice like skiing or swimming, we would practise more and theorise less.

Instead of treating the many named therapeutic approaches as unassailable mini-faiths demanding reverence, I suggest all should be relegated to the status of working hypotheses, regardless of length of existence. If this cannot be done at any formal level, we can at least as individuals (and hopefully within all non-dogmatic trainings) doubt the right of any approach, so-called evidence-based or not, to hold itself up as anything but an enthusiastic, well-meaning set of ideas and practices. Even in those cases where a sizeable volume of confirmatory research has been conducted we have a right to hold them in doubt, given the many problems associated with research in this field. What might we fairly subject such hypotheses to before elevating them to the status of either scientific or philosophically coherent?

Smith spells out the tests he believes psychoanalysis should face if its proponents wish it to be considered scientific, as many of them do.[24] Freud's 'necessary conditions thesis' is based on the two conditions: that psychoanalytic insight is indispensable, and that *only* psychoanalytic treatment can bring about such insight. Similarly Rogers' necessary and sufficient conditions require unconditional positive regard, empathy and congruence. While humanistic psychology theorists wish to avoid scientific pretensions, perhaps they will nonetheless agree that their approaches should be made as *clear and credible* as possible. Could we ask that all discrete therapeutic hypotheses be submitted to the following tests?

1. Their claims should be clearly stated in plain language.

2. They should define clearly the scope and aims of their described approach (i.e., in terms of client population and presenting problems, and extent of envisaged success).

3. Their therapeutic claims should not be so vague or complex as to evade the tests of falsifiability.

4. They should accept the principle of predictability, that is, that their hypotheses will always be borne out by practice.

5. They should consider carefully the legitimacy of seeking exceptions to the rules of predictability.

6. They should show transparently how their ideas were arrived at, and make their reasoning and practice as open to examination and critique as possible.

7. An account should be given of the claimed uniqueness of their approach and of how it does or does not duplicate and improve on pre-existing theories in the field.

8. They should describe in detail all approach-specific practitioner attitudes, skills and techniques.

9. They should spell out why their new hypothesis and its practice is *necessary*.

10. Where they believe criteria such as these are based on a paradigm unsympathetic to their approach and its validation, they should be willing to fully elucidate their objections and propose alternative tests of credibility.

This is a tentative and not exhaustive list. Some requirements may be seen to be more readily fulfilled than others. For example, it should be relatively simple to explain matters in straightforward language (1), to identify the factors that make an approach unique (7) and necessary (9). Others however might prove extremely challenging. Who is willing to state categorically that his or her approach guarantees a (well-defined, enduring) successful outcome with everyone who is moderately depressed, say (4)? Who will avoid or minimise use of the common 'escape clause' whereby poorly trained or errant practitioners, or non-compliant clients are blamed for every failure (5)? How will a psychodynamic counsellor account for the successful outcomes of other approaches where insight was not a feature? How does the person-centred counsellor explain the uniqueness of the PCA and its success compared with others not explicitly utilising the core conditions?

Of course we do face a chicken-and-egg problem here. Nobody dreams up a new hypothesis, subjects it to such tests and only then tries it out on clients. Disaffection with existing models, combined with whatever personal motives, usually stokes an enthusiastic new creation which is gradually and cautiously tried out under another name, until there is confidence about launching the new product. (One under-analysed historical phenomenon in the field is precisely what practitioners like Berne, Beck, Ellis, Janov et al. were doing with their clients as they moved from the approach they were disaffected with to another of their own making.) Talking therapies cannot legally be held up in their small-scale informal trials with the public in the way drugs are. Often they are not so much designed as discovered (or allegedly so) by the spotting of a primal scream, negative automatic thoughts, or a felt sense. Here, we might still usefully theorise about why a novel technique or client experience apparently cannot be subsumed under existing approaches, why the creators of new models are driven to launch discrete approaches and so on.[25]

Endnotes

1. The figure of 600 is taken from Newnes, C. (in press). *The Toxic Industry: Deception and diagnosis in the mental health professions.* London: Palgrave.

2. See, for example, the following books: Hall, K., & Iqbal, F. (2010). *The Problem with Cognitive Behavioural Therapy.* London: Karnac; House, R., & Loewenthal, D. (Eds.). (2008). *Against and For CBT: Towards constructive dialogue.* Ross-on-Wye: PCCS Books; Loewenthal, D., & House, R. (2010). *Critically Engaging CBT.* Maidenhead: Open University Press. One of the signs that CBT's so-called evidence-based dominance was beginning to crack was the Swedish Government's ending of its policy of massive economic support for CBT, following a large-scale review in 2012 finding damningly negative results.

3. Hall, K., Godwin, N., & Snell, I. (2010). *The Problem with Psychoanalytic Psychotherapy.* London: Karnac.

4. Noonan, E. (1983). *Counselling Young People.* London: Methuen, p. ix.

5. Borch-Jacobsen, M., & Shamdasani, S. (2012). *The Freud Files: An inquiry into the history of psychoanalysis.* Cambridge: Cambridge University Press.

6. Smith, D. L. (2003). *Psychoanalysis in Focus.* London: Sage.

7. *Ibid.*, p. 142.

8. Wilkins, P. (2003). *Person-Centred Therapy in Focus.* London: Sage.

9. Thorne, B. (1992). *Carl Rogers.* London: Sage, p. 27.

10. Sulloway, F. J. (1980). *Freud: Biologist of the mind: Beyond the psychoanalytic legend.* London: Fontana.

11. 'Conditions of worth' lie at the heart of the Rogerian aetiology of later psychological problems. The infant (or even baby, or foetus) senses threats and disapproval which are then internalised in the self-concept, acting as self-protection.

12. Blanton, B. (1994). *Radical Honesty.* New York: Delta.

13. Ellis, A. (1997). Rational emotive behaviour therapy. In C. Feltham (Ed.), *Which Psychotherapy? Leading exponents explain their differences.* London: Sage, pp. 51–67.

14. Halmos, P. (1978). *The Faith of the Counsellors.* London: Constable.

15. Kirschenbaum, H., & Henderson, V. L. (Eds.). (1990). *Carl Rogers: Dialogues.* London: Constable, pp. 41–63.

16. Davenport, D. S. (1992). Ethical and legal problems with client-centered supervision. *Counselor Education and Supervision, 31*(4), 227–231.

17. Reed, D. (1976). *Anna.* New York: Basic Books.

18. Levitt, B. (2005). *Embracing Non-Directivity.* Ross-on-Wye: PCCS Books.

19. Sanders, P. (2004). *The Tribes of the Person-Centred Nation.* Ross-on-Wye: PCCS Books, p. 13.

20. Lazarus, A. (1990). Can psychotherapists transcend the shackles of their training and superstitions? *Journal of Clinical Psychology, 46,* 351–358.

21. Aldridge, S., & Pollard, J. (2005). *Interim Report to the Department of Health on Initial Mapping Project for Psychotherapy and Counselling.* Rugby: BACP and UKCP.

22. Garfield, S. (1995). *Psychotherapy: An eclectic-integrative approach* (2nd ed.). New York: Wiley.

23. Orlans, V., & van Scoyoc, S. (2009). *A Short Introduction to Counselling Psychology.* London: Sage, p. 19.

24. Smith, D. L. (2003). *Psychoanalysis in Focus.* London: Sage.

25. Feltham, C. (Ed.). (1997). *Which Psychotherapy? Leading exponents explain their differences.* London: Sage.

CHAPTER 4

Problems of counselling practice

On the face of it counselling is a rather simple matter. A person who is in distress or need (designated the client) sits on a chair and talks to another seated person[1] (designated the counsellor) who listens attentively and responds helpfully. This remains the core of counselling. It does not of course require a 'counsellor' or anyone with any other title to do their best to listen deeply and respond appropriately. This is to some extent what any good friend or partner will instinctively and compassionately do. It is also what doctors, nurses, teachers, priests and anyone else in caring interpersonal roles will sometimes do in the course of their work. There are indeed good reasons to think that some people in these circumstances may be very helpful, skilful, compassionate and possibly as competent as a trained professional. However, we are probably well aware that friends, partners, family members and untrained professionals often have limitations. They may be biased, impatient, have vested interests, fail to put aside their own concerns, lack confidentiality, fail to recognise severe problems, unintentionally or otherwise exploit or harm the distressed individual. You may not want your wife to know that you have doubts about your marriage, your friend may panic if you disclose your cancer diagnosis, or may want to drink alcohol while you talk, your doctor has only seven minutes to spend with you, and so on.

For all these reasons we seem to accept that a designated, trained, confidential helper is often necessary. Many of us, in spite of the ubiquity of self-help books, do not find what we need there. Most of us find self-analysis insufficient or impossible. For some, meditation or prayer or other practices help. Curiously, co-counselling, an egalitarian, amateur and cost-free arrangement, has never become a widely accepted practice. I think we must posit the idea that not only do practitioners promote a positive image of their profession with all its benefits and necessary components but it is what punters want or allow themselves to be persuaded into. Although only two or three decades ago many in the UK perceived counselling as something somewhat strange and unnecessary, it is now fairly widely accepted and even demanded. A certain level of private practice thrives and counselling is supported reasonably well in the NHS. Surveys of those with mental health problems commonly reveal a demand for counselling, often in preference to antidepressant medication. But counselling, like all similar social phenomena, has a history, tradition and set of expectations. The individual client, for all his anxiety or uncertainty, comes only to unburden himself, whereas the counsellor or counselling psychologist meets every client with a set of professional preoccupations and protocols in mind. Counselling paradoxically is both a fuzzy, complex and unpredictable business and a process crowded with self-conscious expectations. It is sometimes said that every client brings his family into the room with him (mentally) but the counsellor, too, brings her trainers, supervisors, theoretical authorities, employers, and shadowy professional overseers into the room.

Getting into practice

All trainees must work in some sort of placement or practicum during their training before they can even qualify, and many rely on such arrangements to consolidate their practice while they are accruing hours towards accreditation and before they can get paid employment. Placement opportunities are variable in supply and quality, with the worst offering a patchy throughput of clients and hit-or-miss (or no) supervision. In principle, trainees should gain experience of a variety of clients and of short-term and longer-term work, but in practice they often have to simply take what they can get. Nevertheless, many trainees benefit greatly, as do service providers and their clients, particularly since most such provision is free. A huge conundrum here is that many trainees struggle to complete their hours (100 for BACP course accreditation purposes) in order to gain their qualification. Some need an additional year or more to do this. Sometimes this time lag causes a blockage in the system as the next cohort of trainees awaits placements. This level of delay and frustration is one thing, but consider a more absurd logistical problem. Thousands of newly qualified counsellors are annually disappointed to find very few job opportunities and, even worse, sometimes struggle to find voluntary counselling work. The greatest absurdity here is that there is an over-abundant supply of counsellors and a huge demand from distressed people, with no effective mechanism for bringing them all together. Whatever the failings of counselling, it can certainly bring some basic comfort, yet lack of funding and will, combined with bureaucratic obstacles, frequently prevent this.

Theory into practice

Most counselling training courses deem it necessary for students to learn and internalise certain knowledge and skills before commencing practice. Some have experienced counselling as a client and some have not. BACP and BPS requirements differ on this. Most will, during the earliest stages of training, practise the use of counselling skills with fellow students, often following demonstrations by tutors and observing videos of distinguished practitioners in action. Some courses permit or even encourage students to begin practice immediately in order to get real experience and also to clock up hours towards accreditation. Most, however, consider it important to observe trainees closely, to give feedback, to study trainees' recordings of sessions with fellow students, all in order to ensure fitness to practise. Oddly enough, psychoanalytic training puts an emphasis on the trainees' own analysis but de-emphasises explicit skills training. For trainee counsellors it is the placement that signifies their readiness to begin to practise, that is, to work with their first 'real' clients.

Trainees gain their early experience in placements in a variety of counselling agencies, many of them in the voluntary sector, or in the NHS, educational and corporate settings. Such counselling should be of a standard suitable for the clients involved, hence some agencies assess clients and allocate those they consider appropriate to trainees. But assessment is not a science and clients who may at first appear suitable can turn out to have complex difficulties. Trainees will take all their concerns to supervision, however, and where necessary supervisors will identify inappropriate referrals or help the trainee to make their way through it all – learning on the job, being thrown in at the deep end, is how much of it is experienced. Clients are supposed to be made aware that their counsellor is a trainee, indeed their consent should be sought before counselling begins. But how the trainee presents her or his inexperience to the client can be problematic. A majority of clients seem happy to be seen at all and are agreeable. There is even some evidence that trainees may sometimes work with greater enthusiasm than more experienced practitioners and one of the associated conclusions (supported by some research) is that training may not in fact be necessary.[2] Along with this 'interesting' question is the matter of whether theory is necessary, or if it is deemed necessary, exactly what should it consist of?

Exactly what trainees bring to early practice depends on a number of factors. They may fortuitously have already worked as social workers or in another helping profession that has sensitised them to the counselling process. They may be mature in years and have relevant 'life experience' under their belt, including parenting, being a survivor of abuse or alcoholism, for example; that is, they may start out as 'wounded healers'. Some will have read extensively or have a voracious appetite for reading; others will not. Some will probably have a natural gift for counselling, a personal warmth, intuitiveness, insight, sensitivity and so on. In my experience any class of trainees contains variations in aptitude, articulateness, interpersonal and academic skill, attractiveness and so on. When you think about trainee variables as well as client variables, and depth and complexity of client problems, plus client motivation and readiness, alongside the trainee's readiness to practise, you may agree that a certain hit-or-miss dynamic is involved. Actually, one piece of counselling folklore here is that as a trainee counsellor you get the clients you deserve or need, or those who are mysteriously drawn to you. Counsellors of humanistic and psychodynamic persuasions often seem to believe that some sort of psychic attraction mechanism is operating. Hence 'I don't know how this client came to me' I have heard some say, in tones of awe and mystery, as if somehow the client is magically matched up with the right counsellor by unknown ethereal powers.

Against this kind of thinking (not, I must say, true for all) it is easy to see that for many trainees the theories taught in class and the associated academic assignments are rarely the most loved or valued aspects of becoming a counsellor. Not only do some trainees find parts of theory difficult to comprehend but they are also sometimes unconvinced by it. Imagine anxiously meeting your first clients when all your attention is probably focused on paying attention, tuning into your new role and not making a mess of things, and then on top of that, feeling that you are supposed to *apply theory*. It is unsurprising that trainees in this position would resent the burden of trying to believe in something that is not immediately useful but tutors too can struggle to explain exactly when and how theory should be applied. If, for example, a course is based on object relations or transactional analysis principles, it may not be at all clear how the trainee is to respond to her first clients presenting with problems of PTSD, OCD and other problems that are not obviously about relational difficulties. One wonders why courses are not more designed around presenting problems and variable clinical needs rather than generic theories of personality structure and change.

Attention to the client *in the moment* is crucial and undermined by theoretical preoccupation. Theory is to be referred to after sessions, between sessions and in supervision, according to one justification. But critics have long said that a large role for theory is about socialising trainees into a professional mindset. Supervision, case discussion and written case studies all require the theory-into-practice manoeuvre. BACP accreditation applications in fact demand case studies in which the applicant demonstrates how theory was applied, and of course it is not acceptable to argue that theory was added on after the event as a belated rationale. Hence, the fiction of theory as essential, useful and a lynchpin of training and practice becomes alleged non-fiction. The 'model' becomes reality. And most strangely, even theory-sceptical counsellors come to believe the fiction.

I am being unfair here to those trainees who deliberately choose a particular theoretical orientation, who do substantially believe in and grasp its theory and who do find themselves applying it in sessions and find it reassuring and stimulating. But it is hard to tease apart these from trainees who succumb to a myth propagated by some tutors that all trainees must begin their training like dependent, trusting acolytes. In this way of thinking competency comes developmentally by (uncritically) learning basic skills and theory first, being immersed in theory, and only gradually and at higher academic levels being permitted to think critically like a mature practitioner. Unfortunately it is true that in counsellor training there is no level playing field. To put it bluntly, some trainees/students are more intelligent than others, quicker to grasp subtle concepts, more articulate. This is evident to all tutors who must assess students' work. Strangely, tutors may agonise over whether to award a mark of 58 per cent or 59 per cent but on graduating, students on most courses appear equally well qualified.

We must at least pause to consider what parity exists between a student struggling on a Foundation degree course, say, and another enrolled on and confident within a doctoral programme in counselling psychology. The latter does not necessarily equate to a better practitioner but will probably have a firmer sense of theory and praxis. As I have said elsewhere in this book, it may be distasteful to make such comparisons but to avoid them doesn't banish them from reality. I won't, however, tackle the extremely sticky question of matching, say, a relatively inarticulate client and counsellor on the one hand and a highly educated and articulate client–counsellor pair on the other (always remembering that articulateness isn't the whole story regarding competency).

Counselling as unnatural

Counselling is asocial and asymmetrical. Traditionally it has been said to be neutral as to personal, religious and political values, with no clues forthcoming from the counsellor as to her beliefs. Critics suggest this posture is neither possible nor wise. But as Kahn puts it, one often finds 'a therapist mask, a therapist voice, a therapist posture and a therapist vocabulary'.[3] The client (I am never sure the word is really any better than the supposedly medically inappropriate term 'patient' but many counsellors recoil in horror at the latter usage) must quickly learn her or his role. You must talk about yourself with unfamiliar honesty and avoid small talk and rambling conversation. You must be punctual (not to be so may be considered pathological resistance), you must not expect to know anything personal about your counsellor. Do not bring your counsellor any gifts. If you have any strong negative or positive feelings about your counsellor, this is transference. Get used to filling an hour with meaningful utterances, emotional disclosures or uncomfortable silences. If you should wonder about your counsellor's competency or their mental health, or if their habit of repeating your words back to you seems irritating, you'd have to be a brave or insensitive soul to voice it, in spite of the counsellor's apparent openness to your feedback. But if you do get into the swing of it, if you find you appreciate the opportunity to offload, to have someone's completely nonjudgemental attention and allow yourself to become emotional, say, and recall painful events from your past, time this well. 'It's time to stop. Same time next week.'

Some counsellors secretly love the role of confidant, psychic explorer, diagnostic hotshot or trauma detective, psychological tough guy or saviour, and the not-uncommon client statement 'You're the first person who's ever really listened to me' can be enormously seductive. Who knows how many counsellors harbour a prurient interest in the details of others' lives? Silence to some comes naturally but some have to bite their lip not to blurt out their great insights into your behaviour, some force themselves to sit on their hands instead of throwing their arms around you when you cry. For many, spontaneity is constrained by training. Some must experience confidentiality as a muzzling of the natural gossip instinct. Sometimes the enormity of the client's suffering seems overwhelming and the counsellor barely knows how to begin to respond. Silences, reflections and clichés can rescue a counsellor from such awkward moments. Counsellors are, after all, only human. It may be that some of the best, for example, some deeply congruent person-centred practitioners, allow themselves to be fully human. Up to a point, that is, but not including giving the poor client money or free sessions or telling the one with low self-esteem and poor body image how much you fancy them. A few risk-taking counsellors might do this but only a very few. Years ago, at the height of humanistic therapy's popularity, more practitioners would have been confrontational when it felt right – letting the client know what a jerk he's being, how fucked up she'll be if she stays with that jealous guy, and so on. Today, along with the success of counselling in the NHS and other settings, counsellors are probably more cautious and defensive. In some clinical settings you would hardly want the client to sob too loudly lest nearby colleagues became alarmed or a client complained that you had made them cry. The old adage sometimes passed on to clients that things may get more painful in counselling before they get better is probably heard rather less these days.

Following Freud, we have become used to the idea that clients come to the practitioner's room for an hour (or 50 minutes) at a time. The medium is mainly verbal, with many approaches expecting the client to set the agenda, which may typically comprise a little updating of the week's events, feelings and sense of progress, followed perhaps by an emergent focus on significant memories or present-day preoccupations. The client inevitably selects what she presents in any session, with the counsellor sometimes challenging or bringing back a past topic, say. Above all, the counsellor gets an edited picture of the client's life and cannot know accurately what their everyday experiences and interactions are like, what their partner and family members are really like, and so on. The emphasis on consulting room boundaries prevents the counsellor from learning much directly about the client. One can imagine that if the counsellor were able to accompany the client on a typical day in their life, a modified picture would emerge; you would see your client's habits of waking, hygiene, eating, dressing, interacting, and passing time. This might conceivably enable you to see more accurately where the client is 'going wrong' and what might help, for example, in terms of time structuring, nutrition, reacting to others. But this kind of ambulatory therapy is hardly conceivable, given the tradition of the office-bound, verbal interchange, reflective ritual that is the uncritical habit and tradition of most therapy and counselling.

Counselling is unnatural too when compared with everyday life and relationships. It is unnaturally attentive, warm and nonjudgemental. Think of the counselling psychologist who works in a prison or other criminal justice setting. I worked in a probation hostel for some years and remember clearly the somewhat wry and dismissive reaction of some clients/residents receiving counselling: 'the outside world is not like this, the people I know are not like you, my circumstances are not like yours'. Such clients may face constant pressures to commit crimes, to act tough and cynical, to drink, to shut off painful feelings. One hour weekly of asocial counselling for a limited period, from a middle-class counsellor, is not enough to turn around the effects of a lifetime of abuse and acute daily difficulties.

Counselling as cure?

A major assumption of early psychoanalysis was that the uncovering of unconscious conflicts teeming beneath the symptoms would remove symptoms, in other words that the client would be 'cured' of the form of distress that brought him to analysis. This expectation came over the years to fade into a set of fuzzier aims such as addressing symptoms, helping the client or facilitating the client's own growth process. Halmos frankly refers to 'the mirage of results'.[4] Conversely, Arthur Janov was one of the very few who promoted his approach in the 1970s – primal therapy – as the cure for *all* 'neurosis', and the *only* cure. NLP proclaims that it has an effective 'phobia cure'. Counselling traditionally avoided any expectation of cure, partly due to its medical connotation and partly out of awareness that any promised cure could lead to complaints and potential law suits on its not being forthcoming. But dropping the terminology of cure was also strongly linked with the psychodynamic aim of insight and the person-centred aim of helping the client to achieve self-acceptance, congruence and actualisation. In other words, putative underlying or accompanying process factors were valued by counsellors more highly than 'cure' or outcome. Practitioners were, and still are, fascinated by the therapeutic process, the moment-by-moment micro-interactions, the subtleties of intersubjectivity, the wrestling with meanings, the work of making the unconscious conscious.

In the 2000s, with the growth of counselling in the NHS and the expansion of research, the promotion of evidence-based practice, and then with the advent of NICE, a sea change occurred. Although the term 'cure' wasn't used, concepts of effectiveness and outcome became commonplace and counsellors in employment had to accommodate to this new culture.[5] Practitioners in private practice were less pressurised, but clients/consumers were becoming more savvy. Newspaper articles began to summarise research and recommend CBT as more effective than other approaches. Not only had the ideas of consumer discernment as to the clinical and cost effectiveness of therapy and counselling arrived but the wisdom of discriminating between competing methods was on the agenda. Clients were being urged to shop around and indeed a shift was detectable between the expectation of one committed shot at therapy (for all ills) and multiple attempts.

It's possible that a mixture of fudged research evidence, positive public relations and letting people believe what they want to believe has created the fantasy that a majority of clients generally achieve all their desired outcomes. Standard textbooks present chapters on the main conditions, treatment approaches and case studies that reinforce the fantasy of total and permanent cure. Clients who were not helped at all, who went from counsellor to counsellor (or therapist or psychologist), suffering for years, relapsing time and time again, may be airbrushed from the picture or briefly discussed in terms of anomaly or noncompliance. Read client accounts or attend user meetings to discover how frequently attempts to halt obsessive compulsive disorder or insomnia, for example, fail. Yet official records may well show some of these as therapeutic successes. Gayle Green, for example, is a lifelong insomniac who tried everything, read everything, attended high-level specialist conferences, interviewed sleep experts, and found occasional relief and fallible coping strategies but overall no real improvement.[6]

Alongside the image of talking therapy as cure- or outcome-focused practice there has been for decades the notion of therapy or counselling – of *being in* counselling – as a normal cultural practice, indeed a rite of passage or fashion. The British have mocked Americans for their lifestyle choice of being in lengthy therapy (New Yorkers in analysis, Californians in encounter or personal growth groups) but have now also succumbed to the same phenomenon to some extent. 'Perhaps you should see a therapist/counsellor', a friend or colleague may say. One no longer has to have sharply defined problems to be 'cured', it is sufficient to feel that one's life is in a mess or that certain problematic behaviours are repeating themselves. For some, entering therapy or counselling is also like a faith in stripping away the internalised false values of society (or at least of one's parents) in order to discover the holy grail of authenticity. Even more grandiose is the idea that all citizens should have therapy as a way of transforming society, a fantasy that can be found even in the earliest days of psychoanalysis. Perhaps in a conscription-free era and culture we have almost taken on a myth of voluntary and courageous self-purgation, fighting our own demons, as a service to our country. Paying for five years in analysis, or even two years in counselling, with nothing visible to show for it, must mean something after all.

Counselling context

Counsellors and counselling psychologists work in an array of settings – mostly the NHS, voluntary sector, education, commercial organisations – and frequently in private or independent practice. A majority of counsellors have a mixed portfolio of work which may include a part-time unrelated job, part-time or sessional counselling, supervision, training and consultancy. Some enjoy this diversity and some do not but have no choice. Some counsellors are privileged to be semi-retired or have a well-remunerated working partner and therefore do not rely entirely on an income from counselling; many of these work in the voluntary sector. Given the paucity of funding for counselling agencies and jobs, many voluntary organisations such as Cruse, Mind, Relate and some eating disorders, domestic violence, rape and sexual assault, drug and alcohol agencies traditionally support trainees on placement and may continue to use some trained but unpaid counsellors. Counsellors in this position are every bit as trained and qualified but questions can hang over them about their status and how their 'working for nothing' undermines counselling as a profession. Nevertheless, many clients, who cannot afford to pay for counselling or cannot access free statutory services for their particular needs, depend on counselling provided by the voluntary sector. Often humanistic and psychodynamic approaches are espoused or supported. Longer-term counselling may be available, diagnostic categories are probably avoided, and the environment may be private even if not always well furnished.

Counsellors working in the NHS, particularly in primary care, may find themselves in various less-than-ideal medical offices used for other purposes. Case notes and records are usually stored along with other medical records manually or on computer systems. Usually counsellors are obliged to use brief questionnaires and instruments for evaluation purposes (GAD7, PHQ9, CORE, etc.) and there are mixed feelings about this practice which until recently was alien to counselling practice and theory. While some counsellors value this exercise, more reluctantly go through the motions of doing it because they value their jobs and need the money. On the ground one hears that many clients dislike the practice or just go along with it. Attention to (or is it anxiety about?) suicidality and child protection issues is heightened in this sector. Counselling in these settings is usually time limited (typically six or eight sessions, sometimes extendable) and often counsellors see pre-assessed clients who are deemed suitable, such as those who are bereaved, separating or divorcing, stressed, mild to moderately depressed or anxious, and so on. Again, on the ground, one hears of many referrals to counsellors that are complex (e.g., sexual abuse, post-traumatic stress, eating disorders) because there is no one else available to see them or they may have been judged too non-compliant or otherwise unsuitable for cognitive behavioural therapists or other mental health professionals. Counsellors in these settings may be acutely aware of their lower status and pay (especially in relation to their high caseloads) but a job is a job in a weak domain like counselling, all the more so in rough economic times. Most ironically, it is not uncommon to hear of counsellors experiencing job-triggered stress going off sick.

Counsellors working in further and higher education, usually in small teams, often part time, tend to see a full range of client-presenting problems, with depression, anxiety, losses, issues of sexuality, addiction and identity being uppermost. The age range is younger than elsewhere, the environment often informal and exciting, and such jobs are sought after. Although job security is now far from predictable, counsellors in universities are often on relatively high salaries and good conditions of employment. Despite the egalitarian ethos of counselling, university counselling teams usually have hierarchies in terms of seniority and pay, probably reflecting the overall structure of universities. My impression is that in spite of the good work done with vulnerable young people, such counselling teams are often the site of rivalries, grievances and unhappiness. Organisational stress and conflict are hardly a novel phenomenon, the Tavistock Institute and other psychoanalytic institutions having analysed, consulted and published copiously on such matters. But it is a curious finding that teams of counsellors – people dedicated to the understanding and amelioration of mental health and interpersonal problems – sometimes create and cannot resolve intense interpersonal problems.

Counselling within or for commercial companies (and non-commercial organisations providing staff counselling) has grown significantly over the last three decades. Driven by a combination of genuine care, concerns for staff efficiency, particular risk factors in certain occupations (e.g., airline pilots, train drivers, frontline staff exposed to violent assault) and awareness of litigation possibilities, some companies create internal counselling departments, subcontract to others or sometimes hire counsellors on an ad hoc basis. Employee assistance programmes (some of which are American owned) pay private practitioners to see employee-clients for a strictly limited number of sessions for work-related concerns.

In practice, it is difficult to separate work-related concerns from entirely personal issues and this can present dilemmas for counsellors whose clients have only three or six sessions available to them. (In fact I know of some employee counselling services where valued senior staff are permitted a greater number of sessions than lower grade staff.) Probably the greatest criticism of counselling in this context is that those who engage the counsellor are often also the source of the client's problem. An impossible workload, a constant threat of redundancy, bullying or harassing managers, depressingly boring work routines are not alleviated by counselling. Even when a counsellor hears repeated stories about workplace horrors, and even when hypothetically the company says it wishes to get feedback and act on it, in reality things rarely change. The counsellor is then left feeling ignored and impotent. But why would counsellors for toxic companies ever fantasise that their individual work with clients would overthrow the inevitable damage they do to employees? Most organisations will continue to perpetrate damage on employees, which can be 'unconsciously' welcomed by counsellors since it promises an infinite stream of clients. Cavil at the presumed cynicism of such statements, or object that many employers are benevolent and most employees happy in their work, if you will, but this problem is unlikely to go away. The mismatch between the bottom-line motives and ethos of corporations and the naïvely reformist or utopian fantasies of counsellors is vast.

It is at the private (independent, freelance) counselling and psychotherapy sector that the wrath of critics is often aimed.[7] Many counsellors maintain very small part-time practices charging modest hourly fees to clients (sometimes spending more on mandatory supervision than their income from clients) but some practitioners in large urban areas, especially affluent parts of London, charge high fees and make substantial incomes. Obviously intensive psychoanalysis over many years for the affluent 'worried well' is what pays best and most reliably. Short-term counselling in low income areas is clearly a poor relation. Indeed, given the prevalence of private practice being conducted from counsellors' own homes (the overheads are very low), it is no surprise that clients are more impressed by private practices located in smart middle-class homes and areas. The experience of being seen by a highly articulate, highly qualified counselling psychologist living in an expensive, well-furnished house can act like a placebo, a trick that the working-class counsellor living on a council house estate cannot hope to pull off. Actual competency is not necessarily related to class, qualifications and setting but is likely to be perceived as such. It is for some of these reasons that individual and group practices in settings apart from the practitioner's home have been used increasingly, because this is (perceived as) 'more professional' (not to mention more expensive for clients).

There are other reservations about private practice. It is possibly the most risky in terms of the client not getting a good return for her money (especially in long-term therapy), arguably the site of most practitioner abuse, and the least regulated or monitored. Although practitioners may well have regular supervision, they usually choose their own supervisors, are likely to make convenient choices, and such is their dependence on every paying client for their livelihood (especially if this is full time) that they are extremely likely to want clients to stay in therapy for some time. Subtle pressure on clients to do so is understandable in these circumstances and there is usually no obvious point at which therapy is clearly over. Psychodynamic and humanistic approaches are those most oriented to in-depth long-term work. But the biggest criticism is simply that counselling in the private sector discriminates against the poor. Counselling has an overwhelming ethos of caring and egalitarianism but when the chips are down even the most unconditionally positive regarding of counsellors is unlikely to continue to counsel many clients who have lost their jobs and incomes.

Some counsellors manage to convince themselves and others that because counselling is a valuable service like any other in the kind of economy we happen to have, self-respecting counsellors should value themselves appropriately and charge high fees accordingly. Two problems present themselves here. First, against which other professionals should counsellors compare themselves in order to determine their fee levels – cleaners, shelf stackers, plumbers, teachers, psychiatrists, brain surgeons, corporate CEOs? What is reasonable – £30, £40, £50, £70, £100, £150 or more per hour?[8] The stock response here is that counsellors pay dearly for their own training, supervision, CPD, insurance, etc., that they have a unique set of high level skills, and as professionals have to cover all their costs. Second, it is often heavily implied that charging low fees (a) does a disservice to your colleagues/competitors by undercutting them, and (b) reflects a problem you may have with low self-esteem. I have even heard the argument that poor clients could very well pay your fees *if they really wanted and valued counselling*, for instance, by stopping smoking, drinking or other predominantly working-class habits. A counter argument sometimes put here is that you could invite a good friend out to dinner on several occasions and pay the bill, in return for them listening to your concerns, instead of paying the same amount or more to a counsellor or therapist. Money is such a pivotally difficult issue for counsellors and therapists that it is usually avoided as a subject for analysis or teaching.[9]

From the counsellor's point of view, from the time of considering training to post-qualifying decisions about careers generally, the most serious problem for all but those fortunately supported by partners or other income streams is reliable income from counselling. The early fantasy of a meaningful career helping people in distress can come crashing down to the reality of few or no jobs available, high competition for those that do exist, and chasing and maintaining a sufficient number of paying clients in private practice. In this scenario, apart from the principle of *caveat emptor*, we have the long-ignored problem of culpability lying with course providers and professional bodies who have failed to make responsible links between annual training places, qualifying practitioners and actual jobs and clients. For all the straining off of the midges of professional ethics, those stakeholders responsible continue to gulp down the camels of unethical profiteering from hopeful trainee counsellors. One paradoxically good sign in recent years has been that a small number of university providers of counselling training, hit by changes in government subsidies, have had no ethical compunctions about closing such courses.

Brief and time-limited counselling

Traditionally, for the best part of the 20th century, counselling and psychotherapy were conceived and practised as open ended and long term. Psychoanalysis might take many years at several times a week, psychoanalytic psychotherapy might take two years at once or twice a week, and counselling usually took a few months at once a week. But sometimes psychotherapy would be terminated after a few months and counselling would continue for several years. In the USA the question of how long therapy should take came to the fore in the 1960s with Health Maintenance Organisations. In the UK a number of factors conspired to bring this question on to the agenda only around 1990. American-style employee assistance programmes (EAPs) imported into the UK typically limited sessions to anywhere between 3 and 12. The growth of counselling in the NHS and the problem of waiting lists began to cause service providers to consider limiting sessions. The growth of CBT and of some humanistic approaches also contributed to a critique of the assumption that counselling must or usually would take a long time.

Initially there was massive resistance. Counsellors and therapists protested that this was unethical, that clients would be short-changed, that damage would ensue, and so on. To some extent these objections remain in some quarters. However, in light of the paucity of employment, many psychotherapists and counsellors of a psychodynamic and humanistic persuasion found themselves willing to take on short-term therapeutic contracts with clients, whether opportunistically or intrigued by the challenge. Indeed new models arose – intensive short-term dynamic therapy, brief dynamic therapy, cognitive analytic therapy and others. Neurolinguistic programming, solution-focused therapy, eye movement desensitisation and reprocessing (EMDR) blossomed and many counsellors embraced an 'integrative' spirit of practice. Diehard psychoanalysts and person-centred counsellors continued to resist, the former on grounds of tradition, the latter in the principled belief that it must be left to clients to determine their own therapeutic pace and ending. It is a moot point whether psychoanalysts truly accept psychodynamic counselling, the latter almost always being much briefer than the former.

In all the debate surrounding the advent of time-conscious therapy, brief therapy and time-limited counselling, certain arguments took time to percolate through to awareness. First, within services with finite resources, the more time each client used, the less time was available for new clients and waiting lists would grow. Second, where ex-clients of private practitioners had written negative accounts of their experiences, their complaints often centred on psychoanalytic practice in which they had felt dependent, pathologised and ultimately unimproved but blamed for their own lack of progress. Where long-term practice was or is the norm, problems of this kind seem likely to arise: why not regard short term as the norm and extend therapy or counselling only if necessary? Third, clients benefit from short-term, time-limited counselling in being able to foresee how much time they need for it and/or what they will spend on it. Fourth, some research revealed that, contrary to expectations, a majority of clients of all services used an average of only six sessions even when they had free access to more; in other words, many wanted only brief rather than protracted help. Fifth, psychoanalysts and all other psy-practitioners had learned over the years to take it for granted that clients would have their individual sessions strictly limited to 50 or 60 minutes, even when at the end of their 'hour' they might well be in the midst of deep distress. Is that not reprehensible doublethink? Sixth, and most damningly, it looks as if those most opposed to brief therapy are those most likely to benefit financially from long-term therapy or counselling, in other words those in private practice whose mortgages are most reliably paid by a small number of clients (or 'patients') attending several times a week for several years.

This isn't to ignore the reality that some clients do in fact need more time, sometimes much more time, especially those with deep-seated and complex personal problems as opposed to relatively simple single issues. Where possible, they should get the time they need. But in my experience many counsellors are stubbornly unrealistic, arguing that counselling should be available to everyone who needs it, when they need it. Now, it is perhaps true that in the emotional domain of psychological pain, ideally every one of us would receive the help we need, the counsellor or therapist of our choosing, for as long we need it, regardless of ability to pay. This is not, of course, how the world works. The UK has 42,000 GPs, each of whom gives a typical seven-minute consultation to each patient at each visit, yet an army of counsellors fantasises that employment should be made available for them. One rough estimate has it that there are 70,000 paid counsellors in the UK, and we might struggle to understand the comparative economics involved here.

What counsellors agonise about

Two of the goals or values of humanistic counselling are spontaneity and authenticity. It would be interesting to know what proportion of trainees on entering training possess such lively, outgoing personalities compared with the proportion who are introspective, anxious or even somewhat obsessive. I pose it like this because counselling culture seems saturated with inwardness, rumination and worry about the most detailed of matters. This is, of course, partly natural in a profession focused on distress and the careful and ethical responses to distress. It is probably exacerbated by the nebulousness of so much counselling and the mismatches between this and the infrastructure of theory and fantasies of linear progress. Let's consider now some of the infrastructure.

The therapeutic relationship

Most counsellors will have been exposed in training to the idea that the relationship between client and counsellor is paramount. According to some theories, getting the relationship off to a good start is absolutely key. The therapeutic alliance model of Bordin, for example, argues that strong bonds, clear tasks and explicit goals are crucial.[10] Clarkson's five relationships framework suggests that a working alliance must exist; transference and countertransference are always in play; the person-to-person or I–Thou relationship is always in play; a developmentally needed or reparative relationship is sometimes indicated; and a transpersonal relationship may also manifest itself.[11] For person-centred practitioners the core conditions alone are always central. Yet at the same time counsellors are taught to listen accurately and deeply to clients, and to expect sometimes not to know what is happening, which seems to contradict the above tenets of relational theory. But counsellors must be able to tolerate ambiguity too. So most will perhaps balance or alternate an informed mind with an open and a confused mind. Some counsellors fall into repeating the mesmerising cliché that 'it's all about the relationship'.

Contracting and boundaries

Good practice guidelines have it that clients should know some of what is being offered and what to expect, indeed they can only give their informed consent when they know what they are consenting to. Trainees may be taught to inform new clients about the service and its parameters, confidentiality and its exceptions, record keeping, sessions and timekeeping, cancellations, therapeutic orientation and its meaning and expectations. Clients may also want to know about the counsellor's training, qualifications, experience and supervision, professional body membership and ethical code and complaints route. The counsellor should perhaps mention risks of self-harm and what actions might be taken if suicidality is suspected. We then approach matters of boundaries, for example, an explanation that counselling is not a social or personal relationship but a professional one; that there can be no dual relationships; whether the client can be reached by phone in the event of not turning up; the likelihood that the counsellor will not acknowledge the client if they accidentally meet in public. And so on.

There are big problems with all this. Clients are unlikely to take it in when they arrive and counsellors are often reluctant to bombard clients with information on first meeting them. It often feels indelicate and frightening to mention suicide too early. Spelling out too laboriously the expectations of boundary maintenance can sound unfriendly and obsessional ('I will not touch you, socialise with you, visit you at home', etc.). In the psychodynamic approach it can be very important to stay as minimalist as possible in order to let the client enter into states of fantasy and transference as necessary. A person-centred practitioner may want to begin the person-centredness immediately, which would require avoidance or minimising of such information-imparting and contract making. In rural areas it may be impractical to avoid social contact. In small professional circles the two parties' paths may often collide. For all these reasons few practitioners will give all necessary information or will postpone some of it until it feels right and in practice discretion may often be used. Also, considerable disagreement between practitioners from different therapeutic approaches exists about many of these matters.

It may be due in part to the excesses of several of the founding fathers that counselling has become the scrupulously ethical activity that it is today. Agonise over small gifts, home visits, a timely hug, consider the wisdom of a lifetime ban on relationships with ex-clients, and eagerly embrace lifelong supervision of all your work. Even when ineffective, your counselling will be ethical!

Assessment

It is conceivable that some practitioners, say some radical humanistic counsellors in private practice, might ask new clients no questions about their reasons for beginning counselling and might keep an open mind that entertains no hypothesis about clients that is anything remotely diagnostic. But this seems unlikely since we all form impressions about people we meet, including momentarily pigeonholing them as warm, friendly, chatty or cold and withdrawn. Anyone who has read even a little psychology or psychopathology, or has been somewhat familiar with mental health and counselling discourse, will find it hard not to have words like depression, anxiety, post-traumatic, eating or alcohol problem, delusional, and so on, popping into their mind. Terms like passive aggressive, defensive, paranoid and schizoid have passed into everyday language. Yet some humanistic counsellors distance themselves from the practice of assessment, claiming that it pathologises, labels and dehumanises and even that the so-called psychiatric disorders do not exist. It has also been mooted that 'a feminist counselling psychology approach is rooted in a social-constructionist understanding' and since 'the nature and role of power is central to feminist counselling psychology' assessment is regarded with great ambivalence.[12]

At the opposite end of the spectrum we have a psychiatric tradition that rests on clinical assessment that finds it imperative to arrive at diagnostic decisions. The reason this particular client has come for help or come reluctantly before this mental health practitioner is that he is suffering from such and such a disorder as described in the *DSM*, say. He may be assessed as having no discernible or treatable problem, as having comorbid symptoms, or as exhibiting classic symptoms of a common disorder. Practitioners may well disagree about diagnoses or take a long time to reach one. But a chain of reasoning exists between presenting symptoms and diagnostic assessment, and a treatment plan which may include no intervention, counselling, CBT, medication and hospitalisation. Most clinical psychologists belong within this tradition, and CBT and psychoanalytic practitioners commonly put into action assessment procedures at the beginning of any therapy.

The problems of assessment then include whether it has any value at all; what its terminology and purposes are; how to reconcile different diagnoses resulting from it; who should implement it (including the degree to which it should be co-assessment with the client); how it impacts on the client; how it is linked to monitoring of progress and ultimate evaluation of outcome. In reality many clients now self-assess by Google or other means, or come to the attention of mental health practitioners involuntarily or reluctantly. Again, in reality I know of very few counsellors who do not practise at least some minimal form of assessment, even if covertly in the shape of a working hypothesis. Whatever individual practices exist, most talking therapists probably experience a degree of uncertainty about the necessity and place of assessment. Arguably in the person-centred approach it is simply redundant, the focus being on the whole person and his or her phenomenological field. But the picture is complicated by some clients' preference for a diagnostic label and the reassurance of 'knowing what's wrong with me'. Not only are practitioners in disagreement with each other here but sometimes they are out of synch with their clients' wishes.

Suicidal ideation

The possibility that a client will kill himself is perhaps the greatest fear for most counsellors. It brings up a cluster of anxieties. The counsellor should be able to foresee and prevent it (although this implies some form of assessment). She should be able to discriminate between the common, passively toned utterance 'Sometimes I wish I was dead' and the active plan leading up to it. She should know the difference between attention-seeking or release-effecting self-harm and a serious suicide attempt. If serious suicidal impulses are in evidence, the counsellor should act swiftly and skilfully to alert related professionals (if necessary breaching confidentiality) and to get the client to contract not to commit suicide between sessions, say, by 'closing the escape hatches' in transactional analysis terms. She should liaise closely with a supervisor. Should a suicide be successfully carried out she will probably face some anxiety about whether she did enough to prevent it, about the possibility of official investigations or law suits, about her professional reputation and her very future as a counsellor. She will also be susceptible to feelings of sadness and anger which could cloud her ongoing work with other clients.

Should a suicide bid fail, she may well have to agonise about whether it is a boundary violation for her to visit the client in hospital and whether she can continue to work with the client.

Yet at the same time she is aware that no one can ultimately prevent anyone else from committing suicide. From a radical person-centred perspective (most likely to be found in private practice), it is even defensible practice to empathise with someone's suicidal tendency and refrain from intervention, while in statutory settings the pressure will be on all practitioners to prevent it. Although we have no test cases yet, it is quite possible that counsellors could be drawn into the controversy surrounding assisted suicide, at least in the sense that they might be perceived as psychologically condoning a suicide. But one of the main problems concerning client suicide is the philosophical depths of the matter. Counselling course tutors do not have the facility to include input from moral philosophy on the nuances of suicide. (Is it ever justified? Is it always a result of depression?) Nor do they have the luxury of having trainees reflect much on philosophical or theological views on how good or bad a world this is, which would provide some foundation for understanding suicide and addressing it when it arises as a possibility. The literature on suicidology and specialised suicide prevention techniques alone could fill a course. And counsellors themselves are not immune from suicidal thoughts or actual suicide, as discussed briefly in Chapter 2.

Transference, dependency, and complications

We have looked at transference and countertransference in theory. In practice, some practitioners talk about working in, with or against the transference. A client's transference, if it really exists at all, may be fleeting or entrenched, positive, negative, erotic or whatever. Psychodynamic counsellors expect and welcome it, and have no doubts about its reality; it is the water in which they swim. For others, it may be considered not to arise (for instance in very short-term work), or to be noted but not worked with, or not to exist. In some cases the client–counsellor pair may find themselves entangled in mutual or antagonistic emotions from which it becomes difficult to extract themselves.

A case was reported to me some years ago of a female client feeling sucked into a vortex of dependency on her male person-centred counsellor, into an experience of mutual sexual attraction (without physical contact) that became progressively unhelpful and painful. It was so bad for her that she considered complaining to the professional body but did not because she felt protective towards her counsellor in spite of his perceived incompetency and the pain it caused. He seemed to enjoy the depth and drama of it all, and could justify this with person-centred concepts. Had this come to light, psychodynamic observers might well have enjoyed a quiet moment of *Schadenfreude* at the counsellor's ineptitude in not knowing how to deal with the transference and countertransference. The point of this story is the aggregate conundrum that (a) it could happen to anyone, given the complexity of human beings, the unpredictable interpersonal chemistry involved, and the probability of occasional entanglements, (b) it wouldn't happen to properly trained psychodynamic practitioners, and (c) apparently it doesn't happen to everyone (as far as we know), particularly those practising short-term non-psychodynamic therapies. Finally, if and when such messy entanglements occur, we do not conclusively know if they have anything to do with putative unconscious forces, practitioner incompetency or abuse, and/or the client's manipulative behaviour.

One trend we should probably watch carefully is for immersion in long-term psychoanalytic therapy in private practice to foster the conditions in which damaging client dependency may occur.[13] Combined fiscal and ideological pressures easily result in a therapist continuing to see a client for many years with few if any mechanisms for evaluation of effectiveness. At its worst, this scenario can result in years spent unproductively and sometimes in the client deteriorating, with much money wasted. Unlike the sensationalist cases of therapists sexually abusing clients, mere dependency and therapeutic failure (or an indeterminate outcome) attract far less publicity and concern. This may be due to a tacit recognition that much therapy and counselling has rather vague aims and outcomes, and clients sometimes blame themselves for lack of progress.

All counsellors understand that such entangled and problematic relationships happen. Most are probably conscientious enough to discuss such cases in supervision. But it is a well-known fine balance the counsellor must often face between getting over-involved or under-involved. Some clients keep you at a distance or something in you struggles to connect with them, or on the other hand you feel especially drawn to and deeply connected with certain clients. What a coincidence that your beautiful client gets divorced at the same time that you are single, and you both like each other intensely (or is it always transferential and always wrong?). Is it a chance rapport, a transpersonal meeting of souls, or an unrecognised countertransference and a disaster waiting to happen? The properly trained, more conscious than unconscious psychological therapist can be expected not to fall into such traps, or to wrestle with them with ethical heroism and iron self-control when they arise. Alternatively, the pressure is on for the counsellor to maintain ever-healthy relationships outside of their work so they are never tempted unconsciously or abusively to use clients for their own emotional gratification.

Progress, success, endings

Person-centred counsellors may eschew assessment but they know from studying Rogers' writings that most clients commence on the 'seven stages of process' (from psychological fixity to fluidity) identified by Rogers[14] or that clients begin in a state of incongruence and move towards congruence. By closely tracking clients' descriptions of their own ever-shifting inner processes they get a sense of progress from moment to moment and across sessions, across weeks and months. Just relating to each other is a success and no goal has to be spelled out in advance. Similarly in psychodynamic counselling, defences may be rife at the beginning but will fall as the client gains insights as the unconscious becomes conscious. Since all theoretical dogma dictates that correct understanding and application necessarily lead to progress, then barring stubborn client non-compliance and resistance, progress is what happens in every case. Progress and success are even better guaranteed when a client knowingly buys into a particular approach in private practice after having read or heard about it and deciding to take the plunge. Hopes and fantasies of success may often coincide with actual success (where this is measurable in some way) but cognitive dissonance can also sometimes furnish delusions of success: 'I've spent so much time and money on this, I suppose it must be working.'

Perhaps there are complacent or strictly approach-faithful counsellors who assume that reasonable progress is sure to be made with all clients. But more often counsellors are aware of some undercurrents of resistance and ambivalence, and patches of stuckness, impasse and meandering, not to mention crises and relapses[15] and 'cycles of change'. 'I'm not sure this is going anywhere', the honest supervisee may say, or 'I just don't know what I can do with this client'. A large part of the supervisor's job is to restore the faith. Person-centred supervisors may urge counsellors to 'stay with the stuckness' and remember that counselling is about being-with, not doing-to. The client knows deep down what to do, what pace to move at, and so on. Psychodynamic supervisors may remind counsellors about mechanisms such as projective identification and about the need for constant 'working through'. Cognitive behavioural supervisors are more likely to suggest alternative technical strategies but may also ask about therapeutic alliance maintenance and client compliance. Counsellors are often reminded to 'trust the process', another article of faith. Keep going, in other words. Sometimes reviews with clients are in order, where in principle both are free to voice with complete honesty their views on how well things are progressing or not. Counselling is an arena where high levels of candour are expected but I suspect both parties always harbour some inhibitions about potentially upsetting the other.

Variations in delivery

I have concentrated in this book on traditional, individual face-to-face counselling but now counselling comes in various modalities. One-to-one counselling remains the preference for the majority of clients but couple and group counselling also have a long history. In couple counselling it is often said that 'the relationship is the client', in other words the focus is on the bond between the two clients, who are expected to attend together but do not always do so. The same counselling theories will be applied (although often with a Relate-endorsed emphasis on attachment theory) but the counsellor is frequently faced with *in situ* crisis and anger management issues and with the challenge of attempting to remain impartial. In practice, it is more often the female partner who has initiated counselling, a predominance of counsellors is female, and the milieu is intimacy and communication. It is also an arena for the discussion or concealment of chronic resentments, affairs, differences over money, sex, child-rearing and life values and ambitions, as well as very real heartbreak. It is acknowledged that couple counselling cannot always save marriages (but often does) but can help manage discussion and where necessary, separation, with reduced conflict. Significant success is claimed for couple counselling. It is easy to see the many socioeconomic reasons for higher divorce rates and to appreciate the need for sensitive assistance with the conflict and pain involved. But the same problems as those cited for individual counselling apply here.

Group counselling (more often referred to as group therapy) is often cheaper than one-to-one counselling; it enables clients to learn from others' (peers') experiences and to some extent to 'practise' better communication within the group. Psychodrama and drama therapy are arenas in which enhanced opportunities for observation, experimentation and catharsis are afforded. Group formats are often favoured in the addictions field, for a number of reasons, but remain overall far less popular and available than individual counselling. It is both free of some of the problems of one-to-one work and also burdened with greater complexity. We could add family therapy here but it is seldom included alongside counselling.

Like psychotherapy, counselling originally developed with the expectation that the work would be quite long term, face to face and conversationally oriented. It has taken some time to accept that arts and expressive therapies can contribute to addressing the same range of human problems. Brief and time-limited models of counselling have mushroomed in recent years. Perhaps the greatest challenge to the field is the advent of telephone and online counselling, including Skype, and also computer-based CBT packages and emerging apps for smart phones. These formats are contested by some therapists, even considered absurd as serious alternatives to long-term intensive face-to-face work. However, think about the traditional psychoanalytic arrangement of the analyst sitting out of sight of the patient (as the telephone counsellor is out of sight), think of the work of Samaritans and other telephone helpline services. Consider the experience and needs of blind and deaf therapists or clients. Consider that some people (for example, some who are extremely shy, autistic, or have had traumatic experiences at the hands of others) find the prospect of talking to and being physically with a stranger daunting. Some prefer writing therapy, for example, or online communication. We must reckon with the possibility of such distal forms of counselling being defensive, perhaps being symptomatic of an alienated age. We should also question the effectiveness of encryption mechanisms and risks of compromised confidentiality. But these new formats remind us that nothing stands still and counselling might not remain the predominantly office-based and verbal practice it has always been.

Conclusions

The positive or charitable concise interpretation of counselling practice is that well-trained and supervised counsellors invariably do their best to understand and help their clients in what is tough, complex work with the human psyche, and results, according to official research, are overwhelmingly positive. Although the panacea-like image attached to counselling is often disowned, it isn't necessarily *really* disowned, since it has handy pulling power. And the psychodynamically wise will explain that fantasy (or 'phantasy') and disillusionment are in fact inherent in the process. The more realistic interpretation is that counselling is usually far from being the linear process leading to wonderful outcomes fantasised and reified in most models. Chaos theory probably captures more of the reality.[16] Insecure, non-Pollyannaish and honest counsellors and counselling psychologists may blame themselves or (sometimes) their clients, the limitations of their approach and training, or counselling itself. Inevitably, counselling business will continue as usual, the treadmill of commitment being sustained by the sunk costs of training, and ongoing supervision, continuing professional development, reading and research. An industry of encouragement supports the enterprise and an endless supply of human misery fuels it.

Endnotes

1. Counsellors, like psychoanalysts, certainly agonise about seating arrangements. Most counsellors prefer comfortable chairs slightly angled towards each other and at the same height so as to try to avoid any hint of inequality.

2. For an overview of some research on training, see McLellan, J. (1999). Becoming an effective psychotherapist or counsellor: Are training and supervision necessary? In C. Feltham (Ed.), *Controversies in Psychotherapy and Counselling*. London: Sage, pp. 164–173.

3. Kahn, M. (1997). *Between Therapist and Client: The new relationship* (rev. ed.). New York: St Martin's Press, p. 163.

4. Halmos, P. (1978). *The Faith of the Counsellors*. London: Constable.

5. NICE guidance documents typically employ the language of 'treatment', 'clinical effectiveness', 'effective delivery of interventions', and 'patient responsiveness', etc., rather than anything as committed and precise as cure, complete extinction of symptoms or problems.

6. Green, G. (2008). *Insomniac*. London: Piatkus.

7. Pilgrim, D. (2012). Social class. In C. Feltham & I. Horton (Eds.), *Sage Handbook of Counselling and Psychotherapy* (3rd ed.). London: Sage, pp. 39–43.

8. As noted by Porter (Porter, J. (2012). Working in private practice. In R. Woolfe, S. Strawbridge, B. Douglas & W. Dryden (Eds.), *Handbook of Counselling Psychology* (3rd ed.). London: Sage), the BPS-suggested average hourly fee for counselling psychologists was £80 and upwards. At this time the average fee for counsellors in Sheffield (South Yorkshire, UK) was around £40.

9. See Berger, B., & Newman, S. (Eds.). (2011). *Money Talks: In therapy, society, and life.* New York: Routledge. Also note that within (Jungian) psychotherapy (less so in most counselling but still a factor) 'money, perceived power, and perceived spirituality all flow to the few certified Jungian analysts in the elite at the top in this pyramidal economic system' (Noll, R. (1996). *The Jung Cult: Origins of a charismatic movement.* London: Fontana, p. 283).

10. Bordin, E. (1979). The generalizability of the psychoanalytic concept of the working alliance. *Psychotherapy, Theory, Research and Practice, 16*(3), 252–260.

11. Clarkson, P. (2003). *The Therapeutic Relationship* (2nd ed.). Chichester: Wiley-Blackwell.

12. Tindall, C., Robinson, J., & Kagan, C. (2010). Feminist perspectives. In R. Woolfe, S. Strawbridge, B. Douglas & W. Dryden (Eds.), *Handbook of Counselling Psychology* (3rd ed.). London: Sage, pp. 227–228.

13. Bates, Y. (Ed.). (2005). *Shouldn't I Be Feeling Better by Now? Client views of therapy.* Basingstoke: Palgrave.

14. Rogers, C. R. (1961). *On Becoming a Person.* Boston: Houghton Mifflin.

15. Leiper, R. (2001). *Working through Setbacks in Psychotherapy: Crisis, impasse and relapse.* London: Sage.

16. Chamberlain, L. L., & Butz, M. R. (Eds.). (1998). *Clinical Chaos: A therapist's guide to nonlinear dynamics and therapeutic change.* Philadelphia, PA: Brunner-Mazel.

CHAPTER 5

Problems of counselling research

In Freud's time, although the principle of being able to duplicate results by experiment was in operation, Freud and his followers were fairly cavalier about it. Theorising, alleged evidence derived from case studies, and assertion became the norms for the talking therapies. This should not surprise us given the historical parallel norm in descriptive psychopathology for new diagnostic categories to be created on the basis of tiny samples. But it is small wonder that Hans Eysenck complained in 1952 that no evidence existed to support claims to psychoanalytic or psychotherapeutic success.[1] There was by Eysenck's reckoning little if any evidence of actual success, of durable success over time, or any evidence that clients had not improved due to the passage of time or placebo effects. From about 1940 Carl Rogers and his colleagues began using the available, somewhat primitive recording technology and from the 1950s to the 1970s developed and used measuring instruments to study the counselling process by coding all speech into categories of intention. Influential tomes on research findings such as those by Lambert and Roth et al. have shaped many efforts to direct future research and to prioritise 'evidence-based' therapies over others.[2] As in other areas of the advancement of counselling psychology, research awareness has been led by a small number of pioneers, most notably in the UK by John McLeod.

According to Michael Barkham, research can be understood as developing across four generations of focus: (1) efficacy (does it work?); (2) specificity (which therapy works best?); (3) efficacy and cost-effectiveness; and (4) clinical significance.[3] It is now commonly asserted by the counselling and psychotherapy community that research has fairly conclusively demonstrated effectiveness and, logically, we would presumably not be much involved in subsequent generations of research if significant doubts remained about fundamental effectiveness.[4]

The case for research in counselling

Perhaps in reality it has been mainly the critics like Eysenck who have pushed the need for research in counselling and psychotherapy to the fore; research psychologists have taken it up vigorously and professional bodies have latterly backed it. Research-mindedness has been a wedge between clinical psychology and psychotherapy since Eysenck's time. But a majority of counselling and psychotherapy practitioners have been less than enthusiastic about research and therefore need persuading. Hence a book like Mick Cooper's *Essential Research Findings in Counselling and Psychotherapy* is aimed at just those practitioners who either must or should grapple with research findings.[5] It is worth quoting from this book's first pages on why counselling research findings are so vital:

> They can give counsellors and psychotherapists (as well as clients) some very good ideas about where to start from in the absence of other information. Research can only ever tell us about the likelihood of certain things happening, but that knowledge can be enormously valuable if we have virtually nothing else to go on. So, for instance, if a therapist is meeting a depressed client for the first time, it can be very useful to know that, in general, positive outcomes with depressed clients are associated with empathic, caring and warm ways of relating.[6]

This is a book that overall does its job of explaining and appealing very well. But if we look closely at such statements we can immediately derive some obvious criticisms of research. First, we learn that research is better than nothing, or rather we are entreated to believe that this is the case. Actually, given its typical cost–benefit ratio, we might think about whether we agree that it is invariably better than nothing, or better than educated guesses. Second, we should know that research is useful as a predictive tool only in suggestive or probabilistic terms – it may or may not help practically, clinically, in specific cases. Third, if the example of depressed clients given here is typical, research may well tell us things that we already know because they are pretty obvious. The polemical journalist Francis Wheen has routinely lambasted expensively arrived-at research findings with the phrase 'Who would have guessed it?!'[7] Fourth, we may note a small example of linguistic cunning here: positive outcomes are *associated with* empathic, caring and warm ways of relating. No linear causality is implied. Academics writing about research can be as artful as lawyers in sidestepping definitive statements that might lead them into trouble.

Cooper goes on to show some major discrepancies between counsellors' and clients' perspectives on their experience of counselling in order to argue that without research we might be quite ignorant of such glaring discrepancies. Here he has a strong point. Practitioners, like most human beings, tend often to deceive themselves (a very common finding in psychological research) and clients tend often to defer. Only anonymous research is likely to get a more objective picture of matters. However, as Cooper also later admits, research findings 'will inevitably be influenced by the researchers' own assumptions and agendas'.[8] Bias or the risk of it is ever present, even in tightly controlled quantitative research. Furthermore, 'researchers can even come up with radically different conclusions with the same set of data if they use different tools of analysis'.[9] Acknowledging these and other limitations of research, Cooper nevertheless urges that a research-informed approach to counselling is necessary. Given the volume and complexity of research, its fallibility, and only generalised indications for practice, should we not ask seriously about its value for money and its diminishing returns?

Problems of definition and appropriateness

It is easy to acquiesce in the use of apparent axioms like 'we need more research' and 'there is a lack of evidence'. Rarely do we ask what research actually is, who and what defines the legitimacy of research (and which kinds of research), whether it is really needed, and what constitutes evidence. Presumably we do not want to ape some philosophers and ask questions like 'How do we know the client exists?' that have no practical use. But if, hypothetically, most depressed clients said after a few sessions that they felt much happier, they also looked happy and their doctor and friends reported that they had improved remarkably, we might ask why any further research evidence was needed to verify this. Of course, therapeutic improvement is not usually this clear and uniform, but if it were, would it not render outcome research superfluous? If Counsellor A had many such testimonials while Counsellors B, C and D had more negative results, or Method A had better results than Methods B, C and D, we might well be curious why this was so and look for some means of finding out. In fact the outcomes of most counselling are less clear (there are variable degrees of success and fuzzy definitions) and we might want to know why this is so. But first we should ask ourselves whether the answers might in fact be obvious. We would surely want to establish exactly what it is that warrants potentially costly and time-consuming research.

If research refers to 'finding out' and evidence refers to 'what is the case', then at a basic level we can surely say that often we find out what is the case by observing, asking, comparing, verifying and so on. The client looks and sounds happier, no longer needs medication, can return to work – this is some sort of evidence of improvement.[10] In some cases a client might improve fortuitously and so we might want to discriminate between chance and therapeutically specific improvements. When we speak of research in counselling psychology we seem to mean research that meets rigorous scientific criteria. This may be needed in some complex and subtle cases but the line between these and phenomena that are directly verifiable must be understood. 'Objective' research seeks to find out what is the case beyond reasonable doubt, beyond the self-deception and professional self-interest that might distort subjective and impressionistic observations. Clients too can distort matters: they may want to reduce cognitive dissonance related to financial investment in counselling, they may feel loyal to the counsellor, they may deceive themselves that they are better and ready to return to work, their friends may rely on them, and so on.

As well as scientifically objective criteria (if we agree that these exist) we have to consider the financial, logistical and ethical aspects of any research. Medical authorities, academics and the public all have a stake in outcome research. But all parties can be deceived, or in some cases deceptive, about the niceties of defining research and appropriate methodologies. The fact that psychological phenomena are much fuzzier and harder, perhaps impossible, to be objective about than physical phenomena should not be ignored or hidden. But psychologists have a vested interest in keeping up the appearance of psychology as an objective natural science. Important ethical and epistemological issues are intertwined here. Yet who has the competency, objectivity, integrity and will to get to the bottom of such fundamental matters? Different research methodologies are briefly examined below but here we can suggest that questions of clear definition, explanation, responsibility and costs are paramount. These are under-discussed matters but Sarah Corrie goes some way towards at least raising some of them.[11]

Problems of methodology

Consider the problems involved in conceiving research into counselling that focuses on outcomes. Actual practice is private and confidential and cannot be directly observed. Audio and video recordings can be made but only with client consent and strict safeguards. Even today, 60 years after Eysenck's landmark challenge and a burgeoning of counselling research, it is relatively rare to seek direct permission for such recordings. Some small-scale and short-term studies analyse actual recordings in order to understand insight into counselling *process*. It is also the case that such recording is likely to alter the character of the counselling taking place (the practitioner trying harder than usual, the client wanting to please the counsellor, and so on), and it would require long-term studies to ascertain how well improvements hold up over time, as well as a significant number and variety of studies to strive to get an overall picture. Indeed the more closely you examine the private and subtle nature of counselling (and different kinds of counselling) the more you are struck by a complexity that may well defy definitive research. It is for these reasons that the psychologist Paul Kline in 1992 declared that 19 serious problems could be identified for research methodology in this field.[12]

Kline's list includes: the definitional problem of recovery or cure; variance among practitioners; personal qualities of practitioners; client–practitioner interaction; certain practitioners being attracted to certain therapies; control groups; spontaneous remission; life events during counselling; client problem or diagnosis; variance among clients; validity and reliability of psychological instruments; length of follow-up studies; the problem of symptom substitution; baseline measurements; gender differences; variance in effects of counselling; and the research design itself. No doubt we could expand on this list. Kline argues that in principle sufficiently rigorous research might be designed but would be extremely costly. There is some agreement that no research design is flawless but many claims that large-scale studies have overcome most problems. It is hard to see, however, how the many variables involved can be controlled sufficiently well to produce convincing results.

We have to consider where data on therapeutic outcomes comes (or is said to come) from and how reliable it is. Consider the possible following sources of evidence: client reports (verbal and in questionnaires); direct counsellor observations and inferences; third party corroboration; reduction or termination of medication; clear improvement or elimination of symptoms; and (unusually) in early primal therapy, for example, measurements of blood pressure, core body temperature, and brain wave measurements. Statements and scores derived from subjective client reports do not become more scientific simply because they are numericised. Subjective client reports (including cases of abrupt loss of symptoms and improvements in unrelated functioning such as eyesight and hearing, and euphoria) are important but unreliable. Subjective client reports approved by humanistic counsellors, such as 'I still have my symptoms but I feel more self-accepting' are open to debate as to their usefulness and reliability. Improvement is much easier to detect in cases of recovery from long-term phobia, OCD, PTSD, etc. (conditions with clear behavioural markers), and even here longitudinal studies are required to determine non-relapse. Moderate improvement over a long period is hard to distinguish from improvement due to passage of time and placebo therapy, at least without rigorously controlled longitudinal studies. The more generic (integrative, eclectic, pluralistic) counselling is, the less is one able to determine which ingredients may have been responsible for change.

Of course, we can decide to take seriously and trust subjective client reports, as counselling psychologists and counsellors do on principle. We can think of these as valid but hardly conclusive. There is no ethical problem, perhaps, in trusting client reports on satisfaction with counselling from private practice settings but this is more problematic in funded settings. We all might feel better and report satisfaction if we could receive ample massage or undivided sympathetic attention from NHS services but this isn't cost effective and isn't going to happen. Funders consulting research quite reasonably want to know specifically what they are paying for and whether these methods (and not unrelated or incidental phenomena) are effective. We also need to ask who is doing the research and why more negative or neutral results are not forthcoming, as well as why more research is not conducted into known failed therapies.

Compare the results of years of extensive and costly outcome research with the following statement made by an American gestalt therapist, Brad Blanton:

> Psychotherapy doesn't always work. My estimate is that about a third of the time the results are good to adequate, about a third of the clients make a few half-assed changes, and at least a third of the folks who see me don't get any good out of therapy worth mentioning. Very few people suffer any damage in therapy since it is as hard to do damage as it is to help.[13]

Of course we can immediately retort that this is a crude estimate based on one therapist's practice, not necessarily applicable to others' practice. But how likely is it that any practitioner will *under-rate* his own effectiveness? Blanton is attempting to be honest here; he is not necessarily claiming that these results are true of all other therapists, nor is he saying that the results necessarily reflect on his own competency. We are not told here what the sample size is, nor what his criteria are for judging outcomes as 'good to adequate', 'half-assed' and 'any good worth mentioning'. We can interpret Blanton's statement as rating about 33 per cent of therapy as unsuccessful compared with a typical 20 per cent failure rate commonly suggested by formal research. Crude as this calculation is, the claim that 33 per cent 'make a few half-assed changes' may in fact show greater subtlety of judgement than much formal research that merely measures positive and negative outcomes. Indeed Blanton has four categories of outcome here: good, adequate, half-assed change, and no notable change. We do not know if his clients themselves would come to the same conclusions, nor do we know whether they would attribute their success or failure to themselves or to the therapist. Blanton also shrugs off significant damage here, which is again a relatively large preoccupation for professional body personnel. What if this estimate for all its crudeness actually does reflect typical outcomes in counselling and psychotherapy? I believe it might. Blanton's subjectivity might badly colour his estimate but equally subtle biases and blunt criteria in formal research might badly colour results. Who should we trust?

Qualitative, quantitative, gold standards

A huge problem for counselling research, barely discussed, is choice of focus and aims. Broadly speaking, we have some relatively large-scale quantitative studies, some major and minor randomised controlled trials (RCTs), and many qualitative studies. The differences between formal efficacy and informal effectiveness studies are noted but I have mainly used the common term 'effectiveness' here. We have a great deal of focus on effective outcomes but also on within-session processes. We also have some studies based on client observations and reports. Many studies use phenomenological, narrative and feminist methodology to examine clients' and practitioners' feelings, beliefs and experiences. While there is an implicit aim of learning from research and thereby improving practice, in reality much counselling research merely duplicates the fascination practitioners experience concerning micro-aspects of the impact of life events and subjectivity, intrapsychic processes and the therapeutic relationship. Of course, a lot of traditional scientific research is of this micro-focus and gradual nature, with some observations taking years to coalesce into major new insights and breakthroughs. But as far as I can see most counselling research is stuck in a world of micro-foci with no clear or unifying aims. Put differently, it has no aim remotely comparable with medical research that hopes to identify the causes of cancers and promising avenues towards cures.

Consider the following comment on psychoanalysis and its Freudian take on outcomes and research:

> [The] essentially medical perspective caused a problem because Freud was to see that symptoms did not always disappear, and as a consequence conceived of the analytic process as differentiated from the therapeutic goal: the aim of analysis became rather to apply the method – in short, to analyse – and by the application of this method, *cure* was seen as a (hoped-for) byproduct of analysis as a method of *research* which had to be conducted without any specific goal, except that of making the unconscious conscious and acceptable to the patient.[14]

I suspect this remains the case today not only for much traditional psychoanalysis but for a great deal of psychodynamic and humanistic counselling: often practitioners tacitly suspend concerns with outcomes and delve fascinatedly into a search for biographical detail, suppressed emotion and intersubjective nuances. This is covert case study research, if you like.

For most counsellor researchers the main interest is in process. For many, outcome concerns are either considered proven or tacitly shelved as being merely 'positivistic'. It is the detail of sessions, of the attitudes and experiences of clients and counsellors that fascinates. There is also a wish to harness case material and to argue for practice-based evidence to validate the wisdom believed to already reside in clinical experience. In order to legitimise such qualitative research for higher degrees, journal articles and some funded small-scale research, counsellors typically reach out for grounded theory, interpersonal phenomenological analysis and other methodologies approved within academia. One text containing myriad methods of research, although not dedicated to counselling and therapy, but neatly reflecting the pluralism of schools, is *The Sage Handbook of Qualitative Research,* in its third edition at 1210 pages long.[15] This reinforces counsellors in their anxious war against the hegemony of quantitative research. Most research-equivocal counsellors studying for higher degrees and obliged to produce empirical research follow a fetishistic formula of tedious discussion of methodologies, interview a few people and come up with unremarkable 'findings' that meet criteria that are, in spite of university quality administrators' protests otherwise, often not very demanding. This process is invariably more of a bland ritual than a passionate or ground-breaking enquiry.

Denis Postle makes a passionate case against a Department of Health-endorsed model of psychotherapy research that mimics medical research. Its notion of validity, he suggests, derives from research *on* people, is institutionally funded and expert-led; its methods are autocratic and hierarchical; and its outcome validities focus only on efficacy, cost-effectiveness, treatment protocols, data collection and statistical meta-analysis; with high value being placed on measures of social adaptation, happiness and work functionality. Postle's case for a loving, human form of research emphasises the value of research *with* people; that is co-operative, negotiated, personal, local; that reflects diversity; the outcomes for which are decided between practitioner and client. Postle's chapter heading, 'Love Provides a Better Benchmark than Science' is deliberately challenging, but arrestingly so.[16]

On the other hand, quantitative research often looks at the ostensibly tough questions of effectiveness. Does talking therapy work? (The implicit question here is, of course, 'are we being conned?') Does it work better than placebos, usual GP care, or the passage of time? Which kind of therapy demonstrates effective treatment of particular psychological problems? How does someone fare on a waiting list as compared with someone receiving active treatment? Does one therapeutic approach generally work better than others? On the face of it these are quite important questions. What they have always failed to grasp however is that psychotherapy and counselling are not pharmacological interventions, that is to say that talking therapies do not act like drugs and should not be compared simplistically with drugs. Aping large-scale medical research, particularly in its allegedly gold standard form, the randomised controlled trial, does not serve psychological therapy research well. Medications have specific properties (and even then cannot target for complex individual differences) whereas the largely listening-and-talking processes of counselling contain multiple subtle complexities the operation of which cannot be accurately predicted in advance. Quantitative research in talking therapy is often conducted as if its properties and methods can be broken down into precise physical components (like those of a drug) but even cognitive behavioural therapy may vary widely in its delivery and reception depending on multiple subtle client and counsellor factors.

Another confounding variable is found in false assumptions, and conceptual and terminological misunderstandings. The literature of comparative research abounds with the titles of different therapeutic approaches – CBT, psychotherapy, interpersonal psychotherapy, brief dynamic therapy, systemic therapy, humanistic counselling, etc. – as if these are clearly defined, distinct entities. A little probing usually shows however that vague or biased definitions and innuendo are often in play, or spurious distinctions are made, or assumptions are made that 'counselling', for example, is a largely non-specific, non-directive procedure, whereas in reality it is commonly and integratively composed of elements of person-centred relational attitudes, psychodynamic understanding and interventions, and some modified CBT techniques. Astoundingly, we can therefore find apples compared with fruit. Snobbery is often in play vis-à-vis approaches constructed and researched by medical therapists and psychologists, such as cognitive analytic therapy, interpersonal psychotherapy and acceptance and commitment therapy. It seems that sometimes psychological researchers combine discipline-based bias and lack of familiarity with counselling to produce spuriously clear and emphatic statements about outcomes. Much of this has to do with who conducts the research, from which professional background, sympathies and blind spots, with what vested interests.

Those conducting such research, usually academics in clinical psychology and/or those in NHS positions, must chase large funds that can be secured only by producing spuriously water-tight proposals. Fuzzy procedures and noticeable margins of error must be airbrushed from the picture so that the final submission has an appearance of mythically medical crispness. Although I would not suggest that overt fraud is involved,[17] I think it highly likely that inconvenient loose ends and unwarranted assumptions are routinely extracted from research documentation. Livelihoods and reputations are at stake, associated academics and clinicians, professional body staff and award-granting personnel are all involved in the manufacture of costly research products.

Research points to common factors, or otherwise

A glaring problem for all psychotherapy and counselling is that the multiplicity of theories, put into practice by therapists with their own idiosyncrasies, appear to be equally successful. Logically, this cannot be the case if we take seriously the belief that each distinctive theory (including aetiological, practice guidance and predictive features) is *the* way to proceed and *the* explanation for successful outcomes. Each theory either states or implies that it rests on truer principles, is better than others and should get better results. Otherwise, every creator of these theories is tacitly conceding that theirs is something like a *superfluous alternative*, that anything works equally well. But this is precisely what a whole tranche of research has pointed towards since as early as 1936: If 'all have won and all must have prizes'[18] yet few have drawn attention to its embarrassing – we might say devastating – implications. It surely portrays the field as a mass of contradictions. Yet many have conceded that it must suggest that ostensibly distinct theories and techniques are redundant. Instead, there must be something effective yet previously unacknowledged going on across all therapies and beneath the myriad acclaimed theories. This thing must surely be the factors common to all approaches, the positive features of all therapeutic relationships, the attention, warmth, rapport, empathy common to all competent practitioners and clients' psychological-mindedness, ego strength or resilience, capacity to make and maintain relationships and so on.

For quite some time it was (and still is) proclaimed that common factors must be the key ingredients of the successful outcomes of therapy. Yet by the 1990s copious research on CBT was leading to the conclusion that CBT led the field in terms of successful outcomes. Even when it was recognised that CBT was much more researchable than many other approaches (because more methodical and manualisable) and that lack of evidence supporting other approaches did not equate with evidence of lack of effectiveness, the CBT world was happy to let its superiority be imagined and its services to receive far greater funding. Curiously, CBT's high research profile prevailed alongside the continuing success of research-confirmed findings about the significance of common factors or the therapeutic relationship.[19] Given CBT's reliance on non-relational factors (its many techniques), this glaring contradiction received little attention – the relationship is everything, yet simultaneously CBT techniques are everything, as it were.

Consulting one of the most recent summaries of common factors research by Alan Carr[20] we are told the following: Lambert and Barley's 2002 review concluded that common factors were twice as significant (30 per cent) as specific factors (skills, techniques, beliefs) at 15 per cent. Placebo factors account for a further 15 per cent and the largest relevant phenomenon of all is so-called extra-therapeutic factors (40 per cent), often said to include various forms of social support. Yet another, similar review by Wampold in 2001 had concluded that common factors were responsible for only 9 per cent of successful outcome factors, alongside 3 per cent client factors, a paltry 1 per cent for specific therapeutic techniques and a staggering 87 per cent for extra-therapeutic factors. As Carr states, a great deal may hang on the way in which common factors are understood, client and therapist factors and therapeutic context factors all being significant. But what seems beyond reasonable doubt is the small part played by the much-vaunted specific therapeutic techniques. How are we to square the dissonance here between recurring claims drawn from many extensive research studies that common factors are the primary determinants of positive outcomes, and endless research into the effects of different models? Even worse potentially is the embarrassingly high proportion of extra-therapeutic factors, which remain relatively little discussed.

Professional body promotion of research

BACP has explicitly promoted counselling research since the journal *Counselling and Psychotherapy Research* appeared. As more training courses have incorporated research modules and more courses have been created at Masters and Doctoral levels (particularly but not only for BPS-aligned counselling *psychology* students), so more and more research projects have been conducted. Although no survey of these is available, my own impression gained from nationwide (and in a few cases international) university external examining is that most of these are small scale (often involving no more than six to ten interviewees), almost always qualitative (more often than not using semi-structured interviews to be subjected to thematic analysis of one sort or another). Topics often reflect the student researcher's immediate preoccupations in the workplace or life history and are often chosen on practical grounds (e.g., local services avoiding cumbersome permissions obstacles). While some are very well presented and methodologically correct, few are more than moderately novel or useful. Few doctoral submissions in counselling would stand up to rigorous comparison with those in more traditional disciplines. This is partly due to the early stage at which counselling education and research finds itself within academia but much more pervasively, I think, it is due to the likelihood that most people entering counselling training and employment are from arts and humanities backgrounds. Many value the interpersonal qualities of emotion, intuition and empathy above any scientific knowledge or norms (including psychology).

Counsellors' attitudes to research

Counsellors have an ambivalent attitude to research.[21] On the one hand, a sufficient volume of positive research would help to establish its status, secure greater funding and create jobs. On the other hand, counsellors like psychotherapists and psychoanalysts tend to believe that they already know their work is effective, and that research is probably superfluous except as confirmation and for public relations purposes. Counsellors are mostly ambivalent about seeking scientific status for counselling, or are hostile to it. For counselling psychologists this is not the case, psychology having a decades-long commitment to scientific identity and clinical and counselling psychologists apparently accepting their dual role as scientist-practitioners. Yet most counsellors also seem wary of any close alignment with alternative disciplines like philosophy. If it is true that counsellors relate most closely to emotional, interpersonal and narrative themes, one might ask why they do not at least seek an identity alongside drama and literature. Or if we are being really honest about it, we might argue that the vocation of counsellors is essentially non-professional (not *un*professional), somewhat akin to original priesthood and nursing. Arguably counselling for some has a countercultural identity, even perhaps an anti-capitalist element, with salaries and fees being a necessary evil. For others the belief holds good that counsellors provide a service for which they should be paid a respectable salary. The point here is that research is not supported wholeheartedly and the 'profession' of counselling may harbour divided ideologies indefinitely.

While I have been critical of clinical supervision elsewhere in this book, perhaps I would commend its usefulness in the matter of research. Unless things change significantly, the typical counsellor will never relish the prospect of consulting research findings, and even counselling psychologists more disposed towards them may have quite limited interest. However, if we are determined to retain the professional layer of mandatory supervision, should we not expect a major role for supervisors to be research-aware? If the positive claims on behalf of research have some merit, should we not require supervisors to be fairly well research-informed and to be expected to pass on such information to supervisees? Currently the norm tends to be, I think, that supervisors can duck this kind of responsibility by arguing that they are not educators or trainers but facilitators; they are not in fact expected to have knowledge superior to their supervisees but to act as practice consultants on an egalitarian basis.

I am being a little disingenuous in proposing this research role for supervisors because I know that most of them prefer an exploratory, supportive and relational role. But to take just one major area of research, that on the differential effectiveness of therapies, supervisors should perhaps have at least a minimal awareness of the critical mass of findings. Arguably it is an ethical responsibility of supervisors either to challenge supervisees' way of working with a particular client when it is contraindicated by research findings or to actively inform them that approach X, say, has better evidence in its favour for client A's problem than approach Y has. Such supervisory interventions can be considered not only an ethical imperative but preventative with regard to possible complaints and law suits. A counsellor, who in her ignorance has neither used a specific research-indicated technique nor mentioned it to the client for consideration for a referral, might be susceptible to complaint. But here we would open up a can of worms. Will research ignorance become a legal issue? To what extent are supervisors implicated in such clinical responsibilities? And what of the differential philosophies underpinning supervision from the perspectives of different therapeutic orientations? If research in the counselling field comes to be taken more seriously (on a par, say, with pharmacological or surgical research), we might expect to see some negative consequences in terms of associated charges of negligence and malpractice. Could you (and your supervisor) be sued for using or condoning an approach or technique lacking evidence for its effectiveness or safety, or for failing to suggest or implement another approach?

Scientist-practitioners?

Clinical psychologists have accepted this dual role for quite some time, counselling psychologists too signing on for it, if sometimes with a preference for 'reflective-practitioner'. But the former is arguably both a heavy burden and an unnecessary one. Even granted a necessity for copious research (and this is highly debatable), there is no logical demand that practitioners be the researchers. Even psychotherapy's erstwhile diehard critic Hans Eysenck agreed that since excellent practitioners do not necessarily make excellent researchers and vice versa, the two roles might be best split.[22] Eysenck himself was not a clinical practitioner. It seems entirely probable that the mathematical aptitude and scientific bent required for most (quantitative) research design and execution will be found primarily among those with scientific or mathematical qualifications. Conversely, are not excellent practitioners more likely to possess arts, humanities or social science qualifications (assuming they have and need any prior academic qualifications)? Underlying qualifications, of course, are personality traits, and while it is possible that clinical and research excellence might be found together in one person, it seems unlikely to be common.

I think it is more likely that many trainees are now being obliged to struggle to learn research vocabulary and methodology, to undertake small-scale projects and critique existing research, which they will never enjoy or be good at. A few might, granted. But I suspect most will abandon research rituals as soon as they can.[23] Too many student assignments on counselling research betray signs of merely going through the ritual of using the jargon of reliability, validity, triangulation, reflexivity, data mining, thematic analysis, etc., before going on to a research exercise based on one mundane research focus or another. For counselling psychology students the picture is a little different and is based on the idea that competent practitioners will be competent researchers, with psychology being the science that is a *sine qua non* of counselling practice.

It is a plausible claim that trainees be trained to be able to read and understand published research as an aid to improving their practice. Consider however the same argument being made for medical trainees and practitioners. It certainly makes sense that doctors should be constantly aware of the latest research in medicine and its specialisms, given that much of the field holds life-and-death decisions and responsibilities in its hands. But there are thousands of medical journals worldwide that doctors cannot hope to keep abreast of. Many doctors probably rely on distilled findings and headlines in more popular professional journals, magazines and websites, and on occasional conference presentations. Counselling and counselling psychology have far fewer journals but it could be argued that an awareness of research in psychiatry and clinical psychology should be added to up-to-date knowledge of counselling and psychotherapy. Despite online access to many research summaries, it is unlikely that most counsellors will have the time or inclination to regularly and meaningfully consult even a judicious selection of these. And how many research studies do in fact produce genuinely new, significant breakthroughs that alter practice? Very few, I suggest.

Randomly perusing a current research journal as I write this, I find the following themes: significant client disclosure; attachment styles of psychology students who have not had psychotherapy; students' perceptions of audio- and video-recording of counselling sessions; adolescent clients' perceptions of online therapy; counsellors' experiences of male victims of domestic abuse; young people's experiences of counselling in schools; counselling students' perceptions of altruism; therapists' and clients' perceptions of outcome measurements. These are mainly written by teams of academics and NHS staff, all using small interview samples. All are written with a characteristic balance of crispness and jargon, most include due justifications, careful descriptions of methodology, ethics procedures, clarifying diagrams and copious references. None come to any surprising conclusions and most are clearly oriented around university pressures to produce peer-reviewed research for the Research Exercise Framework (REF) that may attract future funding. We might charitably say that they all add something to our understanding and to practice. Yet who is behind this 'our' and exactly how much will they improve practice? A lot of planning, time and care, reviewing and re-writing will have gone into them and I have no doubt all the authors feel they have worked hard to produce new knowledge. Probably, to some extent these articles will do their careers no harm. Journal publishers are making money here. Some readers may be enlightened (although most colleagues admit they are far from enthralled). I say that none come to any surprising conclusions but this is a subjective judgement. Some authors may have been surprised by what they found and some readers may be fascinated by or enthusiastic about this research. What seems banal to some of us appears precious to others. Could we find some way of weighing the ratio of fascinated-and-instructed to bored-by-banality?

What cannot be researched

It is in the delicate and confidential nature of counselling that certain topics prove difficult to research. For example, clients' misgivings and unhappiness about counselling received sometimes find their way through complaints procedures and/or into publication. But some such clients do not wish to face the unpleasantness of this kind of disclosure. I know anecdotally of one or two dissatisfied ex-clients of counsellors who have legitimate grievances yet refrain from taking action because they do not want to cause trouble for the counsellor. In principle, matters like these might be identified by standard evaluation instruments, complaints procedures or even by counsellors in conjunction with supervisors. The point here is that we do not know the incidence of such occurrences due to their delicate nature.

Supervision should go a long way in picking up problems before or as they develop. Part of the brief of clinical supervision is after all to safeguard against poor practice and malpractice. Supervision should presumably help to reduce practitioners' risk of stress and burnout, and also enhance effectiveness. Not for nothing is supervision a mandatory requirement of the BACP for all practising members, regardless of their length of experience or size or kind of caseload. The normal expectation is a minimum of an hour and a half per month. This incurs time and money. Supervision is also a mini-industry in its own right, with hundreds of practitioners, associated specialised training courses, conferences and publications. For something as important as this quality control function, we surely expect to see some research. There is indeed some research but it mainly consists of enquiries into supervisees' or supervisors' experiences and its main finding is overall subjective satisfaction with supervision.

Bearing in mind the costs and potential outcomes involved, it is often implied that unsupervised practice would be unethical and dangerous in undermining effectiveness and safety. We know that in most states of the USA and in UK psychiatry, psychoanalysis and several other allied mental health professions, there is no equivalent of BACP's career-long mandatory requirement. Should we assume that the clients in unsupervised settings are at terrible risk of poor practice, ineffectiveness and abuse? I doubt it. Now, we could in principle conduct controlled trials of unsupervised and supervised counsellors to ascertain the effects of supervision but of course we cannot do this because it is 'unethical' to practise without supervision, even temporarily or experimentally. We would also run into the same problems of complexity as those for psychotherapy and counselling – supervisees' and supervisors' variable qualifications, experience, clinical population, caseload, work setting. So this looks like a non-starter for a subject of research.

Furthermore, years of tradition and practice folklore stand in the way. Any counsellor who claimed not to need or want regular supervision would come under suspicion. It is an article of faith that supervision 'works', is helpful and even essential. Yet we have good reasons for arguing that it may not be essential (beyond the training period, let's say, or during the early part of careers) or that we do not know quite what it is for. But here is an even thornier angle. It's possible that less confident and even less intelligent counsellors feel a need for regular supervision that at least some more confident and intelligent counsellors do not feel. Again, in principle this could be researched. It is highly unlikely to be sponsored, however, because it goes against a powerful ethos of respect and equality in the counselling world. Indeed it seems impossible to imagine the question being formally posed. My guess is that even were we able to devise ways of researching the effectiveness of supervision in relation to client outcomes and if it appeared that no evidence could be found to support the idea that supervised counsellors are more effective or safe than unsupervised counterparts, such negative findings would be ignored. A combination of tradition, faith, and the lucrative mini-industry of supervision ensures that the practice will continue indefinitely in spite of any calls for evidence-based practice. And where is the historical research to show us exactly how mandatory supervision was decided upon?

We are highly unlikely to even want to research the question of whether clients who have had sexual relationships with their counsellors are all necessarily traumatised by this abuse of power. It is so much an article of moral outrage and common sense (among counsellors) that one can barely imagine the question being seriously posed, and ethical barriers to such research might be formidable. For political rather than scientific reasons we are unlikely to pose research questions about the differential effectiveness of women and men as counsellors, or of those trained at Foundation degree level compared with those trained to doctoral level. Hard to research for very different reasons are questions about claims concerning past life experiences and also about evolutionary psychology. The first matter is in principle an important topic and might fall within the attention of researchers of the paranormal. This area is more likely to be dismissed as nonsense, in spite of the claims of some hypno-regressive therapists. The second is also important but the highly speculative nature of evolutionary psychology makes it difficult to operationalise in research terms. The wish list of topics for research is long but priorities will be determined by practitioner interests and competencies and by the politics of professional bodies and funders, not by purely scientific concern.

When we speak about the effectiveness of counselling and seek to research the topic, we first have to be sure we agree on what is counselling (and not psychotherapy). We then face certain serious conundrums that we rarely face directly and that may present us with insurmountable logical difficulties. Consider that today's analysts now routinely declare that their practice and theory is vastly different from (better informed, more sophisticated, etc.) that of Freud's time. If that is the case, we are entitled to ask whether today's new, improved therapy serves its clients better (is more effective) than the therapy of yesteryear, which logically it surely must be. Presumably too the psychoanalytic therapy or psycho-dynamic counselling of the future must deliver more effective practice than today's, if it continues to improve. Questions arise here about the meaning of effectiveness and just how improvable therapy is.

But we also have different schools of psychodynamic therapy and we know that different practitioners practise variably. In order to test its effectiveness rigorously, we would need recordings of actual sessions of therapy from different practitioners working under the same banner, and we would need recordings spanning a significant time. Research on relatively short-term, manualised psychodynamic counselling (this example would apply equally to other models) provides an utterly artificial slice of practice at one point in time. It is hard to see how Kline's objections can ever be overcome. How are we to confirm that Therapist A's version of Psychoanalytic Therapy B at Point of Time C is effective against Set of Criteria D, even ignoring Variables E, F, G etc.? We seem capable only of proving effectiveness at the level of fantasised predictable practice. It is not surprising that most analysts eschew such research but it is not satisfactory to leave them with their privileged case studies and/or subjective client reports. I think it adds up to a case for therapy and counselling effectiveness being indeed fundamentally unresearchable. The best we can do is spend a lot of time and money demonstrating that something of a fictitiously straightforward kind at an arbitrary point in time appears to be effective, provided that we don't ask too many questions about the meaning and extent of effectiveness.

How far can we say that any such research is actually reliable, generalisable and valid? Temporal slippage is unavoidable between research conception and operation, passage of time necessary to ascertain secure results and to analyse and publish them.[24] Again, putting aside complex confounding variables (putting aside for the sake of the fantasy of a scientific outcome), we still have to factor in the problem of ever-changing practice and theory (as above). It is dubious enough to argue that certain results obtained in artificial conditions should hold good for natural clinical circumstances but doubly dubious to claim these results as valid for years to come. Unlike in, say, the research conducted in the Large Hadron Supercollider at Cern, which is concerned among other matters with the speed of light itself, counselling and therapy research is woefully vague.[25]

Practical quantitative research can and should help us to understand much that we do not currently know. For example, exactly how many training courses exist at any one time, with how many students? How many counselling graduates are unemployed, under-employed or not working as counsellors at all, and for how long? How many counsellors and counselling psychologists of which theoretical approaches are active in which agencies? Exactly how many counselling services exist, where, dealing with which concerns? How many private practices are there, with what number of clients? All these may seem like mundane quantitative issues, yet a strong ethical argument can be put to support them. Given the enormous interest in and self-funding for counselling training, how much realistic opportunity for employment or work do trained counsellors have? Small-scale surveys have been conducted and estimates made but if research can do anything with precision for us, it would be in just such matters. Furthermore, it should be possible to compare the figures for how many people suffer from depression, anxiety and other counselling-treatable problems against services available and needed nationally. It is not that such things cannot be researched but that we lack the will to do it.

Ignoring inconvenient research

We can forgive couples in love for ignoring research alerting them to the trend for most of the intense passion of love to fade significantly after about 18 months to 3 years, and we can forgive newlyweds for ignoring divorce statistics. You do not base your romantic decisions on science. Indeed we might be suspicious of anyone who consulted research in this area before making such personal commitments. But can we so easily forgive counsellors and counselling psychologists for ignoring findings in their field? Perhaps the most culpable here are psychodynamic practitioners. A good deal of psychodynamic theory and practice rests on notions of a 'presenting past', object relations, and negative formative influences from infancy and childhood. Yet these practitioners do not wrench themselves away from psychoanalytic dogma to consult much research on early development. In spite of the prominence given to the live observation of babies in psychoanalytic training and to attachment research, this partial honouring of research principles hardly carries much further.

I am thinking here of the work of Judith Rich Harris, who put together a cogent case for the strong developmental influence of peers in the school years which flatly contradicted the heavy emphasis on the principle of parental influence.[26] In other words, Harris presented pro-nature evidence contradicting the pro-nurture assumptions of much psychodynamic theory. Psychodynamic counsellors can get around this by arguing that the nature–nurture relationship is complex, that pre-school influences are very subtle, that in practice they attend to all phases of development, and so on. But add to this doubts raised by research suggesting that accurate memory does not extend back before the age of about 4 or 5; add in the longitudinal research showing how little many aspects of personality like introversion and extraversion change across the lifespan; and generally raise many awkward questions about research findings that do not support psychodynamic principles. What do psychodynamic counsellors say in reply? Unless they argue that they have been misunderstood, which they frequently do, their favourite tactic is simply to ignore all contradictory research, much as people in love ignore gloomy research. Not for nothing are psychoanalysis and psychology seldom found to be close academic disciplines.

Given the hype surrounding IAPT and the considerable financial investment in it, along with built-in evaluation, one might naïvely think that reported poor success rates of 13 to 16 per cent would quickly spell its death knell.[27] A great deal of anecdotal evidence from counsellors involved in it (always, of course, ignored by academics and other stakeholders in such matters) warned that IAPT would never work, was not working, and clients' word-of-mouth reports soon warned that it was not working. But even the Centre for Social Justice's (CSJ) damning report of an 84 to 87 per cent failure rate seems unlikely to elicit any confession of 'sorry, we got it wrong' from Layard and others who heavily promoted it, largely on the basis of uncritical confidence in research evidence supporting CBT. The CSJ's report condemns the CBT monoculture of the NICE/IAPT approach, its continuing to spend £10 million per annum on training CBT practitioners when 17,000 well-trained counsellors and therapists are available. The Swedish Government's experience of 10 years of heavy CBT promotion and financial investment followed by glaring negative outcome evidence, leading to termination of the CBT monopoly in 2012, at least finally heeded an embarrassing outcome.[28] So much for listening to evidence in the UK, however. And so much for expensive projects and evaluation of them that common sense warned against.

The rhetoric of indignation (or the tactic of 'ignoring to death') is highly likely to be applied by research promoters to the kinds of arguments put forward here. It goes against the grain of research-as-sacred, it threatens (if taken seriously) to destabilise the image of a profession moving forward in a vaguely scientific direction, and it could undermine the livelihoods of researchers. The prosecution suggests that the research agenda is incoherent and the results mostly trivial; the field is too complex and slippery to yield to research; confirmatory bias is rife; flaws in research design are ignored; research methodologies are pitted against each other in a war of attrition; research studies often contradict each other or remain perennially inconclusive. At the current rate of progress and compilation of small projects, in 10 or 20 years' time we may well have a mountain of cumulatively meaningless research. Perhaps worst of all, given the improbability that even heavily research-informed practitioners deliver better therapy, we must doubt the worth of the research edifice and wonder if we couldn't devote the time and resources to far better ends. When we (human beings) are committed to a course of action and can see no alternative we tend to remain in a trance of uncritical commitment until we are really forced to give it up. In the matter of counselling research we cling to small signs of progress: we appear unable to step back and ask fundamental philosophical questions about the nature of psychological suffering and the epistemology of our remedial efforts.

Endnotes

1. Eysenck, H. J. (1952). The effects of psychotherapy: An evaluation. *Journal of Consulting Psychology, 16,* 319–324.

2. Lambert, M. J. (Ed.). (2013). *Bergin and Garfield's Handbook of Psychotherapy and Behavior Change* (6th ed.). New York: Wiley. Also Roth, A., Fonagy, P., Parry, G., & Target, M. (2006). *What Works for Whom? A critical review of psychotherapy research* (2nd ed.). New York: Guilford.

3. Barkham, M. (2007). Methods, outcomes and processes in the psychological therapies across four successive research generations. In W. Dryden (Ed.), *Dryden's Handbook of Individual Therapy* (5th ed.). London: Sage, pp. 451–514.

4. The norm has become for controlled research studies on outcomes to be designated 'efficacy', and field-based, clinically natural studies to be designated 'effectiveness' studies.

5. Cooper, M. (2008). *Essential Research Findings in Counselling and Psychotherapy: The facts are friendly.* London: Sage.

6. *Ibid.,* p. 2.

7. Wheen, F. (2004). *How Mumbo-Jumbo Conquered the World: A short history of modern delusions.* London: Harper Perennial.

8. Cooper, M. (2008). *Essential Research Findings in Counselling and Psychotherapy: The facts are friendly.* London: Sage, p. 4.

9. *Ibid.,* p. 4.

10. Such criteria can themselves be contentious, of course. 'Being able to return to work' may not be an indication of good mental health if the person concerned works in a toxic environment and survives there only by chronic suppression of his true feelings.

11. Corrie, S. (2010). What is evidence? In R. Woolfe, S. Strawbridge, B. Douglas & W. Dryden (Eds.), *Handbook of Counselling Psychology* (3rd ed). London: Sage, pp. 44–61.

12. Kline, P. (1992). Problems of methodology in studies of psychotherapy. In W. Dryden & C. Feltham (Eds.), *Psychotherapy and Its Discontents*. Buckingham: Open University Press. See also Epstein, W. M. (1995). *The Illusion of Psychotherapy*, New Brunswick, NJ: Transaction Publishers, which critiques the research methods applied to psychotherapy as well as its failure to locate the causes of distress in society.

13. Blanton, B. (1994). *Radical Honesty.* New York: Delta, p. xxviii.

14. Sandler, J., & Dreher, A. U. (1996). *What Do Psychoanalysts Want? The problem of aims in psychoanalytic therapy.* London: Routledge, p. 114.

15. Denzin, N. K., & Lincoln, Y. S. (Eds.). (2005). *The Sage Handbook of Qualitative Research* (3rd ed.). Thousand Oaks, CA: Sage.

16. Postle, D. (2012). *Therapy Futures: Obstacles and opportunities.* Available from http://www.lulu.com/gb/en/shop/denis-postle/therapy-futures-obstacles-and-opportunities/paperback/product-20552282.html

17. Broad, W., & Wade, N. (1983). *Betrayers of the Truth: Fraud and deceit in the halls of science.* London: Century.

18. Rosenzweig, S. (1936). Some implicit common factors in diverse methods of psychotherapy: 'At last the Dodo-bird said, "Everybody has won and all must have prizes."' *American Journal of Orthopsychiatry, 6,* 412–415.

19. Stiles, W. (2012). The client–therapist relationship. In C. Feltham & I. Horton (Eds.), *The Sage Handbook of Counselling and Psychotherapy* (3rd ed.). London: Sage, pp. 67–77.

20. Carr, A. (2012). *Clinical Psychology: An introduction.* London: Routledge.

21. Williams, D., & Irving, J. (1999), Why are therapists indifferent to research? *British Journal of Guidance and Counselling, 27*(3), 367–376. Acknowledging this, a special section of *Counselling and Psychotherapy Research* (Vol. 12, No. 3, September 2012) contains five papers focusing on research into practitioners' attitudes. Yet we may ask exactly why so much effort goes into this when any incremental improvement in outcomes is likely to be merely miniscule.

22. Feltham, C. (1996). Psychotherapy's staunchest critic: An interview with Hans Eysenck. *British Journal of Guidance and Counselling, 24*(3), 423–435.

23. Marzillier, J. (2010). The myth of evidence-based psychotherapy. *The Psychologist, 17*(7), 392–395.

24. Writers like Ulrich Beck and Ken Plummer argue that rapid social change means that we often unwittingly study and research 'zombie categories' of anachronistic phenomena, just as education generally is often behind the times.

25. A study by Fanelli (Fanelli, D. (2010). 'Positive' results increase down the hierarchy of the sciences. *PLoS ONE, 5*(4), e10068) demonstrates that space sciences research shows least confirmatory bias, biological sciences next least, with psychology and psychiatry research showing the greatest tendency to produce results that confirm hypotheses. These findings also seem to reflect a precision versus vagueness polarity.

26. Harris, J. R. (1998). *The Nurture Assumption: Why children turn out the way they do.* London: Bloomsbury.

27. Callan, S., & Fry, B. (2012). *Commissioning Effective Talking Therapies.* London: Centre for Social Justice.

28. See *Revolution in Swedish Mental Health Practice: The cognitive behavioural therapy monopoly gives way.* 13 May 2012. Retrieved from http://scottdmiller.com/blog/page/6/

CHAPTER 6

Problems of counselling and counselling psychology as professions

Let us note that critiques of all professions (classically, the clergy, lawyers and doctors) are rooted in the deep historical phenomenon of surplus food supplies and growing populations. In other words, it was only when human beings mastered agriculture, food storage and protection, and thereafter had surplus time available, that state bureaucrats and military personnel became necessary and possible. Priesthood became useful as a means of hierarchical control. Original law emerged from needs for conflict control and property protection, and medicine from attempts to control infectious disease in dense societies. With time all these activities became enshrined and added to. Human beings in most contemporary societies have inherited structures whereby inverted values operate: the most vital activities like food gathering, domestic work, building, maintenance, caring and parenting rank fairly low in terms of status and rewards, while some of the most symbolic, superfluous and destructive, such as the priesthood, bureaucracy, law, academia, accountancy, and the military, have elevated status. Medicine is much more necessary and rewarded highly (but is not without problems) but professions allied to medicine, including nursing and counselling, have relatively low status and pay, and a high female membership. Even those professions with a practical remit often attract the unnecessary, self-glorifying paraphernalia of elaborate hierarchies, qualifications, and other requirements.[1] Critics of the professions note that they are parasitical upon the physical and menial labour of the masses, who remain largely excluded from their ranks. The professions have a long patriarchal history, recent feminist inroads notwithstanding.

Counselling is in the interesting position of not yet being a profession but seeking to become one. Counsellors are very aware that psychiatry and clinical psychology have much higher status and rewards. Yet counselling is also sometimes a ladder upwards for those residential care workers, nursing assistants, hairdressers and others who aspire to a more professional role, as well as being a desired sideways move for many exhausted and demoralised social workers and teachers. It was noted some years ago that so many care staff were gravitating towards counselling training that no one would be left to perform cleaning and other domestic tasks. Rather than retracing the history of counselling here, however, I will simply select a few significant historical highlights to provide context and then go on to critique key aspects of the components of this 'impossible profession'.

Counselling and counselling psychology

We have already encountered the problem (putting aside the psychotherapy overlap) that two apparently distinct professions exist here – counselling and counselling psychology – the former mainly overseen by BACP and the latter entirely by BPS, the former being older (circa 1970) and larger than the latter (with its roots in 1979). Many in this latter group may also call themselves counsellors when employment dictates this, but 'mere' counsellors cannot use the title of counselling psychologist since it is now a legally protected title. Counselling psychologists are regulated by the Health and Care Professions Council. In many cases counselling psychologists earn more than their non-psychologist counterparts. Counselling psychologists sit in a salary scale between £15,000 to £70,000 p.a.[2] Most counsellors have no salary scale but probably average around £20,000 to 35,000 p.a. full time. There is no evidence that those with the psychologist soubriquet practise more effectively, efficiently or safely but presumably the counselling psychologist offers psychology-enhanced counselling while the counsellor without psychology has less to offer. If any of this seems at all confusing or even bizarre this is, I suggest, simply because it is so. Like so many (perhaps all) professions, large elements of absurdity and self-interest are at play.

Although it is difficult to trace the origins of counselling accurately, a line of descent can be seen from American vocational, guidance and educational guidance systems, through the importation of such ideas to the UK, influenced by the psychodynamic psychotherapy tradition and the voluntary sector.[3] Counselling *psychology* came into view when some psychologists saw they ought to be in on the act and urged BPS to form a Counselling Psychology Section (1982). Counselling psychology retains counselling's humanistic value base and its interest in wellbeing enhancement but has added the scientist-practitioner component and inevitably upped academic requirements for training. Everyone will claim that all such developments are entirely nobly motivated but we can also suggest that they are motivated by naked opportunism. Possibilities for new training avenues, new career structures, income streams and enhanced reputations are seized upon. Of course rhetoric about enhancement of quality of care for the nation's mental health will always be used. Critics will be dismissed as cynics. But let's at least ask – just who are the cynics here?

We might reasonably expect to find in the curriculum of counselling psychologists greater theoretical sophistication, say, than in counselling courses. But at least one doctoral programme in counselling psychology uses the 'Egan approach' as an underpinning theoretical model. This is curious when we note that this approach (a three-stage, methodical, skills-heavy model) is so beloved of initial undergraduate certificate tutors and students for its relative simplicity and is frequently used as a basis for counselling *skills* courses that are preparatory (inferior?) to in-depth training courses.

We might also expect to see in-depth use of psychological theory and research on such doctoral programmes. For example, there is an abundance of research on interpersonal influence and perception, personality types, heuristic bias and so on. Yet these do not necessarily form a substantial part of the curriculum for trainee counselling psychologists. Exactly where, we can legitimately ask, is the psychology in counselling psychology?[4]

Training

Training courses in person-centred counselling began in the 1960s at the universities of Reading and Keele. Some non-university radical training was initially based on principles committed to student-centred learning, so there was no assumption that trainers knew best what to offer or had the right to predetermine the content of a training and some courses managed to sneak in student self-assessment procedures instead of tutor assessment. Such ideas have not travelled well into the 21st century. Not only do we now accept (or seem to have no power to resist) rigidly modularised training courses with legalistic documentation spelling out learning aims and anticipated outcomes. In addition, for courses to be BACP accredited, close alignment with detailed requirements must be demonstrated and these include explicit nomination of a core theoretical model and how it shapes the course in terms of theory, skills, personal development and supervised practice. BACP's long-standing alignment with the principle of respect for clients' resourcefulness and counsellors' reflective practice, along with concern for cultural sensitivity, might edge it towards the ethos of a liberating, countercultural critical pedagogy.[5] We might expect to see some convergence of this with Rogers' views on person-centred education in the training of counsellors and counselling psychologists but this is not much in evidence.

A pervasive problem for counselling psychology and counselling 'professional' training is the seemingly unseverable link with academia. Many independent training institutes provide training as good as any in the further and higher education sector but most of these find that for the purposes of meeting professional body criteria, using named awards, perceived credibility and optimal marketing they must secure external validation. This is always justified in terms of 'quality' (with the usual accompanying rhetoric) but such links mainly add to costs and bureaucracy rather than to any guaranteed hike in actual quality. It may well even detract from quality by imposing unnecessary and unhelpful modularisation, unsuitable progression criteria, layers of surveillance and errors and delays in processing awards. For all these reasons some commentators are highly critical of the link with academia.[6] This is perhaps not totally dissimilar to Mafia-style protection rackets: no one will inflict physical violence on errant trainers but indirect economic violence is often a consequence of not coughing up the validation fees. Small training outfits can suffer from low recruitment simply because they lack university validation and awards, even though the quality of their training may be as good as if not higher than some provided within higher education itself. In some cases the trainers are ex-university academics or distinguished clinicians not found in universities. But such is the stranglehold universities have in the capitalist bureaucracy of the professions that little can be done to change this state of affairs.

We should pause to note that for many practitioners counselling is a vocation and its training reflects this. Most training is self-funded. It is training and not 'education', in other words it is primarily about teaching people how to do something. There has been a heavy emphasis on learning certain interpersonal values and skills since the time of Rogers, Truax and Carkhuff. Counselling and its training have always rested on an attitude of faith.[7] So it begins with faith and enthusiasm and training reinforces a sense of mastery and commitment (even if in some cases it also factors in the tantalising mystery of 'not knowing', of 'giving psychology away' and of the 'client as expert').

Although most training now takes place in or alongside the higher education sector that has always espoused an ethos of critical and analytical thinking, counselling training remains heavily invested in imparting or bolstering faith in a circumscribed set of theories, skills and personal development activities rather than subjecting its principles to interdisciplinary scrutiny and critical thinking. This is in contrast to, for example, the clinical psychology training in the USA that explicitly requires the teaching of critical thinking skills, clinical judgement and prediction, awareness of confirmatory bias, philosophy of science, research methodologies and psychology of human memory.[8] Training in counselling and counselling psychology is tacitly and uncritically committed to a humanistic faith in the remedial values of relational intensity and individual autonomy. But could this be any other way? When training athletes, the emphasis must be on immersion in practice of their sport, in techniques for improvement. We do not expect athletes to spend time studying the history, anthropology and economics of sport, or indeed philosophical questions about the meaning of sport. Likewise with counselling, the point of training is to heighten appropriate attitudes and hone skills, not to turn practitioners into philosophers or sociologists.

Consider too the preponderance of women in counselling training and as trainers, an estimated 80 per cent in the first category and 70 per cent in the second. This echoes nursing except that in the counselling world the average age is higher. As I have suggested elsewhere, a great deal of counselling concerns theories of early attachment, close interpersonal relating and emotion and what we can call remedial conversation skills. We may not be able to call these 'natural' to women or harder for men to master but we cannot avoid wondering about the overwhelming female influence in training and the relative lack of male influence. Contrary to frequently voiced concerns about possible heterosexism and homophobia among counsellors, it is quite possible that its training and staffing suffer from a surfeit of women, gay and 'feminised' men who possess little in the way of traditional masculine qualities and who may unintentionally nurture a testosteronophobic culture. Whether or not this is a reality, an inevitability, and a good or bad thing is another matter. As I have suggested in Chapter 3, perhaps we stand in need of the kind of anti-patriarchal values offered here.

The central conundrum of counsellor training lies in there being at least some doubt about the very necessity of training.[9] How much research are we willing to invest in resolving the question of whether and how much training is necessary, with which criteria for entrants, with what curriculum, and at what level? I have posed such questions elsewhere.[10] It is entirely conceivable, if not probable, that an aptitude for counselling lies in innate personality characteristics and lessons learned in the school of life, and that those most suitable to be counsellors are not necessarily those who put themselves forward for training. It is those who wish to become counsellors, who can afford the training and who are in a position to avail themselves of it, who eventually become counsellors.[11] Optimal aptitude for counselling and the wish to be a counsellor do not necessarily always coincide. But again, can research help us out here or not?

At least we need to question the length, intensity and kind of training that is optimal. The pressure for face-to-face training to be three or more years part time or to be (for BACP accreditation purposes) an arbitrarily calculated minimum of 400 hours probably comes from a combination of anxiety to be perceived as a self-respecting profession, snobbery masquerading as concern vis-à-vis short counselling skills courses, and the financial needs of trainers and their institutions. Yet again, we may ask ourselves whether or to what extent the minimally trained counsellor is necessarily inferior in performance to the extensively trained psychoanalyst, say, or to the clinical and counselling psychologist trained to doctoral level.[12] My guess is that some individuals with the right kind of disposition and intelligence might learn what is necessary largely from a course of self-directed study, while some less gifted individuals might spend years in training only to become moderately competent practitioners. How would we know?

Personal therapy for trainees

Psychoanalytic tradition going back over 100 years has set up the demand that psychoanalytic trainees have extensive analysis of their own as an integral part of training and the associated expectation is that all psychotherapists and counsellors should do likewise. We saw in Chapter 3 that psychoanalysis has always issued such dictates on the basis of dogma and tradition. This belief has been maintained in the tradition of psychodynamic counselling, where it is unimaginable that anyone could be licensed to practise without considerable therapy of their own. This belief is held fiercely by many and debates about it have gone on for years. On the face of it, the argument that practitioners must look at themselves, at their own inevitable blind spots, oddities and unresolved conflicts, makes sense. Gaining the ability to discern what is your 'material' and what is your client's, developing resilience or reflecting on the impact your training and your first clients have on you, and what it feels like to be in the client's chair, are plausible enough reasons for this practice. But it is nevertheless deeply flawed in many ways.

To begin with the most obvious objection, if the very edifice of psychoanalysis is seriously flawed, then to compel people to undergo it is hardly a good idea. Compulsory therapy is often thought to be never a good idea. If required to see an analyst or therapist for training, who should this be? Cronies of the trainers, practitioners approved as loyal to the training model? How can we know what good this exercise is, or if it is of any use at all? For the most part it is an exercise of faith, since the training analyst or therapist cannot be asked to report to the training institute on her client. Factor in the considerable cost of such therapy and the overall cost of training escalates, making it inaccessible to anyone on a modest income and/or with the constraints of family commitments. What redress does the trainee have if unhappy with such therapy? Masson wrote scathingly about the training analysis he received.[13] The point in time at which anyone enters therapy or counselling, with what set of preoccupations, is another crucial factor here. And we are mostly basing this case on psychodynamic counselling. A principled person-centred training surely cannot require its trainees to do something that they may not freely choose to do. Cognitive behavioural training courses simply do not make any such requirement. Different professional bodies and courses come up with different requirements regarding mandatory nature and arbitrary number of sessions required (often 40), and a great deal of snobbery attaches to it. None of this is to say that if you are going to train, it may not be reasonable to have some therapy. But when, how much and from whom, with what evaluation? And is it purely a matter of faith or even wholly superstition after all? Again, some research suggests that few if any benefits accrue from it.[14]

Accreditation and chartering

BACP's voluntary accreditation scheme for counsellors, begun in 1983, has often been revised, and remains in operation. There have also been accreditation procedures for training courses, supervisors and services. (One is tempted to make a joke along the lines of 'if it moves, accredit it'.) Accreditation was deemed necessary as a kind of voluntary regulation mechanism setting out criteria for standards of training, qualifications and practice. This quality control, marketing and public relations exercise makes certain demands of practitioners, including completion of a minimum of 400 hours of approved training and also 450 hours of practice. A substantial application pack must be completed and a significant fee is payable.

Accreditation is necessitated by the great variability of training courses. Apart from a bewildering variety of qualifications, it is all that many employers have to go on for judging job applications. Accredited status is desired by many practitioners but applying for it is also feared. The failure rate is not insignificant and a common reason for failure at first application is a case study that does not convince the assessor that the applicant is counselling in a theoretically consistent way. The main objection to accreditation is that it is (perceived by many as) a cumbersome and expensive bureaucratic exercise conducted entirely by post, and assessed according to questionable principles that bear no real relation to practitioners' actual practice. This is not the intention but the inevitable effect of anonymous mass assessment of practitioners' competency. Queries about case studies in particular seem often to rest on misunderstandings about different models and spurious distinctions about practice. The artful and eloquent applicant who knows how to 'give them what they want' is always likely to do better than the applicant who is not a natural bureaucrat or artful writer but is a compulsive truth-teller! The accreditation system probably deters a few rogues and provides an appearance of stringent gatekeeping, but it probably cannot stand up to any close analytic scrutiny. Is it nevertheless 'better than nothing' or even as some would claim 'a professional achievement to be proud of'? Views will obviously differ greatly.

BPS requires members to complete a first psychology degree (or conversion course), plus an accredited doctorate in counselling psychology (or BPS qualification) if they wish to become counselling psychologists. They then have to apply for HCPC membership before being able to use the title of counselling psychologist. The full route to doctoral status might take at least six years, and probably more. We can see how badly the principle of sunk costs fits with critical thinking here: people who have invested heavily in such procedures do not allow themselves to think too deeply and critically if to do so might threaten either their livelihood or sense of integrity.

Many have misgivings about such professional developments. In my book *What is Counselling?* published in 1995 I cited some of these cases, including Rogers' view:

> I have seen the moves towards certification and licensure, the attempts to exclude charlatans, from a vantage point of many years, and it is my considered opinion that they fail in their aim. ... There are as many *certified* charlatans and exploiters of people as there are uncertified.[15]

Presumably Rogers was not basing this on any quantitative research evidence but on observation. But in the 30-plus years since his statement and almost 20 years since I mulled over these matters in my own book, the combined trends towards accreditation, audit and evaluation have continued undeterred by criticism.

Supervision

I have focused on some supervisory issues (not least the lack of evidence that it actually helps clients) in other chapters but will briefly critique some aspects of supervision here too. As with personal therapy, there are the mandatory and financial aspects. Within the training period it seems necessary to include supervision of initial practice as a course requirement, even if it were not a professional body demand. Yet already here we encounter problems. Who is to supervise? (Many experienced supervisors have no supervisory qualification.) Must their theoretical orientation match that of the course? (Often the limited local supply of supervisors reflects a variety of theoretical orientations.) Is it permissible for course tutors to supervise their own students? (Yes it is but it is still frowned upon by many.) Who will visit course placements to check for quality and to meet and approve placement supervisors? (Universities are often unwilling to allocate realistic time for such tasks.) It used to prove difficult to find supervisors but now trainees can find themselves over-supervised; perhaps supervision training (more bums on seats, more cash for training programmes) has produced a glut of supervisors. Students are taught that supervision is a space where they can freely offload their relevant concerns, struggles and doubts, yet there are the grey areas of whether supervisors might report the trainee to course leaders or related professionals. In other words, supervisors are supportive facilitators but always also, to an extent, monitors of ethical practice. It is far from unknown to hear trainees express either some uncertainty about or dissatisfaction with supervisors. In principle everyone has some right to change supervisors but in reality this is not always possible.

In recent years and quite belatedly some attention has been given to improving the way in which the purposes and potentials of supervision are explained to trainees so that they can maximise their use of it (they are, after all, often paying for it). The absolutely essential nature of supervision is invariably conveyed to all trainees, often in almost reverential tones. It is presented as a seamless part of the fabric of the whole of counselling practice. As with other elements of counsellor training, little if any time is devoted to thinking critically about supervision and debating its merits or possible alternatives. Trainees may instinctively sense that their allocated supervisor is a bit authoritarian, eccentric, sleepy or flirtatious, or that supervision sessions sometimes feel more like empty rituals than lively and necessary occasions. (This experience is often the case when the supervisee has seen few clients recently, perhaps due to 'no-shows', but the trainee must still endure an hour or more of supervision, perhaps speculating about the possible reasons for the non-show.) But as beginners they may be a little timid or simply have no ability to make a reasoned estimate of the value of supervision, or any power to object to it. And of course often enough supervisees are happy with their supervisors and report that they gain from their sessions. Here again, we do not know if mutual satisfaction between supervisor and supervisee correlates with practice that is better than it would be without the supervision. One of the functions of supervision, usually unacknowledged, is to socialise trainees into the professional culture and to reinforce the faith. Let's not forget that supervision, like training therapy, is perceived by some as part of the 'pyramid selling' structure of counselling, with course tutors feeding paying supervisees annually to their local peers and cronies and generally stimulating the economy of counselling.

Professional ethics

For all the disagreements about therapeutic theory, everyone seems agreed on the inviolable status of confidentiality and other boundaries. You could say 'We don't agree on what we're doing but we're doing it ethically'. Counselling is private and confidential, involves no friendship or sex between counsellor and client, no disrespect or exploitation, discourages the giving and receipt of gifts, and so on. All such principles are enshrined in respected professional body documents that are periodically reviewed. I will not dwell on professional ethics too much here, beyond making the point that behind their noise lies a mixture of common sense and sensitivity, very broad practice guidance (counsellors often agonise at the lack of specific guidance), public relations, and a detachment from wider social ethics. For example, as in business ethics, it is perfectly possible to behave in ostensibly micro-ethical ways within a culture that may contain macro-ethical failures or that sits within a damaging, dehumanising society. Even the Mafia, for example, has its code of *omerta* or silence.

The problems with confidentiality are twofold. First, it may legitimately be 'breached' if the counsellor judges that the client could harm himself or others, especially children. It is routinely stretched when the counsellor talks about clients in supervision, and where supervision takes place in groups, up to six or so supervisees will hear details, even if not names. Confidentiality can never be guaranteed, only promised and taken on faith. Second, however, when we think about what it is that is confidential we must realise just how universal most client concerns are. Names and details aside, everyone is suffering from some variation of depression, anxiety, conflict. This is attested to by the experience and theory of group therapy, where confidentiality also has a stretched meaning. It may even be that we can learn from the very opposite of confidential settings for the disclosure of intimate personal stories – the radio and television chat show. Another striking example is the therapeutic campaign designed to encourage the client and give her alternative and expanded views of herself by sending a letter to dozens of friends and colleagues requesting their input.[16] Common sense tells us that confidentiality is important (for the client's safety and for public relations purposes) but a little reflection suggests it may consist more of mystery than substance.

Continuing professional development and other accoutrements

It is a feature of most established professions that qualified practitioners are required to maintain an ongoing programme of education and further training. The requirement is usually pegged to an arbitrary time commitment like 30 hours a year, and CPD providers have learned to helpfully issue certificates of attendance that a professional body may wish to check. One can never regard oneself as fully trained and it would be a sign of complacency to think one is, runs the rationale here. Of course there are always new developments, things to keep abreast of, especially in a field like counselling where workshops on the latest techniques, ethical and legal anxieties, and so on, are pushed. Again, we can see this as a colourful, creative and vibrant aspect of the counselling world, even as an ethical imperative to keep ourselves perpetually refreshed. But we might also question the CPD expectation as part of counselling's suspicious pyramid structure. People make money and reputations from offering CPD workshops, courses and conferences.

Counsellors who feel insecure in their knowledge base may address their anxieties by attending workshops on specific techniques or therapeutic approaches. In many cases practitioners who have completed a Diploma or first degree in counselling may decide to commence a Masters degree in order to enhance their CV in the hope of increasing their competiveness in a tight job market. Universities can be very keen to promote modular higher degrees, for example, to get those bums on seats, and lecturers keen to keep their jobs often become promoters of such courses. Fashion-watchers in the sometimes faddish culture of counselling can soon put together a module on PTSD, brief therapy, or whatever looks like selling. People are attracted to counselling as a vocation both for its warm meaningful ethos and also for its employment prospects, but the latter are often much slimmer than they realise. However, once they have realised how scarce jobs are they must face the question of whether they have made the wrong choice of career. One avenue of cognitive dissonance reduction then is to push on and do more of the same on the sunk costs principle. While some are education junkies hooked on the buzz of learning, some are arguably gamblers throwing good money after bad in the hope of eventually landing that dream job.

Professional identity and statutory regulation

Having examined the main ingredients of counselling and counselling psychology as professions, we can now look at the wider question of regulation. Underlying counselling as a social phenomenon is the fear of it being perceived by the public as a domain in which anything goes. In other words, it could be seen as a wild and flaky enterprise comparable to other pseudoscientific, charlatan-ridden and dangerous cons. Psychotherapists were acutely aware of this when seeking to distance themselves from scientology in the 1970s. Among the problems dogging counselling for decades has been its very definition. While the definitional impasse could be put on hold for years, it came to the fore in the machinations of the Professional Liaison Group (PLG) of the HCPC. Quite reasonably, something called 'counselling' must be different from something called 'psychotherapy', and the HCPC eventually came up with the distinction that the former addresses psychological wellbeing, problems in living and normal developmental challenges while the latter can address severe mental distress in depth. This pseudo-distinction simply could not fly and was rejected.[17]

The situation today is that counselling psychology along with its big brother, clinical psychology, is a protected title under the auspices of the HCPC, while counselling has avoided statutory regulation and remains 'unregulated', although at the time of writing, seeking alternative regulatory mechanisms with the CHRE/PSA. This interim uncertainty is regarded with apparent horror by some and with exultation by others. In the first group are those counsellors, allied professionals and interested parties who believe counselling still to be vulnerable to charlatans, to untrained or poorly trained people who pass themselves off as 'counsellors' to an unsuspecting public and who are likely to be exploitative, to do damage, to miss serious problems in clients and to bring the profession into disrepute. In the second group we see many humanistic, integrative and psychoanalytic practitioners who (sometimes for quite different reasons) are relieved that the HCPC cannot dictate to them how they will practise.

The one glaring absurdity in all this is that it makes no immediate difference to practice if counselling is regulated by the HCPC or any other body; and probably it makes no long-term difference either. It does not suddenly or gradually improve training standards, or ethical protection of clients, or the effectiveness of counselling. Indeed it has often been argued that HCPC standards are lower than those of BACP, IPN and others. Are counselling psychologists more competent or safer since signing up with the HCPC? Of course not. Nothing changes in the short term. The gamble is that in the long run it will pay off, as the field becomes more competitive, the NHS even more influential and the public more discerning (or more readily mesmerised by BPS and HCPC publicity). Then the anti-regulation people will be sorry. We have to live in the real world, say the pro-regulation lobby, and whether we like it or not we are judged by credentials and regulatory mechanisms. None of us likes bureaucracy, they say, but we must grow up and accept the reality that this is how things are done.

A compelling case against the HCPC regulation already in place for counselling psychologists is presented by Janet Haney.[18] Haney followed very closely the HCPC hearing against a counselling psychologist and academic with close HCPC links. Attending and recording meetings of this fitness to practise hearing commencing in 2010, Haney shows through actual dialogue the wasteful, persecutory, Kafkaesque (not to say comical) processes involved. The psychologist had been somewhat drunk and silly at a pre-accreditation course dinner that had no bearing on his practice as a counsellor, yet such was the eagerness of the HCPC to establish its recent 'capture' of the counselling psychology sector that many high-ranking professionals fretted over it, and much time and money was spent on this flimsy and shameful case. The clear inference here is that regulation is more about bureaucracy than quality enhancement or public protection.

No one is likely to confuse counsellors with scientologists today but the vast majority of counsellors would not want to be associated with scientology and its reputation for exploitation, far-fetched ideas and cultish behaviour. On the other hand, a few counsellors may have training in astrology (and Jung used astrology on occasion) and many have some vague sympathy with it. Quite a significant proportion of counsellors have some sympathy with complementary and alternative medicine, with Reiki, Hakomi, homeopathy, acupuncture, naturopathy, chiropractic, reflexology, dowsing, meditation, spirit guides, and spirituality generally. I do not mean to lump these all together for the sake of mockery but to bring up an important epistemological question: how do we know which of these healing arts, remedies or therapies to respect and trust and which if any to dismiss? Where does hypnotherapy, for example, sit on the spectrum of therapies, and where hypno-regression to past lives? What are our grounds for these judgements? Why do some of us opt to train in or receive treatment from these modalities? Clearly our judgements can stem from fascination and gullibility on the positive side to prejudice and snobbery on the negative. Some like to think of themselves as open-minded and tuned in to alternative realities where others are closed off by a narrow loyalty to Western rationality.[19] Those who insist on 'empirical evidence' to test all such claims and outcomes may dismiss homeopathy, say, in the light of negative research.

Look at this from another angle. Some psychoanalysts consider counsellors to be superficially trained, to be engaged in mere symptom removal or defence bolstering. Some clinical psychologists also look down on counsellors,[20] as do some psychotherapists, usually on the grounds that they work with problems in depth and of complexity, while counselling addresses mild problems in daily living. But some counsellors regard clinical psychologists as over-intellectualised, as out of touch with feelings, and psychotherapists as long-winded, arrogant or pretentious. It cuts both ways. And the still youthful identity of counselling psychology is partly based on finding a humanistic niche alongside counselling (at some distance from clinical psychology) and a place for academic psychology and empirical research that sets it apart from counselling.

I have no hope of getting anywhere near the bottom of all this. It resembles what is on offer in religion, with dozens of different major religions, thousands of cults and denominations, ranging from colourful evangelical positions to dour fundamentalism and almost agnostic liberalism, from claims to miracles and healing powers to notions of endtimes and the rapture, with the chosen and the heathen. If this all sounds remote from counselling, when I was in primal therapy in the 1970s there was a distinct sense of the insiders having a cult-like belief in their superior grasp of feelings, indeed of truth. I have my own prejudices about which therapies I regard as nonsense and which I like. There are aspects of the counselling world about which I feel a cringing embarrassment and want to disown completely. I am often incredulous that some people I know are fully persuaded by either psychoanalysis or astrology and I am unsure whether one is more credible or professional than the other. Most of us seem to gravitate in belief towards and away from various approaches and most of us seem to need to belong somewhere with or without supporting evidence.

Who are the counsellors?

No accurate figures are available for the numbers employed as counsellors and counselling psychologists but a UK figure of 70,000 counsellors and up to half a million people working with counselling skills has been suggested.[21] We know however that over 80 per cent of BACP members are women. Cohorts of counselling trainees are often overwhelmingly (and sometimes entirely) female. It is not unusual for more men to be in top positions in academic counselling departments. Counselling has traditionally been dominated by middle-class, middle-aged women seeking part-time and often second or third careers. Many entrants come from backgrounds in nursing, social work, teaching and other caring and helping professions. This picture of the mature entrant (reinforced by a now-abandoned practice of maintaining lower age limits in selection procedures) has begun to change somewhat in recent years with the increase in Foundation degrees and counselling psychology routes attracting some younger people into the profession but it remains predominantly female.

We might ask why this is the case and what effects it has. In practical terms women often try to fit a counselling career around or after parenting and other caring commitments. Psychologically and theoretically women may be drawn towards the more emotional, intuitive, empathic, interpersonal, attachment and object relations aspects of counselling – the 'emotion work'. Until quite recently a majority of clients in most counselling services were also female, and many men entering counselling were urged by female partners to get counselling or to accompany them reluctantly to couple counselling. Talking therapies as part of the caring professions still have a marked female imbalance. In spite of repeated complaints from women that their pay remains lower than that of men, caring professions like counselling are on average relatively low paid. The meaningfulness and job satisfaction elements of counselling probably help to explain its continuing appeal.

Some critics have argued that the middle-class bias in counselling seriously limits it. Although counselling is not alone in this position, especially since demands for caring professions to be at degree level, it does have certain unintended effects. Clients who are working class, unemployed or 'underclass' may not find their way of expressing themselves completely accepted or reciprocated by middle-class counsellors, differences in vocabulary and social skills manifesting themselves from the outset and 'politically correct' and predominantly left-wing attitudes prevailing. However empathic counsellors are, and however universal some forms of personal problems and emotions may be, people who experience chronic low status, low pay, debt, poor housing, compromised health and limited opportunities may not be able to prioritise psychological-mindedness over practical need. Clients who are not from the majority white culture, who are older and/or disabled and experiencing loneliness may not always offer counsellors the ready rapport that is part of the idealised therapeutic relationship. Traditional males are often the most reluctant to seek counselling, which is perceived as somewhat female-oriented and emotion-revealing territory, and I have heard some female trainees voicing exasperation at men's difficulty in owning and expressing relevant feelings and insight. Some surveys suggest that certain clients (often men and some from ethnic minorities) prefer goal-oriented counselling and even advice, which are largely anathema to the process-oriented and non-directive ethos of most counselling.[22]

Perhaps it is a good thing that counselling is so female-dominated, perhaps it is even necessary? Some years ago I wrote an article highlighting these gender factors. In the course of researching the topic I discovered that although men made up the much smaller proportion of counsellors, male counsellors (as well as male psychologists and nurses) attracted a disproportionately high number of complaints from clients. I speculated that all this might be partly due to men's presumed lesser sensitivity and empathy. The article was never published, for fear that it might attract vehement complaints of sexist bias against men. I had not suggested that men are always abusive or less sensitive and I sought to keep some balance by asking whether women also have biases. But the experience taught me that some topics are close to taboo: class may be the hardest to examine but gender is probably also something of a hot potato.

The humorous public stereotype of the psychiatrist or psychoanalyst as crazier than his (interestingly usually 'his') patients carries through somewhat to psychotherapists and counsellors. Orlans and van Scoyoc suggest that 'there is something of the maverick in many counselling psychologists'.[23] Having survived and learned from traumatic or negative life events, the counsellor often prides herself on such suffering as a badge of honour. Indeed questions about learning from experience may form part of any interview for counsellor training. The 'wounded healer' tradition runs deep in counselling as it does in the shamanism tradition. It is common to find counsellors in alcoholism recovery work who have themselves recovered (or remain 'in recovery'), and a similar isomorphism can be found in bereavement and other counsellor experiences. Ironically, valued though they are, these experiences are not expected to be often disclosed to clients. While counsellors value these personal experiences and it is a reasonable assumption that painful experiences will sensitise one to others' pain, there is no hard evidence that they lead to more (or less) effective counselling.

Counselling psychologists are overall better qualified academically than counsellors but both groups consist of self-selecting individuals who hope they may be good at counselling (at freeing people from their suffering). There is no evidence however that they stand out from their fellow human beings in terms of level of consciousness. A fair number of well-known guru-like teachers now exist, some of whom may be charlatans and some not. Take Eckhart Tolle, the German author of the bestselling *The Power of Now,* living in Canada, who seems to have entered a state of consciousness free from ego and temporal entrapment. Sometimes billed as a counsellor as well as a spiritual teacher, Tolle has no qualification in counselling. Assuming however that he is not a charlatan, how might we compare his 'counselling' with that of a highly qualified counsellor who is not personally enlightened (as I imagine most are not)? Or we *might* compare the supposedly enlightened Ken Wilber with counselling trainees on integral psychology training courses that rest on Wilber's theories.

Stakeholders

I have made the point throughout this book that the essentially one-to-one private activity of counselling is surrounded by other activities that we might consider parasitical, although those conducting these activities clearly do not think in these terms. Who do I mean by 'stakeholders'? I mean all who depend upon and usually profit from counselling. Practitioners depend directly and visibly on it for their livelihood, although we should remind ourselves that some practitioners profit more than others. The London-based high-end psychoanalyst, psychiatrist or clinical psychologist in private practice, often seeing affluent and sometimes celebrity clients, has an income far surpassing that of a counsellor working for a voluntary organisation in the north of England. High-end practitioners whether in private practice or salaried are fairly sure to assert or let it be thought that what they provide is high quality, effective, safe, well researched and so on, and may overtly or covertly let it be thought that other psy-practitioners are less reliable or less effective. Many clients with no way of knowing otherwise believe the old adage that 'you get what you pay for'. Our high-end practitioners may sincerely believe in their own clinical superiority, or may have snobbish views about their church mouse colleagues.

I have very good anecdotal evidence that in fact you can sometimes pay a great deal for unsatisfactory talking therapy and conversely pay nothing for sometimes excellent counselling. I once interviewed a therapist in shrewdly rented Harley Street premises, charging high fees, who shamelessly told me that she herself received free counselling from an excellent counsellor at the service provided by a professional organisation of which she was a member. I have also previously discussed a colleague's story of being told by a client that her counselling seemed indistinguishable from the psychoanalysis she had once received.[24]

The next tier of stakeholders comprises the trainers and training institutes, academics and colleges and universities that process the raw aspirant into a qualified, accredited practitioner. Commercial, voluntary sector and academic organisations all provide training for counsellors in what is undoubtedly a multi-million pound business. Just a few decades ago only a small number of independent training institutes offered training, usually psychoanalytic, with relatively small annual intakes of students. Counselling too started partly in this way. With the popularity of the talking therapies as a career choice, student/trainee numbers have swelled. University administrators insist on higher student intakes and the battle fought by trainers and lecturers is lost, with larger classes becoming the norm. But larger classes do mean a growth in academic posts, and many counsellors recognise the advantage of having at least some academic employment in a market with insufficient jobs for the number of counselling graduates being pumped out annually. Also, of course, academic employment is both more prestigious and usually better paid than counselling itself. Colleges and universities often provide whole suites of courses from undergraduate certificates to foundation and honours degrees, Masters and Doctorate qualifications. In addition, supervision training is in demand and short courses and workshops keep practitioners' continuing professional development requirements fulfilled. Many universities also validate courses run by commercial organisations. Counselling training may not be massively lucrative for the educational sector and is often regarded as academically lightweight, but educational stakeholders remain a very significant group. Obviously to quite an extent they come to shape the counselling world and even those who are sceptical about the added value of higher education endorsement recognise they may need to 'go through the hoops' in a competitive employment market.

I have heard it said that many trainee counsellors do not much enjoy reading or that when they read they prefer thin volumes that are 'accessibly written'. While this is anecdotal and contentious, there are reasons to believe that many counsellors in training (and subsequently) gravitate towards the field primarily because they enjoy the intimate relationship involved and the sense of emotional meaning within the field. Many have no first degree or, if they do, are less than enthusiastic about pursuing higher degrees. In other words they are not primarily attracted to counselling for its intellectual qualities. In my experience, many prefer training texts that are small, accessible, and based on easy-to-master theories and gratifying case narratives. Students often love Irvin Yalom's *Love's Executioner*, for example, as well as *Counselling for Toads, Dibs,* and Alice Miller's books, but frequently shy away from the heavy tomes of Freud, Rogers and others. This is all complicated by the fact that entrants into the profession who have psychology degrees, and/or who are pursuing a counselling psychology route, either *do* enjoy or simply have to read serious psychological literature. In either case, all students must engage with theory which is still usually found in books.

Publishers then are significant stakeholders in the counselling market. It is not only that they profit financially from the sale of books that should concern us here but that they are gatekeepers for what does and does not get published. I do not suspect any conspiracy among publishers to banish certain texts but they come to recognise that major course textbooks are their most bankable products and they are likely to court and reward those authors who generate what sells. What sells, both as self-help literature to the public and also to trainees, is on the whole that which is easy to read and inspires hope. Theory that is simple, or if not always simple then conveying a sense of special insider knowledge, warm uplifting stories and anything that reinforces commitment to counselling – this is what sells best. Occasionally a sensationalist text like Jeffery Masson's *Against Therapy* may tickle the rebellious fancy of some students. Publishers of relevant academic and professional journals too recognise that corporate subscriptions to publications that academia demands are profitable, in part because authors are paid nothing for their writing. All publishers in this field are eager to promote new editions of favourite texts and to court authors old and new who will deliver saleable goods.

Authors too, of course, are an essential aspect of this stakeholder area. Most derive quite modest incomes from royalties and a very few make good incomes. But there are important spin-off effects involved. Writing for publication about any topic reinforces it, so counselling authors are also by default salespeople and ambassadors for the entire counselling venture. They also profit in other ways – from adding to their CV and enhancing their own employment and promotion prospects (an essential requirement in academia), from promoting a positive public image of themselves that can lead to fuller counselling and supervision practices, invitations to conferences and workshops,[25] participation in high-status committees and so on. Educational and publishing personnel as stakeholders profit enormously from the part they play in the counselling world. It may seem unfair to speak of them as parasitical and I certainly do not intend any likeness with bacteria, for example (I have after all been one of the beneficiaries of all this), but we cannot construct a comprehensive picture of counselling without factoring in these elements – the stakeholders who partly shape counselling and who decidedly benefit from it. We need to bear in mind always, I suggest, the question of to what extent such stakeholders contribute positively and efficiently to the better and happier human lives that are the goal of counselling.

Other stakeholders include all who work within or for relevant professional bodies, government departments, allied academic disciplines, journalists and insurance companies. In the unfortunate hierarchy of counselling, its clients, the suffering and confused individuals for whom counselling exists, are centre stage but not necessarily powerful. The trainees and practitioners who retain a sincere commitment to the alleviation of suffering have, in some ways, more power than their clients. In the hierarchy of power, status and income in the psy-professions, psychiatrists rule, followed by clinical and counselling psychologists and psychoanalysts, then psychotherapists, and mental health nurses and counsellors.

Endnotes

1. Mair, K. (1992). The myth of therapist expertise. In W. Dryden & C. Feltham (Eds.), *Psychotherapy and its Discontents.* Buckingham: Open University Press, pp. 135–168.

2. Orlans, V., & van Scoyoc, S. (2009). *A Short Introduction to Counselling Psychology.* London: Sage.

3. See, for example, Feltham, C. (1995). *What is Counselling? The promise and problem of the talking therapies.* London: Sage.

4. For differing views on psychology in counselling, see Feltham, C. (2012). Contextual psychology. In C. Feltham & I. Horton (Eds.), *The Sage Handbook of Counselling and Psychotherapy* (3rd ed.). London: Sage, pp. 232–236; and van Deurzen-Smith, E. (1993). Psychology and counselling. In W. Dryden (Ed.), *Questions and Answers on Counselling in Action.* London: Sage, pp. 129–135.

5. Giroux, H. A. (2011). *On Critical Pedagogy.* New York: Continuum.

6. See Berry, M., & Woolfe, R. (1997). Teaching counselling in universities: Match or mismatch? *British Journal of Guidance and Counselling, 25*(4), 517–525; and Rizq, R. (2007). On the margins: A psychoanalytic perspective on the location of counselling, psychotherapy and counselling psychology training programmes within universities. *British Journal of Guidance and Counselling, 35*(3), 283–297.

7. Halmos, P. (1978). *The Faith of the Counsellors.* London: Constable.

8. Lilienfeld, S. O., Lynn, S. J., & Lohr, J. M. (Eds.). (2003). *Science and Pseudoscience in Clinical Psychology.* New York: Guilford, p. 462.

9. McLennan, J. (1999). Becoming an effective psychotherapist or counsellor: Are training and supervision necessary? In C. Feltham (Ed.), *Controversies in Psychotherapy and Counselling.* London: Sage, pp. 164–173.

10. Feltham, C. (2010). *Critical Thinking in Counselling and Psychotherapy.* London: Sage.

11. Guy, J. D. (1987). *The Personal Life of the Psychotherapist.* New York: Wiley.

12. Rogers, C. R. (1980). *A Way of Being.* Boston: Houghton Mifflin.

13. Masson, J. M. (1992). *Final Analysis: The making and unmaking of a psychoanalyst.* London: Flamingo.

14. McLennan, J. (1999). Becoming an effective psychotherapist or counsellor: Are training and supervision necessary? In C. Feltham (Ed.), *Controversies in Psychotherapy and Counselling.* London: Sage, pp. 164–173.

15. Rogers, C. R. (1980). *A Way of Being.* Boston: Houghton Mifflin, p. 244.

16. Madigan, S. (1999). Inscription, description and deciphering chronic identities. In I. Parker (Ed.), *Deconstructing Psychotherapy.* London: Sage, pp. 150–163.

17. Carr, A. (2012). *Clinical Psychology: An introduction.* London: Routledge. See pp. 28–29 on curious and contestable definitions of counselling and counselling psychology.

18. Haney, J. (2012). *Regulation in Action: The Health Professions Council Fitness to Practise Hearing of Dr Malcolm Cross – Analysis, history, and comment.* London: Karnac.

19. Moodley, R., & West, W. (Eds.). (2005). *Integrating Traditional Healing Practices into Counseling and Psychotherapy.* Thousand Oaks, CA: Sage.

20. James, O. (1998). *Britain on the Couch: Treating a low serotonin society.* London: Arrow. According to James, a clinical psychologist and media star whose parents were psychoanalysts: 'a counsellor is someone nice to talk to who won't make a lot of value judgements … They can be very supportive during a crisis' (p. 360).

21. Aldridge, S. (2011). *Counselling: An insecure profession? A sociological and historical analysis.* Unpublished PhD thesis, University of Leicester.

22. Feltham, C. (2012). Client experiences. In C. Feltham & I. Horton (Eds.), *The Sage Handbook of Counselling and Psychotherapy* (3rd ed.). London: Sage, pp. 184–187.

23. Orlans, V., & van Scoyoc, S. (2009). *A Short Introduction to Counselling Psychology.* London: Sage, p. 19.

24. Feltham, C. (1995). *What is Counselling? The promise and problem of the talking therapies.* London: Sage.

25. Many representatives of publishers active in the counselling field attend national and international conferences, as do academics, for learned and commercial purposes, but the hedonistic and ego-flattering aspects of the annual conference merry-go-round should not be ignored. Many counselling trainees and clients on low incomes might fairly wonder at all this.

CHAPTER 7

Summarising and answering the critiques

I have attempted to show throughout this book that certain strong cases against aspects of counselling can be made, as well as moderate and weak critiques. In this chapter I aim to summarise and concisely add to these, to show what counter-arguments may be made, and to leave it to readers to evaluate the overall case against counselling and counselling psychology for themselves.

Problems of definition and scope

Exactly what is counselling and what is counselling psychology is far from clear (never mind distinctions to be made against psychotherapy). Satisfactory definitions have never been forthcoming. We must assume that those responsible for providing official definitions are themselves exasperated by the sheer amorphousness of the counselling project as well as by the difficulty of describing the components of counselling non-ambiguously. Indeed many counsellors probably believe that counselling has to be grasped intuitively or not at all. For some practitioners, counselling is self-evidently one among other treatments for mental health problems, while for others counselling is not health-oriented but about personal growth. Psychodynamic counsellors may believe that clients who insist on clear definitions are betraying psychological defences. Many counsellors find it difficult to define their own (humanistic, integrative, psychodynamic) approach verbally and satisfactorily for clients who enquire. But imagine a potential client asking naïvely but justifiably, 'So will counselling cure me?' Many counsellors will find this difficult to answer straightforwardly and non-evasively. Few would say 'It's a harmless "have-a-go" process that may or may not work for you'. I think we must pause to wonder if in fact all counsellors themselves fully understand what counselling is supposed to be and what it can actually achieve.

It seems impossible to give a finite list of the kinds of problems that counselling is set up to address. Whatever objections there are to the *DSM*, it does at least attempt the daunting task of itemising the hundreds of 'psychiatric disorders' that practitioners who use it claim to address. Counsellors have no equivalent, partly due to uncertainties about the suitability of counselling addressing 'severe' conditions (some claim it can, others demur), but partly too due to a philosophical dislike of the non-holistic cataloguing of problems and to resistance to being pinned down to dealing with only problematic states. Many clients love the opportunity to indulge in autobiographical reflection and many counsellors are fascinated by intrapsychic and intersubjective phenomena. Psychodynamic counsellors may well believe that everyone's presenting symptom conceals deeper matters, and that everyone can benefit from making the unconscious conscious. Person-centred counsellors believe that most people can benefit from a little help with their actualising tendency, regardless of whether clients currently have any named problem.

Pragmatically, counsellors with websites frequently give a list containing stress, anxiety, depression, bereavement and relationship difficulties, and many include more specifically phobias, OCD, PTSD, eating disorders, sexual problems, etc. No one is required to demonstrate specific competency or qualifications in each of these areas and those who practise humanistically or psychodynamically probably see themselves as equipped to *address* (but not, note, remedy) all these areas by virtue of the generic nature of their training model.

Practitioners of CBT may feel competent to address most of these conditions on the basis of faith in confirmatory research.

It is not unusual to read claims that counselling leads to greater insight, relief from stress, wellbeing, better functioning, improved relationships and enhanced self-esteem. Such terms are broad or vague enough not to be easily measurable. Counsellors practising existentially or from certain humanistic, psychosynthesis and other transpersonal positions may claim to work with issues of decision making, authenticity, life values, life paths, past lives, the inner child, dreams, and higher states of consciousness. Practitioners here will be strong believers and clients attracted to such advertising will likely be similarly oriented. All such work is almost entirely a matter of faith. Those involved, and paying for such experiences, may be getting real, new and desired experiences or they may be deceiving themselves, since this is the area where counselling has the greatest overlap with complementary and New Age therapies and spiritual beliefs. The problem is not that these are necessarily wrong or even spurious but that they cannot be verified. Actually, there is a further problem here, which is that while fully informed consumers are entitled to buy into these, it is ethically questionable whether uninformed consumers and those wanting 'down to earth' help with, say, smoking cessation, panic attacks or relocation decisions are best served by these approaches.

Problems of sprawling pluralism

Psychopractice spans the professions of psychiatry, psychoanalysis, psychotherapy, clinical psychology, counselling psychology, counselling, mental health nursing (and arguably coaching). This multiplicity of overlapping and uncoordinated services is highly confusing, inefficient and wasteful. Overlying much of this are competing clinical philosophies and treatments. The talking therapies are divided by hundreds of competing theories. This state of affairs has come about for various historical reasons. Its disadvantages are obvious but it is hard to justify its continuing existence unless one believes that all diversity offers richness and choice. Left to chance, this situation is unlikely to rectify itself but there are no obvious, strong champions of the kind of rationalising and simplifying that would be required to reverse this trend towards ever greater pluralism. Perhaps we realise that the vested interests involved are mightier than the forces of reason.

Very typically, many textbooks covering different therapeutic approaches contain uniformly enthusiastic testimonies to the invariable efficacy of each approach, each written by an authoritative and sincere practitioner/academic.[1] Remembering, however, that these approaches all differ significantly from each other in rationale, we might pose the following explanations to account for all this apparent transtheoretical success regardless of alleged specifics:

1. The writer/counsellor consciously exaggerates about successful outcomes, some degree of exaggeration being quite likely when in effect defending one's livelihood and representing one's community of therapeutic belief.

2. The writer/counsellor consciously lies about the extent of successful outcomes.

3. The writer/counsellor is sincere but mistaken in his judgement of extensive positive outcomes.

4. The writer/counsellor is subject to cognitive dissonance reduction mechanisms, believing himself to be a good judge of theory and therapeutic outcomes which he therefore cannot square with significant clinical failures.

5. Each counsellor mysteriously, invariably attracts clients who happen to suit his therapeutic approach and who are therefore successful.

6. Each counsellor attracts informed clients who know and prefer his approach.

7. All such experienced, authoritative practitioners deliver highly competent therapy that may be more idiosyncratic and less faithful to espoused theory than they realise.

8. All or most successful outcomes may be due to unrecognised common (transtheoretical) factors.

9. Most counselling is broadly made up of positive client–counsellor collusions whereby it is in everyone's interests to emerge feeling better about themselves.

It seems unlikely to me that 2 or 5 are much in play. Instances of 3 may occur sometimes but presumably not often among the very experienced. Number 4 may be quite common. Number 6 may happen quite often in private practice (especially with the cognitive dissonance in 4 also applying to clients who have invested belief and money in therapy). Numbers 7 and 8 seem to me to be the most likely explanations, with 1 being difficult to dismiss entirely, even if undiplomatic to say so, and 9 possibly accounting for many moderately successful outcomes. Few of these writers have the irreverent and reckless honesty of Brad Blanton (see Chapter 5). Even if 8 is the best explanation – as I suspect it is – it must leave us with doubts about our experts' judgement or candour. What we cannot logically accept is that one approach-specific practitioner out of a variety of 16 approaches, say, is a good judge who speaks the absolute truth about the efficacy of his approach and all the others are liars, poor judges or self-deceived.

Perhaps it is time for us to ask penetrating questions about how all such accounts are actually constructed. Some information is factual, such as the history of the approach and its key figures. But some of it is philosophical, and usually loosely so. How did its creators observe the links between the developing clinical approach in practice and its links with such broad concepts as human nature and psychological functioning? On how many real cases are accounts like these based? What minimum number of successful cases should we expect to see accumulated in order to take an approach seriously? On the clinical work of how many approach-specific counsellors with how many clients (and how many sessions) focusing on which conditions, with what means of evaluation? How do we know that such accounts of clinical cases and their theoretical summation are not simply, or partly, made up, or exaggerated, or edited so as to eliminate or reduce inconvenient details that might undermine the strong public relations effect the authors wish to create? The answers must surely converge in this statement: *we do not know*. All such material is taken on good faith. We have no way of knowing whether any self- or other-deception, unwitting or otherwise, major or minor, is involved. Due to confidentiality, transparent records cannot be kept. Due to the uniqueness of every client, no theoretical generalisation is ever quite valid. Given the natural optimism of the authors and the credulousness of many readers, the danger of inadequate critique is high.

Problems of professional organisation

Assuming that the above problems will not be addressed any time soon, here I refer to problems in the organisation of counselling provision – training, supervision, research, ethics, accreditation and regulation. Our dilemma is whether to continue with business as usual, making small refinements according to needs, fashions and pressures, or to instigate some sort of radical review. Such reviews might entail concrete upheavals in organisation or major philosophical challenges. For example, it would be possible to lengthen training, standardise curricula and agree on a research agenda for a certain time span. But a more radical challenge would entail entertaining the questions of whether training is needed at all, or the idea that limiting training places and better identifying the most talented trainees would vastly improve counselling services.

Regulation is clearly a stubborn problem for counsellors, unresolved after many years, yet apparently resolved for counselling psychologists. This differential situation at least may allow us to make comparisons between HCPC regulation and regulation otherwise (by the CHRE/PSA, or professional or voluntary self-regulation), or no regulation. It is a very large step but Richard House among others argues passionately that only a post-professional therapy seems possible if we are to take criticisms seriously.[2] In fact if we recall Freud's advocacy of (non-medical) lay analysis,[3] Rogers' ambivalence about licensing, questions about the place of psychology in counselling and research casting doubt on many aspects of training, we can detect a long-standing trend of scepticism regarding professionalisation.

The problem of effectiveness

Astoundingly, much more time seems to be devoted to ethical agonising over boundaries and their infringements than about the more fundamental question of whether clients are getting what they pay or sign up for. Those pushing for clarity about effectiveness are the funders, those accepting the mantle of scientist-practitioners, and consumers. Rather more disingenuously, most counsellors and counselling psychologists claim to be concerned to gather evidence for effectiveness while rarely intending to change their practice should research indicate any serious problems with what they are doing. Let's not pretend that establishing criteria for measuring effectiveness is easy or that agreement will soon be reached on research methodology found congenial to all parties. We cannot say confidently that CBT 'works' (leaving open the question 'with whom and for what?') if there are significant groups of clients who are so-called unmotivated, non-compliant and 'too severe' to have been included in research. We should be able to observe that, and understand how, neurolinguistic programming works in the case of its acclaimed phobia cure. That is, research should establish effectiveness in a majority of cases (unless claims are incorrect or fraudulent) and analysis should establish the mechanisms by which therapy works (unless it is to be considered magic or inexplicable).

Let us also accept that effectiveness is not a central concern for practitioners from all therapeutic orientations. Counsellors and their clients may well disagree on what constitutes an effective outcome and who is responsible for it. If the counsellor believes in long-term therapeutic work that may entail confusion and trigger pain before eventual resolution, and the client terminates counselling before that 'promise' is delivered, there is no agreement about the status of this sort of outcome. In many cases it is not clear whether the client actually gets what she came for, or all she would hope for, 'realistic disappointment' being regarded by some counsellors as natural and even a sign of maturity.[4] I suspect that much counselling has indeterminate outcomes: clients feel a bit better about some but not all aspects of their lives; it is unclear how much change results from the counselling itself; and clients and their counsellors may well have different views about it. Some statistical research using CORE attempts to answer some of these knotty problems as they occur in routine practice but it is limited to NHS settings and does not reflect 'on the ground' evidence that many clients and counsellors fill in CORE forms with a sense of contempt.[5]

Counselling is in some ways like religion, adherents of the latter usually insisting on its truth rather than its effectiveness, while at the same time being happy with any research suggesting that it effectively creates happiness and lengthens the life span.

Problems with socioeconomic, cultural and political perspectives

Counselling addresses the concerns of individuals (and in some cases couples, families and groups). It is certainly true that Freud, Reich, Fromm, Rogers and many others have proffered views and theories on damaging societal mechanisms. Additionally, some clinicians have written analyses of the putative psychopathology of political leaders and there have been some attempts at concretely operationalising therapists' critiques of social structures in, for example, feminist therapy, multicultural counselling, re-evaluation co-counselling, social therapy, sociodynamic counselling and critical psychology. However, the major focus of all counselling work is on individuals, their experience and functioning. In most training, some attention is given to relevant sociological inputs on power, race, gender, disability, sexual orientation, religion and culture, and class. Most trainees are aware of the notion that counselling addresses the so-called downstream effects of social ills, for example, problems caused by underclass phenomena, unemployment, poverty and debt, chronic low morale and so on.

Counsellors cannot do much directly about the upstream causes of problems for families and individuals, unless they also work in some form of political activism. There is a vocal critique among black and minority ethnic communities of mental health workers' lack of professional understanding of their needs. Some counsellors believe strongly, however, that they can help to empower all clients to survive and challenge circumstances of social difficulty, and some promote the 'social ripple effect' view whereby clients' changes positively affect others in their lives. A moot point is whether counselling adds to the sum total of emotional intelligence in society or subtracts from it by, for example, undermining friends' trust in their natural abilities to listen to each other empathically. It seems that a sizeable proportion of counsellors is either indifferent to social oppression or believe that clients can rise above oppressive circumstances. The radical element in the person-centred community considers itself revolutionary, yet I have read no account that demonstrates how the non-directive principles of the person-centred approach lead to practical anarchism. If anything, anarchists and other political radicals tend to be scornful of therapy as a bourgeois distraction from necessary social upheaval.[6]

Arguing from the point of view of often intractable conditions like OCD, Ronald Conway suggests that 'there is little doubt countless sufferers, removed from the pressures of our clock-watching hyperkinetic culture and dropped inescapably into a tropical jungle or even a layabout hippie commune, would show a notable improvement'. He further cites Fromm: 'there is no medication or hormonal correction which can cure the ills of a rancorous family life or a moribund civilization'.[7]

Worse still, a minority, perhaps, hold the view that clients 'create their own reality' or are responsible for everything in their lives. Clearly the emphasis in all counselling is on clients' own experiences, thoughts, feelings and actions. Psychodynamic, humanistic and cognitive behavioural approaches all work to get clients to look inside themselves and at their personal orbits with a view to making relevant emotional, cognitive and behavioural changes. Some forms of feminist counselling include educational and activist components designed to raise political awareness and eliminate women's guilt. But most counsellors have opted to work in this field because they are interested in inner lives rather than social and political realities. There are reasons to think that many counsellors are politically and economically naïve. Even if most counsellors have somewhat passively left-wing views, it is doubtful if much sustained thought goes into matters of capitalist oppression and the links between social structures and mental health problems. Little explicit thought is given in counselling training to the economics of private practice and class, or to the negative effects of free market capitalism or patriarchy on individuals. The idea that counselling is a mopping up of casualties and a propping up of an immiserating economic system is not entertained seriously. Lucy Costigan argues that most counselling is 'mainstream counselling' that altogether fails to take in learning from liberation psychology.[8]

If we attempt to look into the future a little, I think we might see further complications. The demographic profile of the UK has changed enormously since the original advent of the major counselling approaches up to about the mid-20th century. Multicultural heterogeneity, gender and sexual orientation factors, an ageing population and as yet poorly understood epidemiological changes in obesity, OCD, autism, ADHD and so on, make for challenges that hardly existed in the mid-20th century. Economic, environmental, scientific and technological developments will have to be faced.[9] As society becomes ever more complex it is possible that individuals will become more stressed in their attempts to cope with it. Our traditional religions, politics and therapies tend to splinter and fragment over time. Models of counselling are corrupted or weakened in ways similar to drugs – they no longer work as we become desensitised to them and they lose their novelty value. Just as the NHS (created in 1948) has to adjust to an ageing population, to new medical discoveries and new economic realities, so the counselling movement has to adjust, yet its conservative core resists this.

Philosophical problems

'Philosophical problems' is not the best way to express this but I am mainly referring to serious epistemological problems in our field. We face many problems of definition, as discussed above, of fuzzy language use, of conceptual vagueness, of scientific identity, judgements concerning research, making evaluations among competing knowledge claims (clinical philosophies) and ethical matters. As I have said elsewhere, it is not surprising that most counsellors, who are interested in interpersonal intimacy and communication, are not philosophers, and vice versa. But even in those areas where philosophy is employed, such as existentialist and (Stoical) cognitive behavioural therapy, 'philosophical counselling' and ethics, we do not usually expect or find any rigorous philosophising. At most we can find occasional references to phenomenological research and anti-positivism or anti-Cartesian views. But there is little sign of an appetite for philosophical analysis of assumptions about human nature underlying different models, of different aetiologies of mental health problems, or analysis of criteria for deciding on effectiveness claims. We rather blithely swallow the professional ethics served up by professional body documents but spend no time posing related questions of the social ethics of counselling.

There is a creeping exception to what I have said above. A small group of therapists (mainly psychotherapists but also a few counsellors) are enamoured of Lacanian theory and by the writings of Wittgenstein, Foucault, Derrida and other postmodernist and poststructuralist, mainly continental philosophers. I suspect the vast majority of both clients and counsellors have no interest in or understanding of such writers, most of whose publications are fairly impenetrable and possibly nonsensical. Certain texts asserting that 'the client is the expert' that claim to seek to deconstruct therapy and make it more accessible to ordinary people unfortunately read as anything but friendly towards ordinary people, being saturated in the linguistic contortions of Derrida and Foucault.[10]

Perhaps the largest and most persistent of philosophical problems here is embedded in the nature versus nurture debate, now more usually called the determinism versus free will debate. Counselling is overwhelmingly on the side of free will, or if not exactly free will, at least a large element of freedom of personal choice. If our behaviours (and thoughts and feelings) are predetermined by genes and neurology, no amount of talking therapy is likely to change our problems.[11] On the other hand, if we were truly free, we would not need counselling – we would simply decide what we wanted to change, and change it. Most of us cannot believe that we have no free will. It feels counter-intuitive to deny that we have considerable freedom. Yet we all know how difficult it is to change stubborn and damaging habits. But most counselling theory and practice is predicated upon there being significant room for manoeuvre, given the counsellor's special input of one kind and another. Many counsellors fiercely and romantically defend the notion of individual freedom, yet a great deal of evidence suggests that much depression, OCD, obesity and a range of other problems are probably driven by genetic factors. If in the course of time we were to discover specific biological causes for some of these problems, would we look back and apologise for the incorrect counselling we administered, the misspent money and client guilt induced at failure to change? I doubt it. And I suspect that many counsellors simply find it impossible to believe in such discoveries, so wedded are they to a 'philosophy' of freedom and an antagonism towards the supposedly power-abusing scientific ethos.

More widely than philosophy, I refer to all those academic disciplines that would inform a better understanding of human distress and its possible alleviation. Guidance is needed, I suspect, on what would be required for an optimal study of such matters and the social policies and clinical philosophies that would flow from it. Counselling is already partially informed by fragments of psychology and sociology (as social work training has been for decades) but the challenge is to consider how much it would improve by more rigorous inputs from, say, women's studies, evolutionary psychology, anthropology, genetics and neurology. A relevant critical discipline of mental health and human condition studies would also have room for subjectivity and personal politics, for transpersonal and religious considerations. The autonomous self (or ego) so important to psychology and counselling in the 20th century may benefit from a shift to the environmentally aware self (or 'eco') of the 21st century.

Problems of dissonant values, beliefs, and styles

While I might push for greater awareness in the categories outlined above, there is a major paradox here. The kind of mentality required to analyse and apply philosophical, sociological and political themes pertaining to counselling psychology is suggestive of intellectuality and academia. Various professional body and academic stakeholders would be quite happy to see such a development in line with requirements for practitioners to gain doctorates. But as some critics of the professionalisation of counselling and psychotherapy have pointed out, there is no evidence that intellectuality makes for better, more relationally oriented practitioners.[12] It would not work for warm and emotionally intelligent trainees to be forced to read texts and complete assignments on extra theoretical material that they dislike and can see no immediate use for. But it would also not work to try to turn theory-loving intellectuals into warm and emotionally intelligent counsellors. Is there a middle ground? Indeed, am I exaggerating the gulf between these positions?

We are not merely discussing some fuzzy expectation that counsellors be 'reflective practitioners' engaging in rituals of clinical rumination in supervision and continuing professional development. Many love adding layers of mystique and 'parallel process' to the counselling enterprise. Nor would it be helpful to add academic rituals that have no real bearing on practice. Rather, I have in mind practitioners who are relationally attuned, interpersonally flexible, yet also genuinely passionate about theorising. I suspect this combination is rare.

One huge area of challenge concerns the somewhat anti-medical and sometimes stridently anti-psychiatric stance of many humanistic and psychodynamic counsellors. It is not unusual to find strong remnants of the psychosomatic faith among psychodynamic practitioners.[13] For example, the idea that cancer is caused by suppressed anger lives on in spite of its dangers, its insult to cancer sufferers and its having little evidence to support it.[14] The tendency to see matters in psychological terms instead of more nuanced, bilateral terms means that some counsellors are at risk of ignoring, being ignorant about or dismissing serious medical conditions that present with psychological features like depression or anxiety and that may have exclusively physical remedies that are superior to counselling. (The reverse is also sometimes true, and ideally a comprehensive training might include some history of the failure and abuses of the medical and psychiatric worlds.) We cannot expect counsellors to have in-depth medical knowledge but we can ask for a responsible and open attitude towards medical problems. We could also inject some epistemological element into counsellor training requiring analysis of pro- and anti-biomedical attitudes and practices (just as some medical training has included an injection of critical thought from the humanities).

The problem of rhetorical trance

Let me explain what I mean by rhetorical trance. Counsellors and counselling psychologists are inevitably enmeshed in texts, mainly professional body documents, training literature and promotional texts. All those writing about counselling, including academics, students, professional body staff and service personnel, become habituated to a certain set of assumptions and styles. Read any official document or standard textbook to see what I mean. A large part of such texts comprises a kind of automatic, public relations style of writing that uncritically reinforces an image of counselling as meaningful, coherent and good. In other words, writers learn to 'stay on message', to 'sing from the same hymn sheet', to use a standardised professional language. Its repetition across many texts and many years has a mesmerising effect; a momentum of orthodoxy carries it along. Examples include, say, 'the therapeutic relationship is the key factor in successful counselling' and 'supervision is essential for supporting good practice'.

The overriding effect of such belief-reinforcing language use is to silence natural curiosity and numb our critical faculties. We can unwittingly become ciphers, transmitting institutional scripts. If a potential client asks what counselling is, we can easily go into promotional institution-speak. Once internalised, we may barely notice that we have become automatic mouthpieces. We can believe unquestioningly what we once would have paused to think about. The greatest danger is that we may inadvertently inflict this way of talking on clients, leading to a mesmerised facsimile of improvement instead of genuine improvement. The kind of 'narrative smoothing' that counsellors can get into when reflecting in case studies on their work with clients can also flow in the other direction. Clients can pick up therapy-speak – 'I'm nurturing my inner child', 'I'm changing my script'. We are all susceptible to rhetorical trance, from family scripts to political whitewash and religious behaviours. Reality is, I think, characterised much more by patches of doubt, roughness, friction, chaos and hiccups than by the cliché, the glossy and predictable.

The problem of premature celebration of success

The focus of enquiry underpinning counselling and all other mental health disciplines is psychological suffering. Why do human beings universally suffer from a surfeit of aggression, deceit, anomie and (for want of a better term) neurosis? Why is depression now found at such epidemic proportions? Freud and his circle at the end of the 19th century and many around the middle of the 20th century considered themselves to have discovered effective means to address such problems even if the reasons for them were more elusive. This aetiology problem is closely bound up with the problems of effectiveness and sprawling pluralism. Proponents of the psychological therapies have been borne by enthusiasm to ignore or overrule nagging doubts about these matters. Consolidation of therapeutic enterprises has come to matter much more than sustainedly addressing the roots and reinforcers of suffering and distress. Assertive defence of one's chosen therapeutic approach has pushed these more fundamental questions to the sidelines. We have several professional bodies representing the interests of counselling and psychotherapy (the touted solutions), we have voluntary organisations like Mind speaking for sufferers (or survivors or victims) and we have the disciplines of psychiatry, neurology and psychology researching possible causes of varieties of distress as well as defending their professions. But we do not have much macro-cooperative convergence.

The talking therapies and their representatives are mired in controversies and conflicts and entrenched in fixed belief systems. Public relations are probably more important to them than serious enquiry and genuine rapprochement. What they cannot acknowledge is the tentative nature of their theories and practices.

When certain therapeutic approaches and practices lose support and become part of the history of counselling and psychotherapy, we do not mark their demise or learn from them. Arguably they are an embarrassment. It may seem only natural that we fully support and celebrate current theory and practice rather than declaring it provisional, the half-hearted sound of which will not inspire confidence. Modesty, humility, tentativeness and agnosticism are not good selling points. We do not honestly say to potential clients or funders 'We don't know with any certainty what the causes of psychological distress are, and we are divided in our views and practices, but we do the best we can with the hypotheses and techniques we have faith in'. I suggest this is the honest position but obviously it is not a common or effective marketing strategy. But the ethical objection to following an enthusiasm and marketing route while playing down or concealing the true level of our ignorance is obvious.

The motivation of the client to end or ameliorate her distress or confusion conspires with the good intentions, need for positive self-image, and economic needs of the practitioner. Who wants to tell people in distress 'Come back in 50 years when we may have made significant inroads on understanding and curing your obsessive compulsive problems'? Or 'Well, the chances are 50–50 whether we can help you significantly given the obduracy of your condition'? Perhaps we are right to hold out hope and even to charge money for often giving comfort and illusions of progress, or hopeful 'strategies for managing your condition' rather than effective cures. But there is an alternative to fudging these matters. Much more attention could be given to agreeing a probabilistic aetiological account (integrating evolutionary, genetic, neurological, experiential and social factors), along with efforts to rationalise mental health professions and to collapse the best of the hundreds of therapeutic models into one. We could move in that direction rather than continuing to peddle the myth that the aetiology problem has been solved and the rainbow of psychological therapies are all equally effective.

And so ...

We face some daunting questions. If counselling is really so riddled with the problems outlined in this book, and if many of the critiques come from within the counselling profession itself, what credibility can it retain? If, as we are told, about 80 per cent of clients are satisfied with their experience of counselling, how can we square this with these criticisms? If counselling is completely enmeshed in capitalism or capitalist realism, a milieu which causes distress and distorts human relationships that include counselling, what, if anything, can be done about this? These questions are not at all as daunting as they might appear when we shift our attention from critique of the counselling profession to critique of the counselling phenomenon. If we look at counselling as a reciprocal supply-and-demand, client–counsellor, unitary phenomenon (like the two-backed beast of copulation that transcends the two lovers), instead of practitioners as artful, wicked peddlers of psychological trickery and fakery and clients as the gullible exploited, we get quite a different picture. Counselling then becomes more like a sociocultural phenomenon to be studied as objectively as possible, like religion, democracy, education or marriage. Many people like it, approve of it, proclaim its huge benefits, advance arguments to support it, and can see no alternative to it or future without it; others mock or despair of it, deconstruct it and declare it invalid and dishonest. Counselling, like other social institutions, may or may not be built on positive illusions. If it is, this may or may not matter. Below I suggest six ways of categorising responses to critiques:

Vigorously refute all critiques

Counselling can fairly be portrayed as invariably well-intentioned, usually comforting and more often than not effective. There are arguments that it has strong virtuous effects on society and provides help available nowhere else.[15] It is possible that all charges and criticisms advanced against counselling have flaws, and can and should be refuted. Did Freud lie or did he not? Are concepts of the unconscious, transference, the actualising tendency and non-directivity among others merely articles of faith, or not? Can the hundreds of differently named therapeutic approaches be credible? Is most counselling practice in fact a good-hearted, moderately helpful, eclectic, female-dominated phenomenon surrounded by unnecessary, parasitical theoretical and professional smoke and mirrors? Is related research telling us much of any real use at all? Will regulation make a fraction of positive difference to actual practice?

It is possible that most critiques are based on malignant motives, hearsay, and inaccurate portrayals of theory, practice and profession. All anecdotal evidence might be banished, along with opinion, stereotypes and misinformation. Rigorous philosophical analysis could be brought to bear on all contentious topics. Empirical evidence could be marshalled against many criticisms. Indeed, it should be expected that such refutation would be widespread and vigorous. I imagine that we find far less of it than we might expect because committed practitioners, theorists and researchers feel they have better and more urgent things to do with their time but also because critique is not valued, is seen as irritating rather than valid, does not rank high on the business agendas of the professional bodies, and frankly has little serious impact on the business of making a living as a counsellor. To some extent all such criticism is mainly a public relations problem for those whose job it is within professional bodies to deal with it if necessary. It would only be when it came to bite acutely in terms of falling memberships, a serious decline in applications for training courses and for counselling itself that serious refutation and action would come to the fore.

Critiques of a philosophical nature such as those put forward by Wittgenstein, Popper, Gellner, Grunbaum, Erwin and others do not get the responses they may warrant because probably few within the world of the talking therapies have the necessary philosophical skill and knowledge to construct duly rigorous responses. Likewise with sociological and political arguments. The average working counsellor and also the public relations representative probably cannot meet intellectual specialists at their own level, even should they muster sufficient interest to try to do so. It seems likely too that a disconnect exists between such intellectual analysis and practical counselling on the ground. The practitioner is sincerely immersed in each client's arduous iterative endeavours, with therapeutic theory and research at some distance and critique even further away. For the counsellor who has invested heavily in terms of hope, faith, self-respect, money and livelihood, the prospect of entertaining serious critique might well only cause an unwelcome cognitive dissonance between these investments and her or his self-image as an honest worker and intelligent person.

Ignore critiques, do nothing, let time decide

Perhaps it is part of human nature to ignore that which we do not like. Particularly when critics are perceived as motivated by ignoble negative motives (for example, their own undeclared envy, projection, hatred, unresolved early conflicts) or wilful misrepresentation of counselling, counsellors and counselling psychologists, their critiques will be ignored. Or it is not uncommon now to read texts on different theoretical approaches that include a token chapter on critiques that makes it appear that the writer is generously considering them but in reality is irritated by them and gives merely a bland analysis. It was found during the course of sincere and passionate objections to statutory regulation, for example, that the most effective way of steamrollering on with the professionalising agenda was for the pro-regulation lobby to ignore objections, a tactic sometimes referred to as *Totschweigen,* or a silencing of objections by 'ignoring them to death'.[16] A less cynical version of ignoring critiques is the pragmatic stance of continuing business as usual and only facing objections as serious when or if they attain critical mass that cannot be ignored. Apart from cognitive dissonance we can suffer from an understandable inertia in relation to calls for change.

Actually the uncritically pro-counselling may instinctively realise that they do not have to do anything but wait their critics out, since the mass of pro-counselling stakeholders now vastly outweighs the critics. As Rob Weatherill puts it:

> Modern counselling and therapy [have] hardened up into a growth industry that has expanded beyond all expectations and projections. Therapy has no natural predators. It has its critics, but they are no match for the whole sentimental ideology that devours all values, all difference, as it joins hands and sends hugs across every former frontier, every former domain of otherness.[17]

Again, we should be wary of critics like Weatherill whose Lacanian-inspired, intellectually sophisticated 'radical psychoanalysis' appears to raise them above and distinguish them utterly from others in the 'therapy culture' they despise. The line taken here – 'counselling and psychotherapy are deeply flawed but we are different, deeper' – assumes that critiques of talking therapies somehow exclude them or fail to discern their superiority. Such deconstructivist, often Lacanian writers do not ignore those who critique them, indeed they probably relish the chance to engage in battle, yet effectively they do ignore or fail to understand the ways in which their identity is enmeshed with the other talking therapists they despise.

It may broadly be human nature to ignore what is unpleasant to us but talking therapy claims to confront and work through psychological unpleasantness. It is my suggestion that there are several elephants in the counselling psychology room, as identified in this book, that can no longer be ignored if counselling psychology wishes to retain credibility. We might stretch a point about some unavoidable 'inattentional blindness' on the part of busy professionals: perhaps the faithful have been too busy to see the wood for the trees. But surely this position of denial cannot persist for much longer.

Initiate serious reforms where necessary

What is a reform and when is it serious? Practitioners in principle constantly evaluate their work and improve it where necessary in supervision, continuing professional development and research. Training organisations and professional bodies also constantly review and update their practices in the light of feedback from trainees and members. One infamous example is comedian Bernard Manning's prank in 1996 of gaining membership of BACP (then

BAC), as a counsellor specialising in racial and sexual issues. Well known for his racist and sexist humour, Manning had mischievously exposed a looseness in membership procedures, which after initial embarrassment were subsequently tightened up. Criteria for accreditation have been changed from time to time. Complaints procedures now make it possible for clients who believe themselves to have been abused by unethical counsellors to receive a fair hearing and for practitioners to face sanctions where necessary.

The kinds of reforms that may be impossible, impractical or simply unpalatable might include the following: seeking to ban the promotion of all newly minted therapeutic approaches until they have some empirical evidence to support them; initiating a survey of the overlaps and duplications in theory and practice of the many psy-professions and radically reorganising them; estimating and limiting the number of training places needed so as to prevent people spending money on training that may well lead nowhere; devising means of evaluating the effectiveness of individual counsellors. On this last point, one can envisage a consumer-led website, along the lines of Tripadvisor or American students' ratings of college lecturers, evaluating individual counsellors based on client experiences; this of course might not be free of bias or potential litigation but the system of aggregate scores could give a reasonable picture of overall client satisfaction or of any persistent problems.

Interestingly, the reform that many would have wished for – the statutory regulation of counselling and psychotherapy via the HCPC – failed in 2011. While clinical and counselling psychologists came under HCPC's auspices, counsellors and psychotherapists remained unregulated. What some saw as a necessary and inevitable reform, others regarded as anathema, which demonstrates that often there is no consensus on such matters and that reform can go in different directions, towards perceived tightening or loosening, towards control or freedom. As I write it seems probable that BACP will now go for a form of regulation with the CHRE/PSA. Alternatively, reform in the direction of greater peer accountability as advocated by the Independent Practitioners Network (IPN), remains an open possibility.

Beyond reform, one can of course speak of a revolution. Indeed Rogers and those who follow him have often referred to the PCA (unconvincingly to my mind) as a quiet or gentle revolution in society and in the professions. But it is possible to argue for a true revolution of values among therapists that would probably upset all current assumptions and vested interests, a revolution towards the meta-professional, post-capitalist and non-egoic.[18] However, since the vast majority of us are neither in receipt of private incomes nor ascetically inclined, the chances of any such revolution coming about are extremely remote.

Call for acceptance of the imperfect

It may be admitted that counselling, like other social phenomena, represents an imperfect set of practices designed to address mental health problems, problems in living, confusion, and aspirations towards better individual psychological functioning. If it is conceded that human beings and all their projects are fallible, we should not expect counselling to be flawless. We might reasonably argue that counsellors simply do their best, that training, theory and professional developments are no more than the best we have been able to come up with so far and that improvements are inevitable but take time. Indeed, if we agree with Arnold Lazarus (see Chapter 3, this volume, p. 66) that therapy is still in the dark ages of its development, we might see it as a set of hypotheses or at best probabilistic theories and provisional techniques for ameliorating distress. We might even accept counselling psychology as an unavoidable ongoing tension with competing theories and practices.

Meanwhile, the task of professional or regulatory bodies, or indeed of consumers, is to help establish minimal standards and expectations. We might apply some of the wisdom of the therapeutic models here and speak of 'good enough' counselling; of the importance of the reality of disappointment in all human affairs; of REBT's advocacy of anti-intolerance, anti-damning or anti-low frustration tolerance; of being compassion-focused.

Agree with critiques and abandon counselling

This is the most radical and least likely position to be adopted, at least for anyone with an established stake in counselling. But if one is struck by the sheer volume of criticism, by its logic, validity and persuasiveness, then it is possible that one might abandon any vested interest in counselling, in the same way a Christian, say, *might* weigh up atheist arguments and associated scholarship and then abandon Christian faith. (This does in fact happen to a significant number of priests exposed to analytical theologies and implicitly faith-critiquing life events.) This might apply to someone considering having counselling or training in counselling, or even an experienced practitioner. Possibly, one could opt to abandon counselling but embrace an evidence-based clinical psychology, say, or abandon belief in person-centred counselling and take up CBT. Any permutation of choices is possible. But the radical position, such as that espoused by Jeffrey Masson, is to denounce and abandon all talking therapies and instead embrace peer support or mutual aid projects. Actually a more radical position still would be to accept the possibility that genuine 'cures' for distress are as rare as distress is ubiquitous. 'You're on earth, there's no cure for that', as Samuel Beckett said.[19] But this is also to abandon hope and perhaps compassion.

Orlans and van Scoyoc, on reviewing their examination of counselling psychology, declare that 'We have become much more aware of some of the madness in our personal debates, as well as the broader madness in discussions, for example, of psychopathology'.[20] Some decide, no doubt because few economic alternatives present themselves, to remain with the madness of this profession. Another possibility is that anyone who had been considering counselling training and has the flexibility to do so might instead turn to some form of radical political or spiritual activism. Depending on how deeply one feels about the human condition, how well informed one decides to become and how committed to action, it is entirely conceivable that some might opt for pathways to achieving a better society with less distress than opting for counselling training.

Question everything and transcend

This may be an unlikely contender and one that perhaps I should omit. However, in all seriousness, I suspect that the problems facing counselling psychology are not ultimately different from those facing religion, philosophy, politics, and everything else that attempts to address the painful riddles of the human condition. The Buddha considered all life as suffering, and this formed the basis of his own transcendence. Everything seems to have some truth in it, and everything offers a buzz for a while before fading, inviting critique and moving in cycles of reinvention until finally burning out. Each of us has her or his favourite remedial recipe that may sustain us briefly or long term. Counselling and psychotherapy in some forms hint at and aspire to a deep uncovering and overturning of individual distress and suffering. Some approaches, particularly the transpersonal, suggest they may hold the keys to transcendence of the human condition. It looks as if a few outstanding spiritual figures have themselves done just this. What if, instead of hoping for deliverance (if it exists) from counselling or therapy, or from any other institution or thought system, we refused the addictive power of such hope? What if counselling, much as it has offered hopes and means, is itself severely limited by all the institutional folly involved in it?

It may be that truly great religious, political and psycho-therapeutic figures are as scarce as geniuses but equally that all those who follow them (that is, most of us) paradoxically move further from deliverance by the act of following. Rather than following or despairing, might there be some way of trusting our own resources? Most of us are poor epistemologists, that is to say we do not know how to evaluate knowledge claims and we typically opt impulsively for belief in whatever feels right, turns us on, agitates some part of our personality. But a few have suggested that it is not only the case that we flounder among competing thought systems, it is that *thought itself is a system* and this system misleads us. Wittgenstein has to some extent pointed us in this direction, but people like Jiddu Krishnamurti and David Bohm have argued that there is something fundamentally redundant, misleading and destructive about thought that constantly searches for solutions to deep human problems.[21] Only by attaining 'freedom from the known', in this view, do we have any hope of transcending our perennial, collective negative condition. This is not where counselling looks for 'truth', since counselling thrives on stimulating ideas and novel techniques, not on surrendering our preciously cultivated minds. There are fragile signs of the mindfulness movement in counselling approaching transcendence but in all likelihood this will become another circus of reified practices and theories.

It is likely too that in the myriad counselling sessions that take place, sometimes a 'meeting of souls' may occur. What I mean here is that within, perhaps because of, the genuine and messy struggle of one fallible human being trying to reach, understand and help another, occasionally the usual social and professional roles will melt, the tricks of the trade, the mutual defences will give way to the underlying reality. This may be spoken of as a transpersonal moment, an I–Thou meeting, or as heightened inter-authenticity.[22]

Can millions of people be wrong?

We are familiar with the argument that the majority cannot make the wrong judgement and we sometimes speak of the wisdom of crowds. In the world of counselling, historically millions of ordinary people used to condemn the talking therapies as self-indulgent nonsense but now it seems there is quite widespread acceptance. Now we do not have millions of practitioners to speak of but clearly the thousands of therapists in the UK (and probably millions worldwide) believe their work is necessary, effective and ethical. Perhaps some of it isn't necessary, or effective or ethical, but most of it probably is: can we say this? Most counsellors are decent, warm, caring people who mostly bring much more comfort and help to their clients than anything negative. Obviously I know many counsellors and I do not consider the vast majority of them to be unprofessional, devious mavericks. Indeed I am struck by how sincere, energetic and dedicated most are, and I am forced to ask myself (as any critic is) if the critiques of counselling and counselling psychology are really fair. After all, the sum of critiques does make it appear that the edifice of the psychological therapies is thoroughly riddled with problems and therefore presumably its practitioners are complicit. But things are not this black and white.

Consider the person who has suffered a lifetime of difficult relationships and who finally sees a counsellor to talk about her memories of sexual abuse in childhood. She allows herself to trust the counsellor and the counsellor sensitively helps her through the recall of painful memories and accompanying cathartic release. The counsellor does her best, endures through doubts about her competency, feels drained at the end of some particularly harrowing sessions. The client moves forward, descends into the depths of pain, retreats, has spells of withdrawal and mistrust. But after some months she feels ready to end the counselling, she feels quite a bit better, yet her life is still far from perfect. The counselling has made a real difference. Admittedly, some practitioners have shown too much prurient interest in such cases, and some have unskilfully pushed for recall and catharsis beyond the clients' readiness; some minority have even implanted false suggestions. If we can put aside gratuitous and incorrect theory and occasional malpractice, we must still reckon that the benefits of such counselling overall may outweigh doubts about it. Compassionate pragmatism may in some cases win out against both pro-counselling dogma and anti-counselling criticism.

I listen to a supervisee reflecting on her therapeutic work with children, most of whom have had very damaging, disrupted early lives and who are enmeshed in the anxieties and powers of various statutory agency professionals. My supervisee has nothing pretentious about her, she brandishes no flag for the therapeutic faith, she is not ambitious, not very highly paid. She is extremely sensitive, warm, intelligent, fluidly intuitive, creative and ethical in her work. She does not insert gratuitous theory into her practice and her use of skills and techniques is tempered by simple humanity and concern. I am quite sure her 'clients' benefit greatly from her work. How could we criticise her? Perhaps it is in her profound humanity and near-indifference to personal advancement that we can see reflected some of the faults of her profession and society. Senior colleagues work in the same mini-hierarchy as her, the psychiatrist, clinical psychologists and psychotherapists earning significantly more for no good reason. She is subjected to constant bureaucracy and agency reviews which limit the time she can spend with children. The good that she does is not measured and would be very difficult to measure, yet it has both immediate and probably long-term positive effects. Why does the counselling profession make such a fuss about so many things yet ignore the value of individuals like this? Could we not proactively find and value people like her instead of churning out thousands of less gifted counsellors?

Personally, I can see a worthwhile role for counsellors in the NHS or other health or voluntary organisation settings offering short-term support and intervention at critical times in the manner of Cummings' 'intermittent psychotherapy across the life cycle'.[23] Such a practice acknowledges that many of us will run into personal difficulties in the same way we run into medical crises, and counsellors and doctors can practise in similar and complementary ways, offering timely help, with local knowledge of the communities in which they live. Current, politically faddish and bureaucratically poisoned IAPT schemes providing CBT, psychological wellbeing and associated services in the UK unfortunately lack the humanity necessary to initiate and support such work.

Inevitably we compare counsellors with religious believers, of whom there are billions. Religion is almost always dedicated to a morality of love, care and truth. Diverse religions share the same altruistic visions and aims. Religious liberals and counsellors alike might say that they only wish to make the world a better place. However, such is historical attachment to (male) founders, hierarchies, scriptures, frameworks of good and evil, and rituals, that religion as we know all too well is also hugely divisive or, to use the Jungian metaphor, religion has its terrible shadow side. And ultimately most religions are predicated on belief in the existence of God, a belief that for millions is unshakeable. But to atheists God is a human construct with spent validity. The world of therapy is likewise divisive, and organised around male founders, hierarchies (the psy-professions, professional body oversight, academic tiers), scriptures (theoretical canon), frameworks of good and evil (actualising tendency, readiness for change versus defence mechanisms, acting out, etc.) and rituals (practice constraints, supervision, annual conferences). Therapy has no God as such but it has its unconscious, its overriding therapeutic optimism, and belief in individual autonomy.

Human nature being what it is, none of us has perfect powers of reasoning, nor complete commitment to objectivity, nor freedom from deep-seated emotional and conceptual attachments. All of us use flawed heuristic means of making everyday and career decisions and all are pragmatic, even when we couch our rationales in overarching grandiose belief schemes. It is a mystery to me why people believe in God, the unconscious or the actualising tendency – people I often know and like – but they do. And of course it is a mystery to others how I can be an atheist and a critic of counselling. Somehow, for the most part, we all get along with each other reasonably well, most of the time. We rarely find ourselves as counsellors in a position where our beliefs are directly challenged and as 'nice people' (both genuinely so and often as 'people pleasers' in a muzzled, politically correct culture) we are inclined not to make religious wars out of clinical or theoretical disagreements. Covertly some will think me cynical, or perhaps humorously accuse me of it, or in a book review seek to destroy me and my critiques. Some will have hypotheses about my presumably authoritarian father or disappointing mother and so on. (Masson received many such analyses from distant despisers.) And I have my covert suspicions about the doggedly faithful.

We could claim that little or any of this actually matters. Many individuals are distressed and eager to try anything, and believe in anything that makes them feel better. One is turned on by Islam but not Buddhism, another by transactional analysis but not NLP, and so on. We can choose between therapy and religion or between religions or therapies, and we can also mix some aspects of religion with therapy, as well as bits of politics and philosophy. 'Whatever gets you through the night', as they say. A huge problem for the dogmatic critic is the risk of falling into a fundamentalist rationality: I think that reason is everything and I believe I hold the reins of rationality. Irrational or suprarational realities may exist, or I may be 'right' in logical terms, but unsympathetic in interpersonal terms. In other words, there is no guarantee that even the most purely motivated critiquing will lead to better results than the phenomena it purports to critique.

Conclusion

I have often found that critiquing counselling can earn me the label of 'cynic', which I reject. Very commonly the most pro-counselling readers appear to misinterpret radical criticism as wholesale rejection of counselling. Since I may sometimes inadvertently give this impression, I wish here to state as clearly as possible my current position.

Much about counselling is flawed. The vast noise that surrounds it detracts from what is at the heart of it. A great deal of its theory fails to stand up to much scrutiny. Some of what it strives to do would be made redundant by better social policies and the causes of many of our stubborn psychological problems may yet be laid bare by future science. None of the problems facing counselling should be surprising in the human world of mixed motives, flawed epistemologies, egoic needs and machinations, and capitalist pressures. Counselling is no more free of such faults than any other enterprise. But this does not amount to an accusation that counselling is total nonsense, completely unhelpful or frequently harmful. At its heart counselling is a compassionate, I–Thou attempt at understanding and responding to painful elements of the human condition. Such attempts can also be made outside of 'counselling' under other names and none. If as seems extremely likely we remain unwilling to revolutionise our mental health professions, counselling may remain a low-ranking member of those professions (which may not matter). Many counsellors will opt for work in the voluntary and private practice sectors, even where this is unremunerated or poorly paid, in order to offer the heart of counselling. Some tricks of the trade derived from different models are sometimes useful in practice. But we should not fool ourselves that the large and pretentious infrastructure of counselling amounts to much, even when we may be forced to 'play the game' by the pressures of making a living.

Endnotes

1. Dryden, W. (Ed.). (2007). *Dryden's Handbook of Individual Therapy* (5th ed.). London: Sage.

2. House, R. (2003). *Therapy beyond Modernity: Deconstructing and transcending profession-centred therapy.* London: Karnac.

3. Freud, S. (1959). *The Question of Lay Analysis* (J. Strachey, Trans.). New York: Norton.

4. Craib, I. (1994). *The Importance of Disappointment.* London: Routledge.

5. Barkham, M., Stiles, W. B., Connell, J., & Mellor-Clark, J. (2012). Psychological treatment outcomes in routine NHS services: What do we mean by treatment effectiveness? *Psychology and Psychotherapy, 85*(1), 1–16.

6. See Zerzan, J. (2002). *Running on Emptiness: The pathology of civilization.* Los Angeles: Feral House; The Invisible Committee. (2009). *The Coming Insurrection.* Los Angeles: Semiotext(e). Less radical but similarly challenging is Cloud, D. L. (1998). *Control and Consolation in American Culture and Politics: Rhetoric of therapy.* Thousand Oaks, CA: Sage.

7. See Conway, R. (1992). *The Rage for Utopia.* St Leonards, NSW: Allen & Unwin, pp. 11–12. The Fromm quote (original untraceable) is also in Conway, p. 13.

8. Costigan, L. (2004). *Social Awareness in Counselling.* Lincoln, NE: iUniverse. See also Balmforth, J. (2009). 'The weight of class': Clients' experiences of how perceived differences in social class between counsellor and client affect the therapeutic relationship. *British Journal of Guidance and Counselling, 37*(3), 375–386.

9. Coyle, K. J., & Van Susteren, L. (2012). *The Psychological Effects of Global Warming on the United States.* Reston, VA: National Wildlife Federation is one of an emerging number of surveys predicting large-scale fallout from climate change.

10. Parker, I. (Ed.). (1999). *Deconstructing Psychotherapy.* London: Sage.

11. See for example Flint, J., Greenspan, R. J., & Kendler, K. S. (2010). *How Genes Influence Behaviour.* Oxford: Oxford University Press.

12. Mowbray, R. (1999). Professionalisation of therapy by registration is unnecessary, ill advised and damaging. In C. Feltham (Ed.), *Controversies in Psychotherapy and Counselling.* London: Sage, pp. 206–216.

13. On psychoanalytic theories regarding cancer causation and cure, see Leader, D. & Corfield, D. (2007). *Why Do People Get Ill?* London: Hamish Hamilton, pp. 228–246.

14. Lilienfeld, S. O., Lynn, S. J., & Beyerstein, B. L. (2010). *50 Great Myths of Popular Psychology.* Malden, MA: Wiley, pp. 129–134.

15. Wright, K. (2011). *The Rise of the Therapeutic Society: Psychological knowledge and the contradictions of cultural change.* Washington, DC: New Academia.

16. See Postle, D. (2007). *Regulating the Psychological Therapies: From taxonomy to taxidermy.* Ross-on-Wye: PCCS Books.

17. Weatherill, R. (2004). *Our Last Great Illusion: A radical psychoanalytical critique of therapy culture.* Exeter: Imprint Academic.

18. Feltham, C. (2009). Revolutionary claims and visions in psychotherapy: An anthropathological perspective. *Journal of Contemporary Psychotherapy, 39*(1), 41–54.

19. Beckett, S. (2009). *Endgame.* London: Faber and Faber.

20. Orlans, V., & van Scoyoc, S. (2009). *A Short Introduction to Counselling Psychology.* London: Sage, p. 107.

21. Bohm, D. (1994). *Thought as a System.* London: Routledge.

22. Friedman, M. (1992). *Dialogue and the Human Image: Beyond humanistic psychology.* Newbury Park, CA: Sage.

23. Cummings, N., & Sayama, M. (1995). *Focused Psychotherapy: A casebook of brief, intermittent psychotherapy throughout the life cycle.* New York: Brunner/Mazel.

INDEX

A

acceptance 62
  of the imperfect 182
accreditation 67, 77, 143–4
  chartering 143–4
actualising tendency 57–8, 59, 162
Adler, A. 29
Aeschylus 6
Aesculapius 5
Against Therapy 157
agape 60
Albee, G.W. 10, 22
Aldridge, S. 75, 160
Andersen, Hans Christian 9
anthropathology 3
anti-authoritarianism 64
antidepressant medication 77
anti-psychiatric Laingians 64
anti-psychiatry 27, 33
Aristotle 6
Assagioli, R. 25, 51
  Assagioli's superconscious, 51
assessment 68, 96–8
  diagnosis 64
  problems of 97
astrology 150
attachment theory 53–5
authenticity 94
  lack of 51

B

BACP (*see* British Association for Counselling
    and Psychotherapy)
'bad faith' 51
Balmforth, J. 190

Barkham, M. 108, 132, 190
Barley, D.E. 119
Bates, Y. 106
Beck, A. 54, 74
Beck, U. 134
Beckett, S. 183, 191
behaviourism 19
belief reinforcement 174–5
Berg, I. Kim 42
Berger, B. 106
Berne, E. 25, 36
Berry, M. 54, 74, 159
Bettelheim, B. 27
Binet, A. 6
biological
    causes of psychological problems 172
    psychiatry 19
Blanton, B. 61, 75, 113, 114, 133, 165
Bohm, D. 184, 191
Borch-Jacobsen, M. 28, 29, 44, 50, 74
Bordin, E. 95, 106
boundaries 56, 95–6, 166
    professional 68
Bowlby, J. 43, 53
Brazier, C. 44
Brazier, D. 44
Breuer, J. 29
brief and time-limited models 104
    dynamic psychotherapy 9
    solution-focused therapy 47
British Association for Counselling and
    Psychotherapy (BACP) 4, 7, 9, 53,
    78, 120, 126, 136, 149, 152, 180,
    181
    accreditation 78, 81, 138, 141, 143

female predominance in 152
British Psychological Society (BPS) 6, 7,
      53, 69, 78, 120, 136
    forming a Counselling Psychology
      Section 137
    suggested average hourly fee 105
    training requirements 144
Broad, W. 133
Buber, M. 63
Buchanan, I. 23
Buddha 9
Burns, J. 21
Buss, D.M. 21
Butz, M.R. 106

C
Callan, S. 134
capitalism 11, 22, 43, 169, 177
    origins of human distress in 3
Carr, A. 119, 133, 160
Carroll, R.T. 22
case
    discussion 81
    material 116
    studies 81, 143
Castaneda, C. 32
CBT (*see* cognitive behavioural therapy)
Centre for Social Justice (CSJ) 131
Chamberlain, L.L. 106
child protection 88
children 134
    conditions for flourishing 64
CHRE (*see* Council for Healthcare
    Regulatory Excellence)
Christianity 12
CIA 31
Clare, A. 23
Clarkson, P. 27, 95, 106
client/s
    ex-, dissatisfied 125
    experiences 160
        negative accounts of 93
        positive 185–9

reports 113
role of 82
working class 153
client-centred counselling 55 (*see also*
        person-centred approach)
    supervision 75
clinical psychologists 97, 123
clinical psychology 6, 8, 16, 139
    a protected title 149
    and research 108, 118
    status of 136
    training in the USA 139
clinical supervision 122
Cloud, D.L. 190
co-counselling 77, 168
cognitive analytic therapy 67
cognitive behavioural therapy (CBT) 7,
      10, 39, 47, 54, 64, 85, 92,
      117, 134
    computer-based packages 104
    is effective for depression 64
    evidence-based dominance (so-called)
      74
    media reporting 85
    negative outcome evidence 131
    problems with 74
    researchable 119
    supervisors 102
    Swedish Government's experience 131
Cohen, D. 31, 32, 44
collective unconscious 51
common factors 119, 120
compassion-focused therapy 4
complaints
    gender bias 153
    procedures 68, 93, 125, 181
complementary and alternative medicine
    150
computer-based CBT packages 104
conditions of worth 58, 72, 75
confidentiality 15, 83, 95, 125, 165
    breaches of 146–7
    compromised 104

gossip instinct and 83
   problems with 146
congruence 59, 60–1, 62
consciousness
   expansion of 2–3
   stream of 6
Constructing the Self, Constructing America
      13, 23
continuing professional development (CPD)
      147–8
contracting and boundaries 95–6
Conway, R. 169, 190
Cooper, H. 44
Cooper, I.S. 22
Cooper, M. 108, 109, 132
Copernicus, N. 28
CORE 87, 167
core conditions 56, 58–62, 73, 95
   necessary and sufficient 59
   non-judgemental warmth 62
core of counselling 76
Corfield, D. 191
Corrie, S. 111, 133
Costigan, L. 170, 190
Council for Healthcare Regulatory Excellence
      (CHRE, now PSA) 149, 166, 181
counselling (*see also* psychotherapy)
   academically lightweight, seen as 151,
      154, 156
   abandon 183
   apps for smart phones 104
   aptitude for 141
   benefits 189–90
   brief 92–4
   for commercial companies 89 (*see also*
      employee assistance programmmes)
   common factors 12, 119, 120
   confidential nature of 125 (*see also*
      confidentiality)
   confusion of terms 9, 16
   context 87–92
   and counselling psychology 136–8
   countercultural aspect of 121

couple 103
core of 76
credibility 177
   is a critique, itself 18
   as cure? 84–6
   definitions of 7, 161, 170
      problems of 161–3, 170
   as a faith 12
   female dominated 140, 152–3
   group 103
   industry 15
   middle-class bias in 152, 153
   models of 102–4, 170
   non-professional, seen as 121, 136
   one-to-one 102
   online 104
   pastoral 9
   practice, problems with 76ff
      transference, dependency,
         complications 99–101
   and philosophy 170–2
   as a profession, problems of 135ff
   professional organisations
      historical paternalism in 136
      problems of 166
   private practice 85, 90, 92, 94, 99,
      113, 155, 170
   process 101–2, 111
   and psychotherapy
      as memes 42
      overlap between 24–5
   research, problems of 107ff
   and scientology 150
   seeking scientific status for 121
   skills 21, 55, 152
      practising 78–82
   statutory regulation, has avoided 149
   theory, problems of 46ff
      cleaning up 70–4
      dogma, facts, dissensus, lacunae
         68–70
   time-limited 88, 92–4
   as unnatural 82–4

variations in delivery 102–4
as a vocation 139, 148
in work settings 87
counselling psychology/ists 38, 110, 136–
    8
    doctoral programme in 81
    the 'Egan approach' 137
    key figures in 25ff
        characteristics of 26–8
    problems with definition of 161ff
    as a profession 135ff
        superior to counselling 151, 154
    regulation of 136
    role as scientist-practitioner 121
counsellor/s
    attitudes to research 121–3
    characteristics/identity of 152–5
    competency 82
    congruence 58, 59, 60–1
    faith of 70, 102, 126, 139, 142
    gender 152, 153
    politically and economically naïve 169
    'reflective practitioners' 173
    personal therapy 53
    trainee 78, 79, 80, 81, 123
    working in further and higher education
        88
    working in the NHS 87 (see also NHS)
countertransference 52–3, 60, 99
couple counselling 103
Coyle, K.J. 190
Craib, I. 190
Crews, F. 15
criminal justice setting 84
critical
    pedagogy 138
    psychology 7, 168
    theory 2, 13, 16, 21
    thinking 139–40
        hampered by sunk costs of training
            144
        how and why 16–17

critics
    dismissed as cynical 137
    various groups of 17
    key, and their perspectives 11–16
critique/s 17, 18, 161
    of CBT 47
    levels and nuances of 18–21
    of a philosophical nature 178
    responses to 177–85
        acceptance of imperfection 182
        agree with and abandon 183
        initial reform 180–2
        question and transcend 184–5
        refute all 177–9
    of therapy, history of 9–11
Culture of Narcissism, The 12, 23
Cummings, N. 187, 191
cure, counselling as 84–6, 112
Cushman, P. 13, 23
cynicism 89

D
Darwin, Charles 28, 57, 58
Davenport, D.S. 75
Dawes, R. 23
Dawkins, R. 56
Denzin, N.K. 133
dependency 99
Derrida, J. 171
Descartes, R. 3
Dessoir, M. 49
determinism vs. free will debate 171
diagnosis 68, 74
diagnostic 97
    categories 107
    label 98
Diagnostic and Statistical Manual of Mental
        Disorders (DSM) 97, 162
Dianetics 7, 27
dissent, pathologisation of 29
distress
    causes in society 133, 168–70
    origins of medicalisation of 14

origins of, in capitalism 3
origins of psychological 2–5
dogma 68
Dreher, A.U. 133
Dryden, W. 41, 132, 133, 159, 190

E
EAPs (see employee assistance programmes)
eclecticism 65–7
    haphazard 66
effectiveness 114, 116
    of counselling 128
    outcomes 115
    problem of 166–8
    studies 114, 132
    of supervision 127
efficacy studies 108, 114, 116, 132 (see
        also research)
Egan-based approaches 47, 67
Ellenberger, H. 6, 21
Ellis, A. 25, 37, 54, 62, 74, 75
empathy 59, 61
employee assistance programmes (EAPs)
        41, 89, 92
Epictetus 6
Epicurus 6
epidemiology 20
Epstein, W.M. 133
Erikson, E. 36
Erwin, E. 178
ethical responsibility of supervisors 122
ethics, professional 68, 146–7
evaluation, instruments for 87
evidence
    anecdotal 131
    -based
        practice 127
            promotion of 85
        therapies 107
evolution 4
evolutionary psychology 3, 57, 69, 70, 127
existentialism 3, 37, 38, 48
extra-therapeutic factors 119

eye movement desensitisation and
        reprocessing (EMDR) 93
Eysenck, H.J. 14, 39, 107, 108, 111, 132,
        134

F
faith, counselling rests on 12, 70, 86, 102,
        126, 139, 176
Faith of the Counsellors, The 12
false consciousness 12
Fanelli, D. 134
Federn, P. 36
fees 91, 106, 121
Feltham, C. 21, 23, 75, 105, 133, 134,
        159, 160, 190, 191
female
    influence in training 140
    majority membership of the BAPC 40
    predominance of counsellors is 103
feminist
    counselling 169
    counselling psychology 97
    critiques 43
    methodology 115
Ferenczi, S. 29, 33
Fisher, M. 22
fitness to practise 79
Flint, J. 190
Fonagy, P. 132
Foster Report 7
Foucault, M. 18, 171
Frank, J. 11, 12, 22, 29
Frankfurt School 16
Freud, A. 42
Freud, S. 2, 11, 15, 21, 22, 25, 28–30, 31,
        32, 33, 35, 43, 44, 48, 49, 50,
        51, 55, 57, 72, 74, 75, 83, 107,
        115, 128, 166, 168, 175, 177,
        190
    falsified some case studies 30, 177
    machinations of 29
Friedman, M. 191
Fromm, E. 33, 168, 190

Fry, B. 134
'fully functioning person' 32
Furedi, F. 13–14, 23

G
Galen 6
Galton, F. 6
Garfield, S. 67, 75
Gellner, E. 178
gender 69
Generalised Anxiety Disorder Assessment 7
    (GAD7) 87
genetic factors 172, 190
gestalt therapy 25, 27, 35
Giroux, H.A. 159
'Gloria' 31, 36
Gluckman, P. 21
Godwin, N. 74
Gomez, L. 21, 34, 44
Green, G. 86, 105
Greenspan, R.J. 190
group
    counselling 103
    supervision 147
Grunbaum, A. 15, 178
Guy, J.D. 27, 44, 159

H
Hall, K. 74
Halmos, P. 12, 13, 22, 63, 75, 85, 105, 159
Haney, J. 150, 160
Hanson, M. 21
happiness 10 (see also Layard, R.)
Harris, J.R. 130, 134
Health and Care Professions Council (HCPC)
    7, 71, 136, 144, 149, 166, 181
    regulation 150, 166
        case against the 150
Heaton, J. 23
Henderson, V.L. 75
heuristics 39, 70, 188
hierarchy of power 40, 42, 158
Hippocrates 6

homeopathy 150
honesty 61, 75
Honig, A. 33
Horney, K. 42
Horrobin, D. 21
Horton, I. 105, 133, 159, 160
House, R. 74, 166, 190
Howard, A. 23
Hubbard, R. 7, 27
human
    condition 3, 12
    development, theories of 47
    distress, understanding of 172
    forgiveness 60
    nature 20, 47, 68, 165, 188
        different views on 47
    potential movement 60
    suffering, origins of 1ff
    tribalism 5
humanistic
    counsellors 80, 97, 113
    diagnostic labels 68–9, 97
    psychology 72, 191
        critics 14, 15
    theorists 25, 32
    therapies 13
        goals 95
hypnotherapy 150

I
IAPT (see Increasing Access to
    Psychological Therapies)
idiosyncratic practice 66
incongruence 56, 60, 69
    origins of 56
Increasing Access to Psychological
    Therapies (IAPT) 131, 187
    scheme/s 10, 187
Independent Practitioners Network (IPN)
    149, 181
individual autonomy 56
integrative approaches 65–7, 75
    practice 93

integrationism 65–7
intuition 39, 40, 43, 65, 121, 161
Iqbal, F. 74
Irving, J. 133
I–Thou relationship 63, 95

J
Jackins, H. 27, 33
Jacobs, M. 41
James, I. 22
James, O. 160
James, W. 6
Janet, P. 29
Janov, A. 25, 54, 74, 85
Jesus 9, 29
Joynson, R.B. 7, 22
Judaism 25
Jung, C.G. 7, 22, 25, 35, 38, 45
    astrology, use of 150
    and the collective unconscious 51
    Cult 44, 45, 106
Jungian analysts 106

K
Kahn, M. 82, 105
Kahneman, D. 39, 40, 45
Kahr, B. 34, 44
Kaminer, W. 23
'Kathy' 31
Khan, Masud 25, 34–5
Kirschenbaum, H. 44, 75
Klein, Erich 33
Klein, Hans 33, 34
Klein, Melanie 24, 33–4, 42
Klein, Melitta 34
Kleinian abstinence 63
Kline, P. 112, 128, 133
Kraus, K. 11
Krishnamurti, J. 184
Kurtz, P. 21

L
Lacan, J. 171, 180

Laing, R.D. 25, 27, 31, 37–8
Lake, F. 9
Lambert, M.J. 119, 132
Lane, H. 22
Lasch, C. 12, 23
Layard, J. 22
Layard, R. 10, 14, 22, 131
Lazarus, A. 32, 66, 75, 182
    multimodal therapy 66
Leader, D. 191
Leiper, R. 106
Levitt, B. 75
life experience 79
Lilienfeld, S.O. 159, 191
Lincoln, Y.S. 133
Linehan, M. 42
Loewenthal, D. 74
longitudinal research 113, 130
love 60, 62, 116
Lucretius 6
Lynn, S.J. 159, 191

M
Mace, C. 23
Madigan, S. 160
Maeder, T. 44
magical thinking 21
Mair, K. 159
male
    disproportionate numbers
        of complaints about 153
        at top of counselling hierarchy 41
    resistance to counselling 153
malpractice 123, 126
Manning, Bernard 180
manualised psychodynamic counselling 128
Marshall, S. 45
Marzillier, J. 134
Maslow, A. 25
    hierarchy of needs 57
Masson, J.M. 15, 18, 27, 32, 34, 44, 142,
        157, 159, 183, 188
May, R. 31

McCall, R.J. 33, 44
McLellan, B. 32, 44
McLellan, J. 105, 159
McLeod, J. 107
Mearns, D. 41
Medawar, P.B. 11, 22
media reporting of research 85
medicalisation of distress 14
medication, antidepressant 77
meditation 77
mental health
    definition of 71
    statistics 4, 10, 68
middle-class bias in counselling 153
Milgram, S. 31
Mind 87, 175
mindfulness 61, 185
Moodley, R. 160
Moreno, J. 25
Mowbray, R. 190
Murphy, G. 21
mythology 5, 35

N
narcissism 12, 15, 33
narrative 115, 121
National Health Service (NHS) 77, 79, 85,
    92, 113, 149, 167, 170
National Institute of Mental Health (NIMH)
    10
National Institute for Health and Clinical
    Excellence (NICE) 85, 105, 131
nature vs. nurture debate 171
Nelson-Jones. R. 41
neurolinguistic programming (NLP) 47, 85,
    167
Newman, S. 106
Newnes, C. 74
NICE (see National Institute for Health and
    Clinical Excellence)
Nietzsche, F. 49
Noll, R. 44, 106
non-directive/ity 56, 62–5, 75

counselling 31, 55 (see also person-
    centred counselling)
ethos of most approaches 153
principles 169
Noonan, E. 74
Nussbaum, M. 6, 22

O
object relations 80, 130
obsessive compulsive disorder (OCD) 80,
    86, 113
organismic experiencing 62
Orlans, V. 69, 75, 154, 159, 160, 183, 191
outcomes (see also research outcome
    factors)
    determinants of positive 120
    negative, CBT 131
    successful 101–2, 119
    tentative nature of 175–6

P
Palmer, S. 22
Parker, I. vii, 7, 22, 190
parrhesia 61 (see also congruence)
Patient Health Questionnaire 9 87
patriarchy 3, 40–3
Pavlov, I. 6
PCA (see person-centred approach)
Perls, F. 25, 27, 35–6, 38, 54
Perls, L. 42
personal therapy for trainees 141
person-centred approach 25, 41, 54, 55,
    61, 64, 73, 182 (see also
    counselling, talking therapy,
    Rogers, C.R.)
    is 'revolutionary' 56
    parroting 56
    practitioners 69, 101
    supervisors 102
    theory 55–65
    therapy 75
    training 138–9
Persuasion and Healing 11–12

pharmacological interventions 117
phenomenology 33, 115
philosophical/social ethical problems 170–2
philosophy/philosophers 20, 37
    of science 70, 140
PHQ9 (*see* Patient Health Questionnaire 9)
Pickett, K. 11, 22
Pilgrim, D. 105
Pinel, P. 6
Pinker, S. 4, 21, 23
placebo
    effect 12, 15, 117
    factors 119
    therapy 113
placement opportunities 77–8
Plummer, K. 134
pluralism 65–7, 163–5, 175
Pollard, J. 75
Popper, K. 178
Porter, J. 105
positive psychology 70
Postle, D. 116, 133, 191
postmodernist 171
post-traumatic stress 51, 80, 113
power 106, 168
    abuse of 127
    avoiding any exercise of 63
    hierarchy of 40, 42, 158
Power of Now, The 154
predictability, principle of 73
Price, J. 21
primal therapy 85, 151
process 102, 104, 111–12, 115
    Rogers' seven stages of 101
professional
    ethics 146–7
    identity 148
        and statutory regulation 148
Professional Liaison Group (PLG) of the
        HCPC 149
professional organisation/s
    problems of 136, 166
    promotion of research 120–1

Professional Standards Authority (for Health
        and Social Care), formerly CHRE
        149, 166, 181
progress in therapy 101–2
PSA (see Professional Standards Authority)
psychiatric
    classifications 68
    disorders, non-existence of 97
psychiatry, high status of 136
psychoanalysis 7, 35, 74, 75, 86, 90, 92
    and Marxism 25
psychoanalytic
    assessment 97
    psychotherapy 92
        problems with 93, 100, 107
    theory 48–55
        criticisms of 11, 14, 28
    training 79, 141
psychobabble 15, 32
psychodrama 103
psychodynamic
    counselling 28–30, 41, 48, 50, 52,
        96, 99, 101, 115
        key figures in 24, 28–30, 33–4,
            41
        manualised 128
    counsellor/s 50, 73, 80, 99, 161
        necessity for personal therapy 141
    supervisors 102
    theory 48, 49, 54
psychological distress 4
psychology 38
    academic 8
    clinical, status of 136 (*see also* clinical
        psychology)
    conventional 54
    in counselling 159
    in counselling psychology 138
    'folk' 7
    history, brief 5–6
    of human memory 140
    mainstream 47
    positive 70

and psychiatry research 134
and psychological therapy, history of 5
as an objective natural science 111
psychopathology 36, 56, 68, 107
psychopharmacology 68
psychotherapist/s
    criticisms of 27
    effective 105, 159
    regulation 7, 148–52, 181
psychotherapy/ies
    common factors 118, 119, 120
    characteristics of leading figures 26
    disputes between approaches 8–9, 24
PTSD (see post-traumatic stress)
Pythagoras 6, 21

Q

qualitative research 114–18, 120
    Sage Handbook of 116
quantitative research 109, 114–18, 123,
        129
    in talking therapies 116–17

R

race and ethnicity 69
radical honesty 61
randomised controlled trials (RCTs) 114,
        117
Rank, O. 31
rational emotive behaviour therapy (REBT)
        37, 41, 75, 182
'real self', pursuit of 60
recovery 14, 112, 113
    'wounded healer' tradition 154
Reed, D. 64, 75
reflective practice/practitioner 138, 173
        (*see also* scientist-practitioner)
regulation 7, 136, 166, 181
    statutory 148–52, 166
Reich, W. 25, 33, 54, 168
relationship, I–Thou 63, 95 (*see also*
        therapeutic relationship)
religion 5, 9, 12, 69, 188

comparison with counselling 15, 56,
        66, 151, 168, 184, 187
research 107ff
    biased 109, 140
    in counselling, case for 108–9
    on CBT 119
    co-operative, value of 116
    confirmatory bias 140
    common factors 118–20
    comparative 117
    counsellors' attitudes to 121–3
    difficult areas for 125–9
    efficacy studies 108, 114, 116, 132
    evidence supporting CBT 131
    Exercise Framework (REF) 125
    findings in counselling 132
    focus, choice of 114–18
    funders 113
    ignoring inconvenient 130–2
    journals 124
    media reporting of 85
    methodologies 140
        different 110–11
        problems 111–14
    model of psychotherapy 116
    outcome factors 115, 120
    into practitioners' attitudes 133
    problems of
        definition and appropriateness
            110–11
        methodology 111–14
    professional body promotion of 120–1
    promotion of 120
    quantitative 123
    questionnaires 87
Retreat, The, York 6
revolution, PCA as gentle 182
rhetorical trance 174–5
Richards, B. 22
Rieff, P. 12, 22
Rise of the Therapeutic Society, The 14
Rizq, R. 159
Robinson, J. 106

Rogerian therapy 55
   necessary and sufficient conditions
      72
Rogers, C. R. 2, 25, 28, 30–3, 38, 40, 44,
      56, 57, 58, 61, 62, 63, 64, 72,
      75, 101, 106, 107, 144, 159, 160,
      166, 168, 182 (see also PCA, non-
      directivity, Rogerian therapy, UPR)
Rose, N. 13, 23
Rosen, J. 33
Rosen, R.D. 23
Rosenzweig, S. 133
Roth, A. 132

S
Sanders, P. 75
Sandler, J. 133
Sartre, J.-P. 51
Sayama, M. 191
scepticism 1, 6, 18, 28
schizophrenia 33
   research in Wisconsin 33
schoolism 72
Schopenhauer, A. 49
science, philosophy of 70, 140
scientific
   criteria 110, 111
   psychology 19
   status for counselling 121
scientist-practitioners 123–5, 167
scientology 7, 27, 47, 148
   associated with counselling 150
secrecy 15 (see also confidentiality)
self
   -analysis 29, 77
   -esteem, addiction to 13
   -harm, risks of 95
   -help books 77
   technologies of the 13
Seneca 6
sexual
   abuse in childhood 186
   attraction, counsellor/client 100

relationships, counsellor/client 127
Shamdasani, S. 28, 29, 44, 50, 74
Shapiro, F. 42
Sieghart Report 7
Singer, M.T. 23
Skype, using in counselling 104
Smail, D. 3, 14, 21, 23
Smith, D.L. 27, 44, 51, 54, 72, 74, 75
social class 105
   differences between counsellor and
      client 190
social/ethical problems of counselling 170–2
Society for the Investigation of Human
      Ecology 31
socioeconomic
   factors 69
   perspectives 170–2
solution-focused therapy 69
Spinelli, E. 45
staff counselling 89
stakeholder/s 155–8
   academic 172
   publishers in the counselling field 158,
      160
statutory regulation 148–52 (see also
      regulation)
Stevens, A. 5, 21
Stiles, W. 190, 133
Stoicism 54
Storr, A. 27, 44
Strawbridge, S. 105, 106, 133
students 123, 124 (see also training)
successful outcomes 101–2, 119 (see also
      outcomes)
suicidal ideation 27, 88, 96, 98–9
suicide
   assisted 99
   therapist 27
Sulloway, F.J. 75
supervision 79, 81, 90, 95, 126, 144–6
   necessity of 105
   to socialise students 146
supervisors, ethical responsibility of 122

Sutherland, S. 15
Swedish Government's CBT experience 131
Swift, J. 9
symptoms 84, 112
    and assessment 97
Szent-Györgyi, A. 57

T
talking therapies 5, 8 (*see also* counselling,
    therapy)
    development of the 7
Tavistock Institute 88
theory/ies
    multiplicity of 46, 70
    putting into practice 78–82
therapeutic relationship 12, 95, 101, 115,
    119, 190
    boundaried 95–6
    creation of successful 12
        difficulties in 153
    idealised 153, 175
    positive features of all 119
therapist
    expertise, myth of 159
    indifference to research 133
    sexually abusing clients 100
therapy (*see also* counselling, CBT,
    psychotherapy, REBT)
    culture, of emotionalism 13
    drama 103
    progress in 101–2
    professionalisation of 190
    -speak 52
    whilst training 141–2
Therapy of Desire, The 6
Thinking, Fast and Slow 39, 45
Thompson, S. 23
Thorne, B. 41, 75
time-limited counselling 88, 92–4
Tindall, C. 106
Tolle, E. 154
Totton, N. 23
training 105, 138–41

academics, seen as for 138–9
analysis 29
    cost of 142
    courses in person-centred counselling
        138
    early practice 79
    gender balance 140
    necessity of 105, 140–1
    personal therapy 141–2
    placements 79, 145
    supervision 144
    voluntary sector 79, 87
transactional analysis (TA) 25, 80
transference 52–3, 82, 99
transpersonal models 35, 70, 184
trauma 51 (*see also* PTSD)
Triumph of the Therapeutic, The 12
Truax, C.B. 27
Tuke, W. 6
'tyranny of the shoulds' 37

U
unconditional positive regard (UPR) 58,
    59, 60, 61, 62, 72
unconscious 48–52, 162
    repressed into the 51
unhappiness 3, 52

V
values, problems of disparate 172
van Deurzen, E. 41, 159
van Scoyoc, S. 69, 75, 154, 159, 160, 183,
    191
Van Susteren, L. 190
Vienna Psychoanalytic Society 27
Vitz, P. 44
Vogt, O. 29

W
Wade, N. 133
Wampold, B. 119
Weatherill, R. 179, 180, 191
Webster, R. 15

West, W. 160
Wheen, F. 109, 132
Wilber, K. 7, 155
'wild analysis' 50, 66
Wilkins, P. 55, 56, 75
Wilkinson, R. 11, 22
Williams, D. 133
Winnicott, D. 24, 34, 38, 43
Wittgenstein, L. 171, 178
women (*see also* female, feminist)
    in counselling 140, 152–3
Wolff, T. 22
Woolfe, R. 105, 106, 133, 159
'worried well' 56, 90
'wounded healer' tradition 79, 154
Wright, K. 14, 23, 191
Wundt, W. 6

Z
Zeno 6
Zerzan, J. 190
Zimbardo, P. 31

Critical Examinations –
new series edited by Craig Newnes

Critical evaluation is an essential element of academic study. Any theory is only as strong as its capacity to withstand sustained critical examination of the assumptions it makes about the world. The individual volumes in this series, written by prominent experts and insider critics in their field, critically examine the theories and practices of the main branches of psychology in an accessible style.

Counselling and Counselling Psychology: A critical examination
Colin Feltham
ISBN 978 1 906254 58 2
(April 2013)

Clinical Psychology: A critical examination
Craig Newnes
ISBN 978 1 906254 59 9
(June 2013)

Psychology: A critical examination
David Fryer
ISBN 978 1 906254 60 5
(Spring 2014)

Psychotherapy: A critical examinaton
Keith Tudor
ISBN 978 1 906254 61 2
(Spring 2015)